ROUTLEDGE LIBRARY EDITION: SYNTAX

Volume 3

EVIDENCE FOR MULTIATTACHMENT IN K'EKCHI MAYAN

EVIDENCE FOR MULTIATTACHMENT IN K'EKCHI MAYAN

AVA BERINSTEIN

LONDON AND NEW YORK

First published in 1985 by Garland Publishing, Inc.

This edition first published in 2017
by Routledge
2 Park Square, Milton Park, Abingdon, Oxon OX14 4RN

and by Routledge
711 Third Avenue, New York, NY 10017

Routledge is an imprint of the Taylor & Francis Group, an informa business

British Library Cataloguing in Publication Data
A catalogue record for this book is available from the British Library

ISBN: 978-1-138-21859-8 (Set)
ISBN: 978-1-315-43729-3 (Set) (ebk)
ISBN: 978-1-138-69969-4 (Volume 3) (hbk)
ISBN: 978-1-138-69972-4 (Volume 3) (pbk)
ISBN: 978-1-315-51617-2 (Volume 3) (ebk)

Evidence for Multiattachment in K'ekchi Mayan

Ava Berinstein

Garland Publishing, Inc. ▪ New York & London
1985

Library of Congress Cataloging in Publication Data

Berinstein, Ava, 1954–
Evidence for multiattachment in K'ekchi Mayan.

(Outstanding dissertations in linguistics)
Thesis (Ph.D.)—University of California,
Los Angeles, 1984.
Bibliography: p.
1. Kekchi language—Syntax. I. Title. II. Series.
PM3913.B47 1985 497'.4 85-7052
ISBN 0-8240-5444-X (alk. paper)

The volumes in this series are printed on
acid-free, 250-year-life paper.

Printed in the United States of America

UNIVERSITY OF CALIFORNIA

Los Angeles

Evidence for Multiattachment in K'ekchi Mayan

A dissertation submitted in partial satisfaction of the requirements for the degree Doctor of Philosophy in Linguistics

by

Ava Berinstein

1984

TABLE OF CONTENTS

PREFACE

FEATURES OF K'EKCHI SYNTAX

PASSIVE

K'EKCHI RESTRICTIONS ON FINAL ERGS: EVIDENCE FOR CLAUSE-INTERNAL MULTIATTACHMENT

SUBJECT FOCUS AND 2-3 RETREAT

ANTIPASSIVE

CROSS-CLAUSAL MULTIATTACHMENT

CONCLUSION

LIST OF ABBREVIATIONS

1 - first person
2 - second person
3 - third person
A1 (2,3) - Set A first (second, third) person
Abl - Ablative
Ag - Agentive
AP - Antipassive
art - article
asp - aspect
B1 (2,3) - Set B first (second, third) person
Ben - Benefactive
Com - Comitative
cont - continuative
Dat - Dative
dbt - doubt
dir - directional
dist - distributive
emph - emphatic
fut - future
imp - imperative
impl - impersonal
inf - infinitive
Inst - Instrument
Loc - Locative
ncl - noun clasifier
neg - negative
nom - nominalizing suffix
p - plural
part - participle
pass - Passive
perf - perfective
poss - possessive
pot - potential action
pr - present or habitual
prep - preposition
pro - pronoun
prog - progressive
prt - particle
pst - remote past
Q - question word
quo - quotative
R - Retreat
rec - recent past
refl - reflexive
subj - subjunctive
sur - surprise
T/A/M - tense/aspect/mood
tns - tense
voc - vocative

LIST OF MAPS

LIST OF TABLES

ACKNOWLEDGEMENTS

Many people helped me to understand K'ekchi so that my words might come out t<u>i</u>c **sa' K'ekchi**, 'straight in K'ekchi'. This was no easy task. It is impossible to name everyone who contributed to my understanding over the years because that would be a thesis by itself. I am particularly grateful to Adelina Ac and Carlota Yalibat. In addition, I would like to thank many other language consultants who aided in checking and rechecking data, they are: Carolin Rut Ac, Ernesto Chen Cau, Manuel Tzib Caz, Eliseo Choc, Roberto Caal Cuc, and Roberto Sacba Tut. I am also very grateful to Francisco Chocooj Paau who gave generously of his time and knowledge in order to tell, and explain, many K'ekchi folktales to me. Pablo Oh' and Carlota Yalibat also aided in the explanation and translation of many texts. In addition, there are two people to whom it is difficult to express my gratitude, namely Francis Eachus and Ruth Carlson. They have both given unconditional support to me in all aspects of my K'ekchi research.

I would also like to thank all of the people who served on my thesis committee: Judith Aissen, William Bright, Edward Keenan, Paul Kroskrity, David Perlmutter, and Stanley Robe. I am especially grateful to Judith Aissen for her careful and perceptive criticism of each chapter, and for the time that she spent with me. I am also indebted to David Perlmutter for many comments that have improved the form of this dissertation, and for the professorial guidance he has offered during my graduate career.

At different times during the development of this thesis, I have had the opportunity to profit from conversations with Stephen Anderson, Donna Gerdts, and Carol Rosen. I am also grateful to Carol Rosen for reading and commenting on an earlier version of Chapter 3.

Some of the research for this dissertation has received support from a UCLA Chancellor Grant, which I gratefully acknowledge.

Finally, I would like to thank all of my family, particularly Edwin Berinstein, Ronald Berinstein, Beverly Mager, Louis Mager, and Mimi Swados for their encouragement and for their confidence in me. I am especially grateful to Grant Swados, my husband, for his unconditional support of my efforts and for his fortitude.

Responsibility for errors, is of course, my own.

ABSTRACT OF THE DISSERTATION

Evidence for Multiattachment
in K'ekchi Mayan

by

Ava Berinstein

Doctor of Philosophy in Linguistics

University of California, Los Angeles, 1984

Professor William Bright, Co-chair

Professor David Perlmutter, Co-chair

This study analyzes aspects of the syntax of K'ekchi, a Mayan language spoken in Guatemala. Working in the framework of Relational Grammar, I find evidence for the constructions of Passive, Antipassive and 2-3 Retreat and provide formulations for the principles of Person Agreement, Number Agreement, Nominal Case, and Aspect Marking. Most importantly, I provide arguments that linguistic theory must countenance the notion of multiattachment (MA). That is, I argue that there exist structures where one nominal bears more than one grammatical relation (GR) in the same stratum (clause-internal MA), and that there exist structures where one nominal bears more than one GR in distinct clauses (cross-clausal MA).

In K'ekchi, Ergatives are distinct from Absolutives in their extractibility. While a final Abs can freely focus

(Foc), question (Q), or relativize (Rel), a final Erg does so only in 'reflexive' clauses. A rule is proposed: for a final Erg to extract, it must head an Abs arc. That Ergs extract just in reflexive and retroherent unaccusative clauses follows from an analysis that posits (clause-internal) MA in these clauses. Evidence from constructions with inanimate subjects provides further evidence for MA. The notions of MA and unaccusative thus find corroboration in K'ekchi.

Cross-clausal MA is discussed in relation to 2-3 Retreat clauses. In K'ekchi, the final subject of a Retreat clause <u>must</u> extract. A rule is proposed: the nominal heading the final subject arc in a Retreat clause must also head a Foc, Q, or Rel arc. It is then shown that the same constraint that governs subject extraction in simple Retreat clauses also governs extraction in complex clauses with Retreat complements. For example, in equi constructions, it is the <u>controller</u> of the Retreat infinitive that must extract, and in ascension constructions, if the retreat subject ascends, it is the <u>ascendee</u> in the matrix clause that must extract. This follows from an analysis that posits MA: the Retreat controller and ascendee satisfy the above condition because they also head the final subject arc in the Retreat complement. It is further argued that a grammar without MA cannot capture these generalizations about K'ekchi extraction.

PREFACE

0.1 K'ekchi

K'ekchi is a Mayan language spoken in Guatemala by approximately 210,000 people. Roughly 90% of the speakers live in townships of the Department of Alta Verapaz. Other departments include: Izabal, Quiche, Peten, and Belice (see map 1).

The K'ekchi dialects of Alta Verapaz are San Pedro Carcha, Cobán, San Juan Chamelco, Senahú, Cahabón, Lanquín, Panzós, Chahal, and Chisec (see map 2). In all of these townships, the K'ekchi population is greater than 82% (Eachus and Carlson 1966:110); in San Pedro Carcha and San Juan Chamelco, for example, it is as great as 97%.

The dialect of K'ekchi that is primarily represented in this study is that of Cobán (the so-called 'prestige' dialect), although I have also conducted linguistic research with residents of San Pedro Carcha and San Juan Chamelco. As there are no known syntactic differences between these dialects (which are said to form a 'group' by Campbell (1977: 24)) I do not distinguish between them in the text.

0.1.1 Genetic Classification

K'ekchi is a language of the Quichean branch. Quichean is the largest single subgroup of Mayan. There are nine

Map 1: Departments of Guatemala

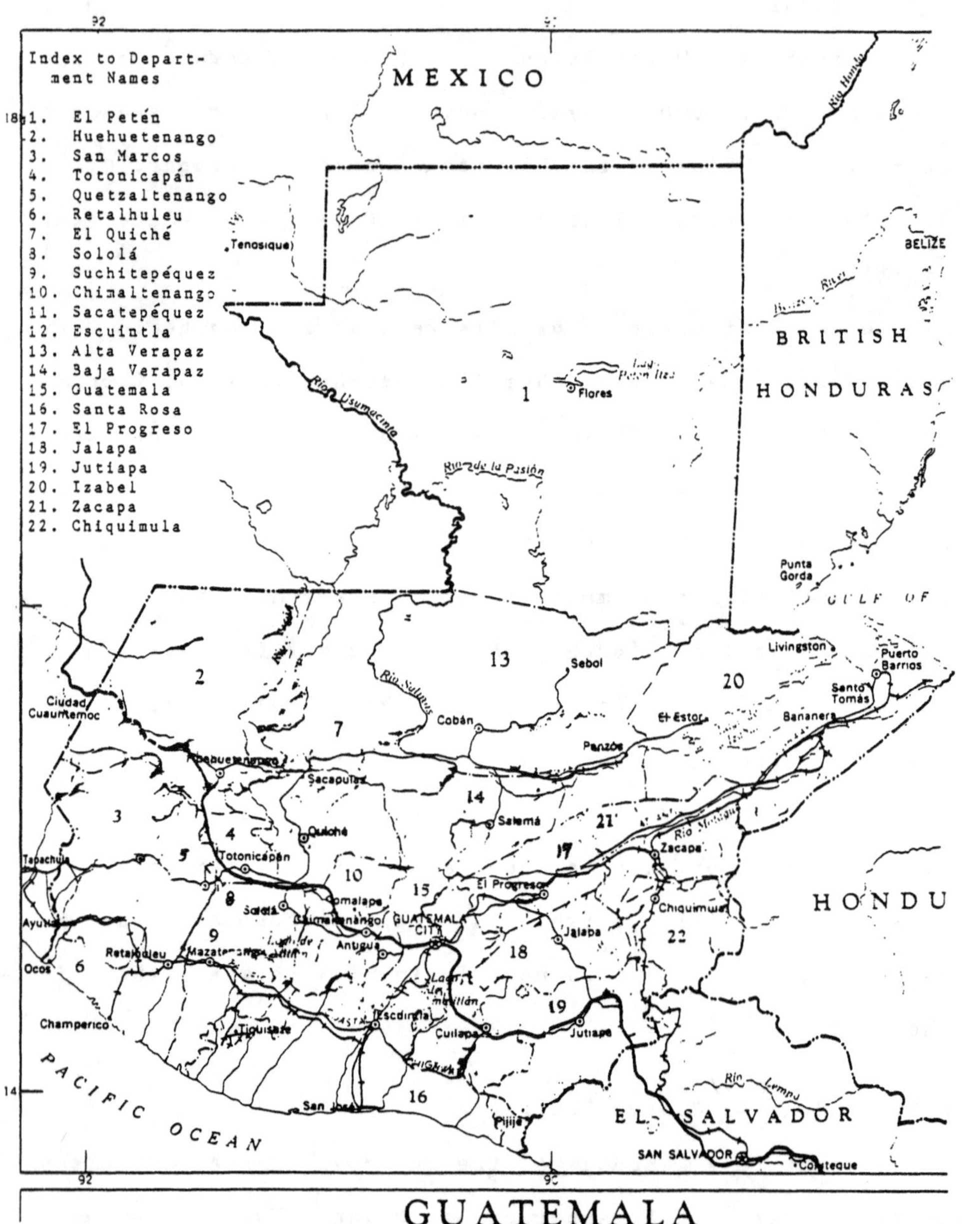

Map 2: Alta Verapaz, Guatemala

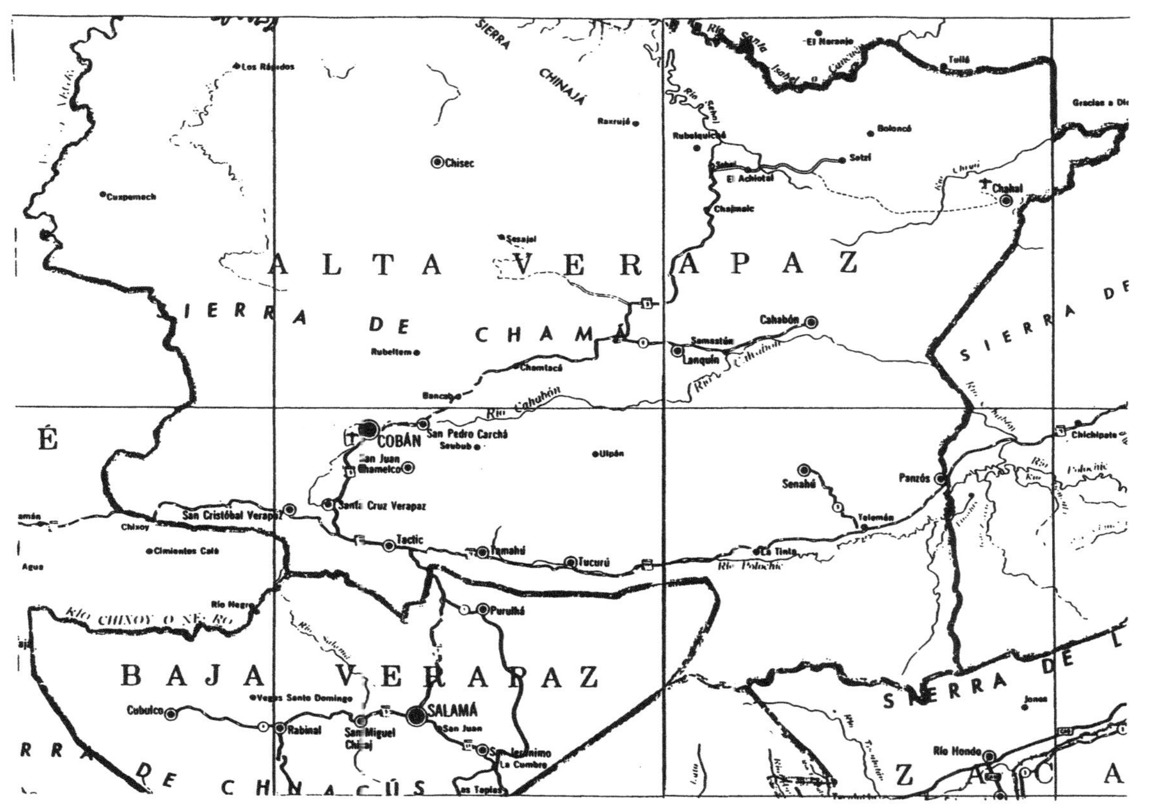

languages with approximately one million two hundred thousand speakers. Quichean Proper includes: Quiche, Cakchiquel, Tzutujil, Sacapultec, and Sipacapa. These latter two languages were previously thought to be extinct, but recently were rediscovered by Kaufman (1976a). In Campbells' classification (1977:19) however, Sacapultec and Sipacapa are treated as dialects of Quiche, not as individual languages. The remaining Quichean languages include: K'ekchi, Uspantec, Pocomchi, and Pocomam.

The diversification of Quichean languages is discussed by Kaufman (1976a). He provides the following classification for Greater Quichean.

<u>Greater Quichean</u>

I. Uspantec
II. Quichean Proper

  1. Quiche (including Achí)
  2. Sacapultec
  3. Sipacapa
  4. Tzutujil
  5. Cakchiquel

III. Pocom

  1. Pocomam
  2. Pocomchi

IV. K'ekchi

Many researchers have also classified Achí (or Rabinal) as a separate Quichean language (e.g. McQuown 1956, 1964, Swadesh 1960, Grimes 1971, Shaw and Neuenswander 1966), others have treated it as a dialect of Quiche (Campbell 1977, Norman 1979, Kaufman 1976a).

0.2 Phonemic Inventory

In the past, researchers and linguists have published K'ekchi material in an inconsistent way. Stewart (1980) bases his orthography on an alphabet proposed by Kaufman (1976b), Haeserijn (1979) bases his on the Proyecto Lingüístico Francisco Marroquín (PLFM) orthography with modifications and Pinkerton (1976) uses the International Phonetic Alphabet (IPA) with modifications. One consequence of this individuality is that there are now two K'ekchi-Spanish dictionaries with distinct orthographies. Amongst the small but growing literate K'ekchi population, there are few who spell words in the same way.

The alphabet chosen to represent the phonemes of K'ekchi is that which has been authorized by the Ministry of Education through the Instituto Indigenista Nacional, as it is described in Alfabeto de las Lenguas Mayances (1977). This alphabet is also used in two major K'ekchi literary contributions: the K'ekchi-Spanish dictionary by Sedat (1955) and the pedagogical grammar by Eachus and Carlson (1980). Hopefully, this choice will facilitate future research.

In Table 1, the International Phonetic Alphabet (IPA) is used to represent the contrastive sounds in K'ekchi. In those cases where the K'ekchi orthography differs from the IPA, the corresponding sound is written in parentheses

Table 1: Phonemic Inventory

	Points of Articulation						
	bilabial	alveolar	palato-alveolar	velar	labio-velar	uvular	glottal
plosives	p	t		k (c/qu)		q (k)	ʔ (')
ejectives		t'		k' (c'/q'u)		q' (k')	
implosives	ɓ (b)						
affricates		c (tz)	č (ch)				
ejectives		c' (tz')	č' (ch')				
fricatives		s	š (x)	x (j)			
nasals	m	n					
central approximant		ɹ (r)	j (y)		w (cu/u)		h
lateral approximant		l					

below the IPA symbol. In addition, it should be noted that the national alphabet represents [k] with qu if it precedes the vowels i or e, otherwise, [k] is represented by c. And, if ' follows a vowel it represents [ʔ], however, if ' follows a consonant it represents a glottalized consonant.

The plosives include the bilabial p, alveolar t, velar c, uvular k and glottal '. There are no (contrastive) voiced counterparts. The glottalized stops include three ejectives: alveolar t', velar c', and uvular k', and one bilabial implosive b. The implosive occurs in word-initial and syllable-initial position, but is unreleased in final position. It is interesting to note that there is no bilabial ejective.

The affricates include the voiceless alveolar tz and voiceless palato-alveolar ch with their glottalized counterparts tz' and ch'.

The voiceless fricatives include alveolar s, palato-alveolar x, and velar j.

There are two nasals: the bilabial m and alveolar n. Central approximants include the alveolar r with tap and trill allophones, palato-alveolar y, labio-velar cu, u and glottal h. There is also a lateral approximant l.

There is a ten vowel system in K'ekchi. The vowels include /a, e, i, o, u/ and /a, e, i, o, u/ where an underline signifies length.

0.3 Previous Studies

The linguistic literature on K'ekchi is not abundant. There exists some early descriptive work (Burkitt 1902, Sapper 1906, and Stoll 1896), two K'ekchi-Spanish dictionaries (Haeserijn 1979 , and Sedat 1955), a K'ekchi-Spanish grammar (Haeserijn 1966), an elementary guide for learning to speak, read, and write in K'ekchi (Haeserijn 1972), a collection of student papers (Pinkerton 1976a), and a pedagogical grammar (Eachus and Carlson 1980). Published folktales include Ac and Pinkerton (1976), Burkitt (1920), Eachus and Carlson (1971), and Freeze (1976b).

Other investigations of K'ekchi include studies in historical reconstruction of the Quichean family (Campbell 1977, Grimes 1971), K'ekchi phonology (Campbell 1974, 1976,), phonetics (Berinstein 1978a, 1978b, 1979), and ethnology (Carter 1969, Carlson and Eachus 1977, Eachus and Carlson 1966).

There have been very few studies concerning particular syntactic constructions in K'ekchi (or the theoretical issues which are raised by them); however, studies of grammatical phenomena include Freeze (1970a, 1970b, 1976a), Pinkerton (1976b), and Stewart (1980).

Freeze presents a thorough description of case morphology (1970a), predicate nominals (1970b), and possessive constructions (1976a) in K'ekchi.

Pinkerton (1976b) proposes an analysis for an 'anti-passive' construction based on a set of elicited material from one language consultant. She posits a rule of 'Focus Shift', but does not distinguish between Focus and Topic, which is crucial to the functional description of the rule (for reviews see Aissen 1980, and Freeze 1978).

Stewart (1980) presents an overview of noun and verb morphology based on previous work of Haeserijn (1966), and others.

It is difficult to compare the present investigation to previous syntactic research because the analyses presented here are based on a different set of theoretical assumptions. Primarily, this is due to the fact that the analysis of syntactic phenomena in this thesis is couched within a Relational Grammar (RG) framework. In contrast, previous work for the most part, has remained atheoretical. Thus, even though Pinkerton (1976b) has proposed a rule of 'Focus Shift' for K'ekchi, her analysis remains noncommittal about the mechanism for detransitivization in a construction that would be analyzed as a relation changing rule (i.e. 2-3 Retreat, Berinstein 1980, 1983a) in RG. An RG analysis of this construction not only provides an explanation for the final intransitivity of the clause and the object marking, it also allows us to compare Retreat clauses in K'ekchi to Retreat clauses in Turkish or Choctaw. This is because the rule of 2-3 Retreat depends on universal notions which can be defined in terms of grammatical relations and syntactic levels (or strata). This leads us to the next section where some basic concepts of RG will be introduced.

0.4 The Framework

This paper is presented in the general terms of Relational Grammar (RG), as developed in Perlmutter (1981, 1983), Perlmutter and Postal (1977, 1983a, 1983b, 1984), and Perlmutter and Rosen (1984). Central to RG, is the claim that grammatical relations are primitives of linguistic theory. _Predicate_ ('P') is treated as a grammatical relation (GR) in a class by itself (Perlmutter 1979). Nominal relations are divided into three types: _term_, _oblique_, and _retirement_. The term relations include subject ('1'), direct object ('2'), and indirect object ('3'). Of these, subject and DO are referred to as _nuclear term_ relations. The oblique relations include locative, benefactive, instrumental, and others, and the retirement relations include chômeur and emeritus. Obliques and chômeurs are referred to as _non-terms_. All of the aforementioned nominal GRs are referred to as _central_ GRs and are also conceived of as being organized hierarchically, as in (1).

(1) 1 > 2 > 3 > non-terms

For our purposes, it is necessary to recognize also, a class of relations referred to as _overlay_ relations such as Topic, Foc, Q, and Rel. A nominal that bears an overlay relation to its clause must also bear a central relation.

A classification of these R(elational)-signs as described by Perlmutter and Postal (1983a:86) is presented in (2).

(2)

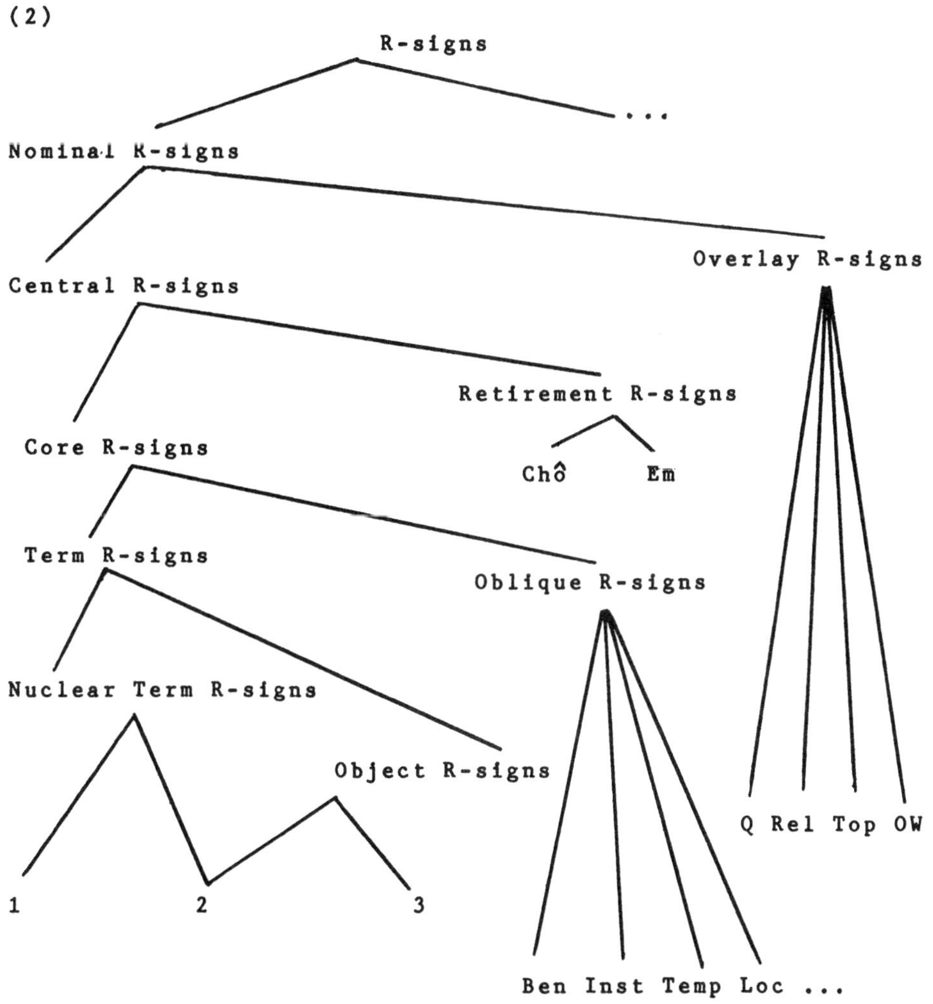

0.4.1 Clause Structure

Clause structure is represented by a set of primitive _R-signs_ (denoting the name of some grammatical relation), as well as a set of _coordinates_ which identify the level of structure at which the relation holds, and a set of _nodes_ representing linguistic elements. It is also necessary to recognize a number of distinct syntactic levels, referred to as _strata_. Strata are referred to by the shared coordinate. The relation that holds between two linguistic elements in a given stratum is represented by an _arc_, and one element is said to govern the other.

In (3) below, the element _a_ bears the GR_x relation to element _b_ at the c_i level. The governor _b_ occurs at the _tail_ of the arc, and the governee _a_ at the _head_. The R-sign occurs to the left of the arc and the names of the strata (c_i, c_{i+1},) to the right of the arc.

(3)
```
           b
           |
  GR_x     |    c_i
           v
           a
```

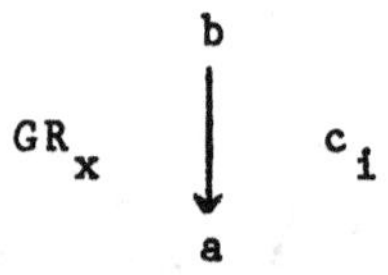

The sentence in (4) is associated with the _relational network_ (RN) in (5).

(4) x - Ø -cu-il li c'ula'al l_a_in.
tns-B3-A1-see the baby I
'I saw the baby.'

(5)

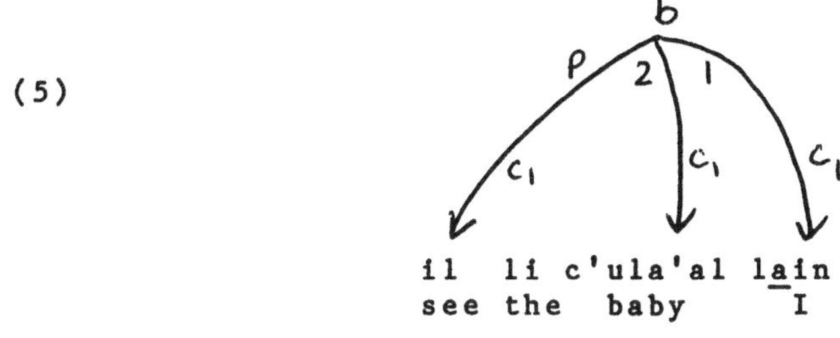

The RN in (5) represents the sentence 'I saw the baby' (agreement and tense not included). In this RN there are three arcs, two nominal dependents and one verbal dependent, which share the same governing node <u>b</u>. All of the arcs in (5) share a coordinate c_1. This is because the arcs of this particular RN all belong to the same stratum. A stratum is defined as the maximal set of arcs with the same tail sharing some coordinate (c_1, c_2 etc.). In (5), <u>li c'ula'al</u> heads a 2-arc in the c_1 stratum and l<u>a</u>in heads a 1-arc in the c_1 stratum. An element which heads a 2-arc bears the 2 relation, an element which heads a 1-arc bears the 1 relation, and so on.

The RN in (5) could also be represented in a <u>stratal diagram</u>, as in (6).

(6)

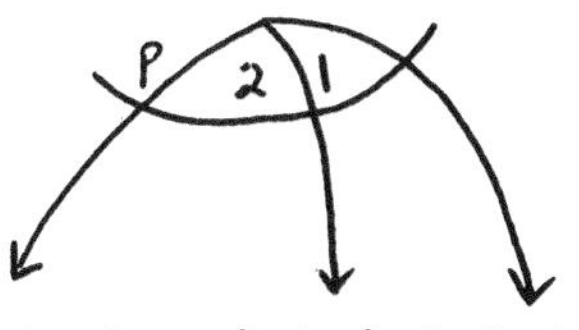

il li c'ula'al l<u>a</u>in
see the baby I

(5) and (6) are equivalent notations for the same linguistic object (RN). In (5) the first stratum is the set of all arcs with tail b which have coordinate c_1. This is equivalent to the stratal diagram in (6) in which the R-signs in the first (and only) stratum are given in a horizontal row. This latter notation, however, is often more convenient when diagraming relational networks with more than one stratum because the arcs belonging to each stratum stand out more clearly.

Consider for example, the passive sentence and its associated RN in (7). In this partial representation of the relational structure, a nominal bears different relations in different strata.

(7)a. x - Ø -il -e'   li c'ula'al (in-ban).
tns-B3-see-pass the baby   by me
'The baby was watched (by me).'

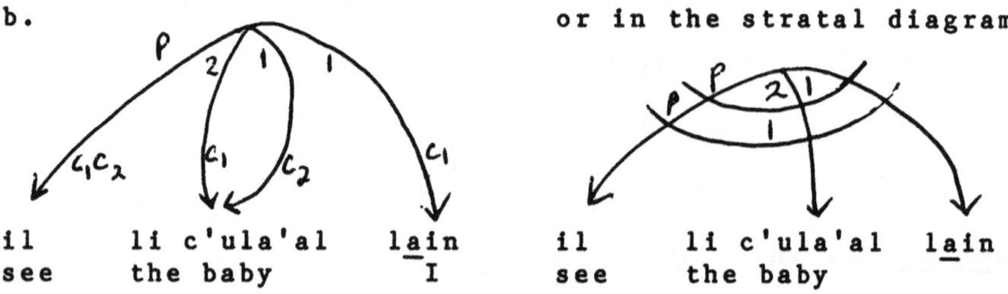

According to (7), li c'ula'al heads a 2-arc in stratum c_1 and a 1-arc in stratum c_2. The c_1 stratum is final if a clause has arcs with coordinate c_1 and none with coordinate c_2. Thus, a final stratum may be defined for monostratal and bistratal clauses. In the monostratal RN in (5), the initial level is the same as the final level. In the corresponding passive clause, as partially depicted in (7), the initial level is distinct from the final level.

So far, I have neglected to say anything about the final GR borne by the nominal that heads the initial 1-arc in a passive clause. This is because the final GR of this nominal is predicted by two proposed laws of RG: the Stratal Uniqueness Law and the Chômeur Law (Perlmutter and Postal 1977, 1983a). Suffice it to say that (in K'ekchi) this nominal must bear the chômeur relation if the conditions of these laws are met. (Discussion of these laws is postponed to later sections.) This means that a clause containing (7b) necessarily also contains (8).

(8) 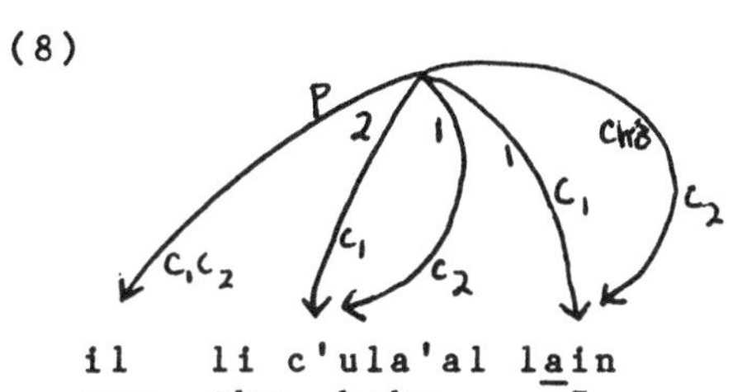

il li c'ula'al lain
see the baby I

or in the stratal diagram

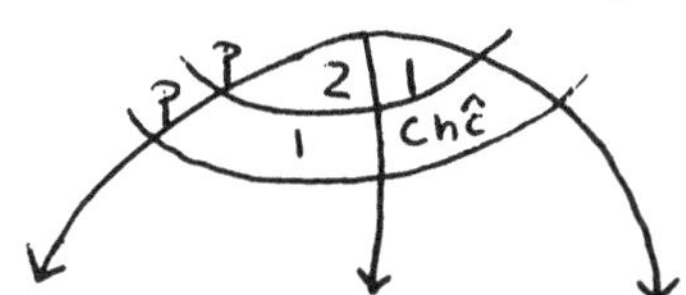

il li c'ula'al lain
see the baby I

0.4.2 Typology of Strata and some Defined Concepts

In this paper, reference will be made to four types of strata. They are defined as follows:

(9)a. transitive - a transitive stratum is one that contains a 1-arc and a 2-arc.

(9)b. intransitive - an intransitive stratum is one that is not transitive.

c. unergative - an unergative stratum is one that contains a 1-arc and no 2-arc.

d. unaccusative - an unaccusative stratum is one that contains a 2-arc and no 1-arc.

By this definition, unergative and unaccusative strata are both intransitive. Also relevant to the present disscussion is the definition of the concepts ERGative-arc, and ABSolutive-arc. These concepts are defined in terms of the notions described above.

(10)a. Erg-arc : The 1-arc of a transitive stratum is an Erg-arc in that stratum.

b. Abs-arc : The 2-arc of a transitive stratum or the the nuclear term arc of an intransitive stratum is an Abs-arc in that stratum.

I sometimes refer to the nominal that heads a (final) Erg-arc as an Erg and to the nominal that heads a (final) Abs-arc as an Abs.

'Ergativity' in RG is thus defined in terms of the information in RNs. There are several advantages to this approach. Most importantly, it gives a cross-linguistically viable characterization of the notions 'Ergative' and 'Absolutive'. Further, it allows rules in a particular language to reference nominals heading Erg-arcs and Abs-arcs (in addition to 1-arcs and 2-arcs) irrespective of case marking.

0.4.3 Multiattachment

As previously stated, a concept relevant to the present discussion is multiattachment (MA). To a certain extent, MA may represent so-called 'coreference', as is claimed by Perlmutter and Postal (1984), Perlmutter (to appear), and Postal (1981). The basic idea of MA is that a nominal can bear more than one grammatical relation in a given stratum. Under the multiattachment hypothesis, the initial stratum of

(11) John understands himself.

would be represented as :

(12)

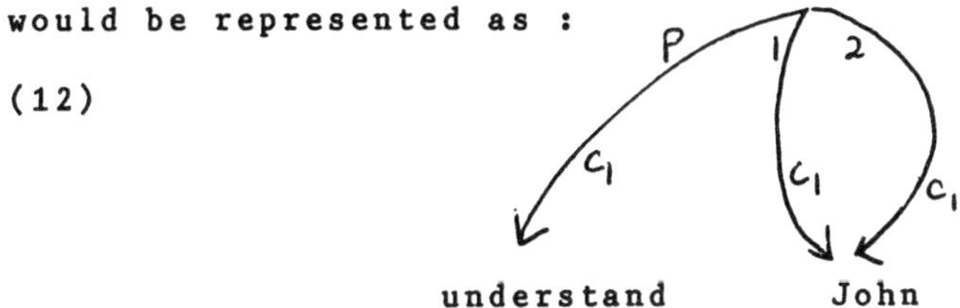

In (12) a single nominal heads two arcs with the same tail in the c_1 stratum. Where the c_1 stratum is a <u>non-final</u> stratum the configuration, as in (12), is well-formed. The question that arises is how to 'resolve' a given multiattachment, such that no nominal heads more than one arc with the same tail in the <u>final</u> stratum.

Two methods of resolution have been attested in languages: 'cancellation' (Aissen 1982, Gerdts 1981, Rosen 1981) and 'birth' (Perlmutter and Postal 1984). The 'choice' of one or the other method to some extent determines the final (in)transitivity of the clause and will be discussed in Chapter Three.

Chapter 1

FEATURES OF K'EKCHI SYNTAX

1.0 Introduction

In K'ekchi, the subject and direct object nominals carry no case marking. Therefore, the primary indicator of grammatical relations is word order (e.g. position after the verb), plus a system of verbal agreement.

1.1 Word Order

K'ekchi is among those few languages in the world which regularly place the subject after the object. The neutral word order of nominals is determined by surface grammatical relations V(erb)-O(bject)-S(ubject).

The major typological study of word order (Greenberg 1963) recognizes only the majority orders SOV and SVO and the minority order VSO. Keenan (1977) in a study of VOS languages, found only eight that he could document. While K'ekchi is not included in his sample, K'ekchi does conform to seventeen of the twenty generalizations concerning the syntactic properties of VOS languages that Keenan proposes. It should be noted that of the languages in the Mayan family, almost all are verb-initial, that is, either VOS or VSO.

In the intransitive sentences in (1a-d) the subject regularly follows the verb. In the transitive sentences in (2a- d) where both the direct object and the subject are presented as full NPs, the direct object regularly precedes the subject.[1]

```
(1)a.  Na- Ø-chal  li  so'sol.
       tns-B3-come the buzzard
       'The buzzard returns.'                          (B,S1.51)

   b.  A'ban nak jok'e ta -Ø-cam- k   l -in-rabin,
       but         when tns-B3-die-asp the-my-daughter,

   t -at- cam- k  ajcui'  laat.
   tns-B2-die-asp also    you                        (E&C,J.51)
   'But, when my daughter dies, you will die too.'

   c.  Cui ta- Ø-yajer- k  l- in-rabin,
       if  tns-B3-sick-asp the-my-daughter
       'If my daughter gets sick...'                   (E&C,J.52)

   d.  Mas nak   qui- Ø- xucuac li  cuink.
       much that tns-B3-afraid  the man
       'The man was very scared.'                      (E&C,RP.40)

(2)a.  Qui- Ø -x- c'oxla a atin a'an li  saj   al.
       tns-B3-A3- think    word that the young boy
       'The young boy thought about her words.'   (E&C,J.56)

   b.  Entonces, qu-Ø -e'x-banu li usilal li ajauchan.
       then         tns-B3-pA3-do  the favor the snakes
       'Then, the snakes did the favor.'             (B,S2.47)

   c.  Ma na- Ø -r -uc'   li  boj        laj David?
       Q  tns-B3-A3-drink the canejuice ncl David
   'Will David drink the (fermented) canejuice?'(E&C,Gr:120)

   d.  Ut chirix a'an  qu-Ø -e'x -mol      li  quic' eb li
       and after that tns-B3-pA3-collect the blood  p  the

       coc'  xul.
       small animals                                 (E&C,MSS.69)
       'And after that, the animals collected the blood.'
```

While VOS is the most frequent text and citation order, other word orders are also possible. For example, subjects and DOs are among the NPs which may appear preverbally. OVS word order is discussed in Chapter 3 and it is clear that while it is less common than VOS, it may occur if the object is contrastive or emphatic, as in (3).

(3)a. **A'an jun li na'leb** na- Ø -ka-nau lao sa' ka-
that one the custom tns-B3-A1p-know we in our-

yankil arin sa' ka-tep Alta Verapaz.
community here in our-land Alta Verapaz
'That is one custom that we know in our community,
here in our land, Alta Verapaz.' (B,S1.94)

b. **Li hu a'in** (li) ta-Ø- r -aj lix Susana.
the book this that tns-B3-A3-want ncl Susana
'This is the book that Susan wants.'

The DOs in (3a) and (3b) are focused, and as such, occur in the immediate preverbal (focus) position.[2,3]

It appears to be a universal that all VOS languages have SVO as an alternate word order pattern (Keenan 1977), and K'ekchi is no exception to the rule. In (4) below, the subject occurs in clause-initial (topic) position.[4]

(4) **At in-na' ut lain junxil** x -Ø-in-lok' chi na'bal li
voc my-mother and I before tns-B3-A1-buy prep much the

tib sa' c'ayil.
meat in market
'My mother, and earlier I, bought lots of meat in the
market.'

As will be discussed in Chapters 3, 4, and 6, nuclear term extraction is complicated by a constraint that to some extent distinguishes transitive and intransitive subjects. Specifically, Absolutive NPs may be focused, questioned, or relativized, and as such, occur in immediate preverbal position. Ergative NPs, however, are restricted in a particular way: An Erg cannot be extracted (i.e. focused, questioned, or relativized) unless it is the subject of a 'reflexive' clause. Thus, SVO word order (where S is in immediate preverbal position) may only occur in clauses with reflexive morphology. The constraint that guarantees this is discussed in Chapter 3. On the other hand, SVO word order (where S is in clause-initial position) is not restricted in this way, as (4) exemplifies. In other words, in 'non-reflexive' (transitive) clauses, SVO word order may occur if the S is Topic, but it may not occur if the S is Focus, Q, or Rel.

1.1.1 Nominal Dependents

It is common for pronominal subject and pronominal object to drop. Nuclear term pronominal dependents are retained only when contrastive or emphatic. For example, x-at-in-sac' (tns-B2-A1-hit) 'I hit you' is a grammatical sentence. Interestingly, if both nuclear terms are expressed in the 'neutral' VOS word order, the sentence is judged by most speakers as questionable, or ungrammatical, usually the latter.

```
(5)a.*?  X   -at -in- sac' laat lain.
         tns-B2- A1- hit   you  I
         ('I hit you.')
```

This is because it is highly marked for two NPs to be contrastive and emphatic in the same clause. In each of the clauses in (5b) below, the DO is retained, and the subject is dropped.

```
                      V                       DO
(5)b.  Cui ta- Ø -a - sac' cui'chic l -acu-itz'in,
         if tns-B3-A2- hit  again     the-your-younger brother
```

```
                V        DO
t  - at -in- sac'    laat.
tns- B2 -A1- hit     you                          (H,D:291)
'If you hit your younger brother again, I will hit you.'
```

In general, most clauses involve Subject-Drop, DO-Drop, or both. Since the verb must cross-reference the final subject and DO, if there is one, clauses with nuclear term Pro-Drop are not ambiguous.[5]

1.2 Verbal Agreement

K'ekchi has a morphologically ergative agreement system. There are two sets of person agreement markers. Set A (also called ergative) is used to cross-reference transitive subjects, and Set B (also called absolutive) is used to cross-reference intransitive subjects and direct objects.

In (6a) below, the second person singular Set B affix at cross-references the final direct object and in (6b) it cross-references the final intransitive subject.

```
(6)a.  X - at -ka- ch'aj.
       tns-B2 -A1p-wash     'We washed you.'

   b.  X - at -yajer.
       tns-B2 -sick         'You got sick.'
```

Notice that the first person plural transitive subject is cross-referenced uniquely with ka (Set A affix) in (6a). This is distinct from the marker for the first person plural direct object of (6c) which is cross-referenced with o (Set B affix).

(6)c. X - o - a - ch'aj.
tns-B1p-A2- wash 'You washed us.'

The Set A and B affixes are listed in Table 1. Set A has two sets of forms conditioned morphologically by the stem. The first column of Set A affixes lists those used with consonant initial stems, and the second column, those used with vowel initial stems. (Vowel initial stems result from initial glottal stop deletion.) There is one set of B affixes. Number in the third person is marked independently by the plural morpheme eb and allomorph e'.[6]

Table 1: The Set A and B Affixes

		Set A		Set B
		___/C	___/V	
Person	1s	in	cu/incu	in
	2s	a	acu	at
	3s	x	r	Ø
	1p	ka	k	o
	2p	e	er	ex
Number	3p		e'/eb	

Because number agreement will be distinguished from Set A and B agreement, the verbal paradigms for agreement in tensed and tenseless, transitive and intransitive clauses, will be given for the Set A and B forms in § 1.2.1 and § 1.2.2, and third plural agreement will be discussed in subsequent sections.

1.2.1 Tensed Transitive and Intransitive Clauses

In verbs marked for tense, the Set A affix is immediately prefixed to the verb stem and the Set B affix is 'suffixed' to the tense marker.[7]

There are two verbal configurations in tensed clauses, 1) Tns-B-A-X as seen in sentence (6a), and 2) Tns-B-X as seen in sentence (6b). The nominal cross-referenced by the Set A affix bears the final Erg relation to the clause, and the nominal cross-referenced by the Set B affix bears the final Abs relation to the clause. I use 'X' to refer to the stem in verbal and non-verbal predications. Whenever, Tns is prefixed to the stem, the stem must be a verb.

Transitive verbs must have both a Set A and a Set B affix. A verb that lacks a Set A affix is not transitive.

1.2.2 Tenseless Transitive and Intransitive Clauses

The position of the Set A affix in tenseless clauses is the same as in tensed clauses. It must immediately prefix to the stem. The Set B affix, on the other hand, is suffixed to the 'end' of the stem (i.e. to the last morphological or aspectual suffix). Thus, tenseless transitive clauses have the form A-X-B, as in (7), and tenseless intransitive clauses have the form X-B, as in (8).

(7)a. **K** - il- om - **at**.
A1p-see-perf-B2 'We have seen you.'

b. **K** - ochben -ak - **ex** nak t -o -xic.
A1p-accompany-asp-B2p when tns-B1p-go
'We'll accompany you (all) when we go.' (E&C,Gr:344)

c. Nak x -at-ki **cu** -il -om- **at**.
when tns-B2-grow A1-see-perf-B2
'When you grew up, I watched/took care of you.'

d. C'a' ta nak inc'a' **k** -il- om- **Ø** chak li raylal
what dbt that not A1p-see-perf-B3 dir the punishment

a'in ?
this (B,S2.32)
'Who says that we haven't witnessed this punishment?'

8) a. Ixk- at laat.
woman-B2 you 'You are a woman.'

b. Sac'-bil- at.
hit-part- B2 'You are hit.'

c. Yak- ak- in.
sick-asp-B1 'I will be sick.'

d. Ch'ach'o - Ø laj calajenak sa' li be.
sprawled - B3 ncl drunk on the road
'The drunk is sprawled out on the road.' (H,D.141)

1.2.3 Summary: Set A and B Agreement

Summarized in Table II are the configurations for the Set A and B affixes in tensed and tenseless, transitive and intransitive clauses.

Table II: Set A and B Affix Positions in tensed and tenseless Transitive and Intransitive Clauses.

	tensed	tenseless
transitive	Tns-B-A-X	A-X-(asp)-B
intransitive	Tns-B-X	X-(asp)-B

The Set A affixes are immediately prefixed to the stem in tensed and tenseless (transitive) clauses. The Set B affixes are suffixed in tenseless (transitive and intransitive) clauses and prefixed in tensed (transitive and intransitive) clauses.

Below is a summary of the generalizations concerning verb agreement and affix positions that we have made so far.

(9) Verbal Agreement:

(i) A nominal heading a final Erg arc determines Erg agreement in the verb.

(ii) A nominal heading a final Abs arc determines Abs agreement in the verb.

(10) Affix Positions:

(i) The affix which is determined by the nominal that heads a final Erg arc is immediately prefixed to the stem.

(ii) The affix which is determined by the nominal that heads a final Abs arc is suffixed to the stem in tenseless clauses and prefixed in tensed clauses.

1.2.4 Addenda: Set A

The Set A affixes have another function: They are used in expressions of possession and prefix to the possessed noun to indicate the person (1st, 2nd, 3rd) and number (1st, 2nd) of the possessor, as in:

(11)a. ka- tz'i' (lao)
A1p-dog 1p pro 'our dog'

b. li x -punit laj Lu'
the A3-hat ncl Lu'
'Pedro's hat' (lit. 'his-hat Pedro')

c. li r - ak -eb
the A3-pig -p 'their pig'

Third plural number is cross-referenced independently by the plural morpheme e'/eb (Berinstein 1981). If plurality is marked, eb must suffix to the possessed noun.

Notice, that the representation of the Set A affixes in Table 1 is applicable to both verb and noun stems. Furthermore, the fact that eb must suffix in nominal expressions to cross-reference the third plural possessor argues that it is functioning as an independent plural marker, not as a Set B form (see footnote 6)[8].

1.3 Tense, Aspect, and Mood

The purpose of this section is to present a brief description of the affixes which mark tense, aspect, and mood. There are six prefixes and three suffixes. In general terms, the prefixes may be treated as tense markers and the suffixes as aspect markers. The tense/aspect system is slightly complicated because certain prefixes may mark mood or aspect in addition to, or instead of, tense. For example, nac- is a present tense prefix. In addition, it describes habitual action. It is in this sense that a particular prefix may sometimes mark tense and sometimes mark aspect. On the other hand, the prefixes mi- and chi-, described below, may some-mark mood and sometimes mark aspect.

1.3.1 Prefixes

The six prefixes and their functions are listed in (12).

(12)a. n(a(c))- present or habitual

b. x- recent past

c. c-/qu(i)- remote past

d. t(a)- future

e. ch(i)- potential action (incomplete), subjunctive and imperative moods

f. m(i)- negative potential action, negative subjunctive and imperative moods

Table III gives the form of each of the six prefixes as they occur before the Set A and B person markers and the number marker. In reading the Table, recall that c (phonetically [k]), is always written as qu when it precedes the vowel e.

(13) is an example of these six prefixes used with the (consonant initial) transitive verb hob 'to maltreat' (E&C, 1980:213). (14) is an example of these six prefixes used with the (vowel initial) transitive verb atina 'talk, speak to' (E&C, 1980:208).

(13)a. N-/niqu- in- e - hob.
pr - B1-A2p-maltreat 'Ustedes me maltratan.'

b. X -in- e - hob.
rec- 'Ustedes me maltrataron.'

c. Qu- in -e -hob.
pst-
'Ustedes me maltrataron (hace tiempo).'

d. T - in -e - hob.
fut- 'Ustedes me maltratarán.'

e. Ch - in - e -hob.
A/M- 'Maltrátenme.'

f. M -in - e -hob.
neg A/M- 'No me maltraten.'

(14)a. N-/niqu -in -r -atina.
pr -B1-A3-talk 'Me habla.'

b. X - in - r- atina.
rec- 'Me habló él.'

c. Qu - in - r -atina.
pst- 'Me habló (hace tiempo).'

d. T - in -r -atina.
fut- 'Me hablará.'

Table III: The form of each of the six prefixes when immediately followed by either a[9] Set B affix, a Set A affix, or a number marker.

a) n(a(c))	1s	2s	3s	1p	2p	3p
Set B	n-in	nac-at	na-Ø	noc-o	nequ-ex	
Set A/C	n-in niqu-in	nac-a	na-x	na-ka	nequ-e	
Set A/V	na-cu n-incu	nac-acu	na-r	na-k	nequ-er	
number						nequ-e' nequ-eb

b) x-	1s	2s	3s	1p	2p	3p
Set B	x-in	x-at	x-Ø	x-o	x-ex	
Set A/C	x-in	x-a	x-x	x-ka	x-e	
Set A/V	x-cu x-incu	x-acu	x-r	x-k	x-er	
number						x-e' x-eb

c) c-/qu(i)-	1s	2s	3s	1p	2p	3p
Set B	qu-in	c-at	qui-Ø	c-o	qu-ex	
Set A/C	qu-in	c-a	qui-x	qui-ka	qu-e	
Set A/V	qui-cu	c-acu	qui-r	qui-k	qu-er	
number						qu-e' qu-eb

d) t(a)-	1s	2s	3s	1p	2p	3p
Set B	t-in	t-at	ta-Ø	t-o	t-ex	
Set A/C	t-in	t-a	t-ix	ta-ka	t-e	
Set A/V	t-incu	t-acu	ta-r	ta-k	t-er	
number						t-e' t-eb

e) ch(i)-	1s	2s	3s	1p	2p	3p
Set B	ch-in	ch-at	chi-Ø	ch-o	ch-ex	
Set A/C	ch-in	ch-a	chi-x	chi-ka	ch-e	
Set A/V	chi-cu	ch-acu	chi-r	chi-k	ch-er	
number						ch-e' ch-eb

f) m(i)-	1s	2s	3s	1p	2p	3p
Set B	m-in	m-at	mi-Ø	m-o	m-ex	
Set A/C	m-in	m-a	mi-x	mi-ka	m-e	
Set A/V	mi-cu	m-acu	mi-r	mi-k	m-er	
number						m-e' m-eb

(14)e. Ch - in - r - atina.
A/M- 'Que me hable.'

f. M - in - r - atina.
neg A/M- 'Que no me hable.'

Since the six affixes are related morphologically (i.e. by virtue of their position), ideally, there should be one cover term for all six. Unfortunately, the affixes in (12e, f) are not 'pure' tense markers or tense/aspect markers; instead they may mark either subjunctive or imperative moods, or potential action. For example, the use of chi- and mi- in (13e,f) is imperative in mood, while the use of chi- and mi- in (14e,f) is subjunctive in mood. Instead of using different glosses for the different uses of chi- and mi-, I use the general cover term aspect/mood (A/M) to describe chi- and neg A/M to describe mi-.

1.3.2 Suffixes

The three tense/aspect suffixes are -c, -k, and -ak. Freund (1976:29) describes these as 'non-future', 'future', and 'future attributive', respectively. This is a good choice of terminology because -c may occur on intransitive verb stems affixed with nac-, x-, c-/qu-, or m-, (i.e. all non-future tenses), while -k and -ak occur on verbs affixed with ta- or ch-. Stewart (1980:63-4) suggests that -k and -ak are allomorphs, written in his orthography as (a)q, thereby collapsing the two morphemes. However, for descriptive purposes, there is good reason to distinguish -k from

-ak. First, ak is realized as -hak after vowel final stems, not as -k (E&C,1980: 341). Second, -(h)ak may occur on finally transitive and intransitive stems, but -k may only occur on finally intransitive stems. Third, -k is obligatory if the (intransitive) stem is affixed with ta- or ch-, but -(h)ak cannot occur (with one exception, see footnote 10). Finally, -(h)ak may suffix to first person imperative stems with a Ø- tense prefix and -k may not. This difference also follows from the fact that -k may not occur on finally transitive stems.

We will first consider the use of -c and -k in intransitive clauses. (15) exemplifies the use of -c in tensed intransitive clauses with T/A/M prefixes from the 'non-future' set.

(15)a. N -at- alina - c.
pr-B2- run -asp 'You run.'

b. X -at - alina- c.
rec- 'You ran.'

c. C -at -alina- c.
pst- 'You ran (awhile ago).'

d. M -at- alina - c.
neg A/M- 'Don't go to run.'
(Sp.'No vaya a correr (usted).')

If the verbal prefix indicates future time or potential action, the T/A suffix must be -k, and -c cannot be used; as exemplified in (16) and (17).[10]

(16)a. T -at -alina- k.
fut-B2-run -asp 'You will run.'

b.* T - at -alina- c. ('You will run.')

(17)a. Ch- at - alina- k .
A/M-B2 - run - asp 'You may go to run'

b.* Ch -at -alina- c .

This difference between -c and -k is also exemplified in verb stems ending in consonants, as in (18a) and (18b).

(18)a. T - e' -cam - k chijunileb li xul.
fut-p - die -asp all p the animals
'All the animals will die.'

b.* T - e' -cam - c chijunileb li xul.
('All the animals will die.')

c.* T - e'-cam - ak chijunileb li xul.
('All the animals will die.')

Notice that if -k and -ak are allomorphs (as suggested by Stewart 1980), and -k is suppose to occur after vowels, then we would expect -ak to occur after consonants, but as exemplified in (18c), it can't.

Finally, it should be noted that -(h)ak unlike -k, may suffix to transitive CV and CVC stems. For example,[11]

(19)a. Ka-bicha- **hak** -Ø li bich.
A1-sing- asp -B3 the song 'Let us sing the song.'
(Sp.'Cantemos el canto.') (E&C,1980:341)

b.* Ka- bicha - k -Ø li bich.
('Let us sing the song.')

(20)a. Ch -Ø -a -cuy - **ak** l -in -mac x -Ø -in-banu
A/M-B3-A2-forgive-asp the-my - sin rec-B3-A1-do

chi jo'can.
like this (B,S3.130)
'May you forgive my sin that I did (like this).'

b.* Ch- Ø- a - cuy- k l-in -mac x-in-banu chi jo'can.
('May you forgive the sin that I did (like this).')

(21)a. Ch -Ø -a -c'am - ak chak l -in asaron li
A/M-B3-A2-bring-asp dir the-my hoe that

x -Ø -in -canab sa' l -acu- ochoch.
rec-B3-A1-leave in the-your-house (E&C,1980:343)
'Bring me the hoe that I left in your house.'

b.* Ch- Ø -a -c'am - k chak l-in asaron li x-Ø-in-canab

sa' l-acu-ochoch.
('Bring me the hoe that I left in your house.')

The sentences in (19)-(21) show that -k may not suffix to finally transitive stems, regardless of their phonological shape. This supports the hypothesis that -k and -ak are distinct morphemes.

The affixes -c, -k, and -ak may also occur suffixed to stems (noun, adjective, positional etc.) lacking an overt tense, aspect, or mood prefix (T/A/M). The presence of -c signifies non-future (22a,b, below), and the presence of -k signifies future (22c,d, below). -Ak may also indicate future, but as Haeserijn notes (1966:75), -ak seems to indicate 'distance in time'- future or past- and may be an element of chak (chi + ak), a distance particle which combines with certain classes of verbs to indicate direction (see DeCormier 1979). Thus, there is a semantic distinction between -ak and -k, even though the two overlap slightly.

In clauses whick lack T/A/M prefixes, as in clauses with overt T/A/M prefixes, -c/-qu and -k T/A affixes may only suffix to stems in finally intransitive clauses, while -ak may suffix to stems in finally intransitive (22e, below) or transitive clauses (as in 19a).

(22) below exemplifies the use of -c/-qu, -k, and -ak suffixes in intransitive clauses that lack an overt T/A/M prefix.

(22)a. Arin cuan-qu-in.
here exist-asp-B1
'Here I am.' (Sp.'Aqui estoy.') (H,D:96)

b. Ma yocyo - c - at?
Q lieing down -asp-B2
'Are you lieing down? (E&C,1980:56)

c. Cuan- k - in.
exist-asp- B1 (H,D:96)
'I will be (in a place).' (Sp.'Estare (en un lugar.')

d. Yo - k - o chi trabajic nak ta -Ø -chal -k
cont-asp-B2p prep work when fut-B3-arrive-asp

li patron.
the boss (E&C,1980:257)
'We will be working when the boss arrives.'

e. Tic - ak - eb taxak x-ch'ol- eb li ka-coc'al.
straight-asp -p subj A3-heart-p the A1p-children
'Hopefully our children will be honest.'
(lit. 'they will be straight hopefully their hearts our children')
(Sp. 'Ojalá que anduvieran en rectitud nuestros niños.') (E&C,1980:342)

1.4 Nominal Agreement

In this section oblique relations and the rules which determine nominal agreement will be described.

1.4.1 Relational Nouns

In K'ekchi, as in most Mayan languages, non-nuclear terms are expressed by a possessive construction. The head noun in this construction, termed 'relational noun' by

Mayanists, is obligatorily possessed and corresponds to the semantic function. The possessor of the noun is the nominal bearing the oblique relation. As in other possessive constructions, the head noun (relational noun) agrees with the possessor and is marked by an affix from (Ergative) Set A. For example,

(23)a. chi r - e li cuink
at his-mouth the man 'with the man' (Com)

b. chok' r- e li cuink
for his-mouth the man 'for the man' (Ben)

c. chi r - ix li cuink
at his-back the man 'behind the man' (Loc)

In these examples the third singular Set A affix r- is prefixed to the relational noun and agrees with the possessor. Most relational nouns are derived from body parts as u 'face', e 'mouth', and ix 'back' and are obligatorily possesed. Relational nouns are used for a variety of semantic case functions as ablative, agentive, benefactive, comitative, dative, instrumental, and locative. Table IV is a list of the relational noun stems, their translation, and the possible semantic functions for their use.

Depending upon the relational noun and its semantic function, it may or may not be introduced by a preposition. There are three prepositions: chi, chok', and sa' which have different distributions. Chi meaning 'at, for, on, with,' or 'from' introduces locative, comitative, agentive, ablative, and instrumental relational nouns. Chok' meaning 'for' introduces benefactive relational nouns, and sa' meaning 'to, in, at', or 'on' introduces locative relational nouns. Of interest is the fact that only the relational noun stems which are derived from body parts are introduced with a preposition, with one exception: e- is not introduced by a preposition if its possessor heads a 3 arc. Iq'uin, ochben, ubel, mac, and ban are never introduced by a preposition. Table V illustrates which prepositions may introduce which relational nouns and under what semantic function.

Finally, Table VI illustrates which relational nouns do not co-occur with prepositions. All relational nouns, whether they are introduced by a preposition or not, have the same syntactic structure: The Set A form is immediately prefixed to the relational noun stem. The possessor of the noun follows the relational noun stem optionally and is cross-referenced by a Set A affix.

The principles that govern person and number agreement in relational nouns are stated in (24) and (25) below.

(24) Nominal Agreement:

(i) The possessor of a noun determines Set A agreement.

(ii) Third plural possessors of a noun determine number agreement optionally.

(25) <u>Nominal Affix Positions</u>:

(i) Set A affixes prefix to the possessed noun.

(ii) If number agreement is marked, <u>eb</u> must suffix to the possessed noun.

Some examples follow:

(26)a. Ma x -Ø - x -si r - e li al li tumin ?
Q tns-B3-A3-give A3-Dat the boy the money
'Did he give the money to the boy?' (E&C,Gr:149)

b. Na -Ø -xic chi cu- u.
tns-B3-go from A1-Abl
'He runs away from me.'

c. Cuan-Ø chi r - u li mex .
exist-B3 on A3- Loc the table
'It's on top of the table.'

d. X- Ø -in-yoc' li che' r- iq'uin li ch'ich' .
tns-B3-A1-cut the tree A3-Inst the machete
'I cut the tree with the machete.'

e. T -in- c'ojla- k ch -a -c'atk .[12]
tns-B1-sit -asp at-A2- side=Loc
'I will sit beside you.'

f. X -Ø -in-lok' li matan a'in chok' r -e -eb .
tns-B3-A1-buy the present this for A3- Ben- p
'I bought this present for them.'

Table IV: A list of the Relational Noun Stems, their Meaning and their Semantic Functions.

Rel N	Meaning	Semantic Function(s)
-u	face, surface	Abl, Loc
-e	mouth	Dat, Inst, Loc, Com, Ben
-c'atk	side, near	Loc
-ix	back, behind, about	Com, Loc
-ben	on top of, 'knee'	Loc
-iq'uin	with,	Loc, Com, Inst
-ochben	accompany	Com
-ubel	under	Loc
-mac	because of, fault	Ag
-ban	'by', because of	Ag

Table V: Distribution of the Prepositions which Co-occur with each Relational Noun Stem and under which Semantic Function.

			Semantic Function			
Prepositions	Abl	Ag	Instr	Ben	Com	Loc
chi	-u	-u	-e, -u		-ix	-u, -e, -ix, -ben -c'atk
chok'				-e		
sa'						-ben

Table VI: A List of the Relational Noun Stems which do not Co-occur with Prepositions.

Ag	Inst	Com	Loc	Dat
-ban -mac	-iq'uin	-iq'uin -ochben	-iq'uin -ubel	-e

In (26f), notice that eb is suffixed to the relational noun stem e to cross-reference the 3rd plural (Ben) possessor. As previously mentioned, I have argued that eb is a marker of number, and is not a Set B (Absolutive) form (Berinstein 1981). As such, eb has several independent characteristics which are atypical of a Set B form. The fact that eb is suffixed to nouns to indicate the plurality of the possessor is an example of one such dfference.

1.5 Case

The Core R-signs include the set of Term R-signs (1, 2, 3) and Oblique R-signs (Ben, Inst, Loc, etc) (Perlmutter and Postal 1982). In K'ekchi, of the Core R-signs, only the nuclear terms (1,2) are unmarked. 3's and Obliques are expressed as possessors of relational nouns.

The principles which govern case marking are stated in (27). Subjects and DOs are unmarked. All other Core R-signs are expressed in a possessive construction as possessors of a relational noun.

(27) Case Marking: (partial statement)[13]
(i) Nuclear terms are unmarked.
(ii) All other Core-R signs are presented as possessors of a relational noun.

The principles governing person and number agreement in relational nouns follow from the statements in (24) and (25) above.

1.6 Third Plural Agreement

Number agreement is not always marked. When it is marked, it is marked by the plural morpheme _e'_/_eb_. The conditioning factors which determine the use of _e'_ versus _eb_ will be discussed in tensed and tenseless, transitive and intransitive clauses. Since previous descriptions of K'ekchi (and Mayan) have treated _e'_/_eb_ as Set B forms (see footnote 6), it is shown that _e'_/_eb_ may cross-reference a third plural nominal if it heads a final Erg or Abs arc. To illustrate this point, the use of _e'_/_eb_ will be broken down by grammatical relation. However, because number agreement with intranitive Subjects and Direct Objects (i.e. nominals heading Abs-arcs) differs, I introduce the notion 'Unerg relation' and define _Unerg-arc_, as follows:

(28) _Unerg-arc_ : A 1-arc in an intransitive stratum is an Unerg-arc in that stratum.

I refer to the nominal that heads an Unerg-arc as a nominal that bears the Unerg relation.

1.6.1 Tensed and Tenseless Intransitive Clauses: The Unerg Relation

To cross-reference a third plural subject in a tenseless intransitive clause, _eb_ must be suffixed. _E'_ may not be used.

(29)a. Ixk- eb.
woman-p 'They are women.'

b.* Ixk- e'

To cross-reference a third plural subject in a tensed

intransitive clause <u>e'</u> must be prefixed, <u>eb</u> may not be used.

(30)a. X - e' -cam
tns-p -die 'They died.'

b.* X- **eb** -cam

c.* X- cam- **eb**

d.* X- cam- e'

Table VII summarizes the use of <u>e'</u>/<u>eb</u> in tensed and tenseless intransitive clauses.

<u>Table VII</u>: 3rd Plural Marking for the Unerg Relation in Tensed and Tenseless Intransitive Clauses.

	tensed	tenseless
e'	prefix	*
eb	*	suffix

This chart may be read as follows: <u>E'</u> cross-references the 3rd plural Unerg relation as a prefix in tensed clauses, and may not be used in tenseless clauses. <u>Eb</u> is suffixed (to the predicate) in tenseless clauses, and may not be used in tensed clauses.

1.6.2 Tenseless Transitive Clauses: The Erg Relation

The verbal schema discussed earlier for Set A and B affixes in tenseless transitive clauses was <u>A-X-(asp)-B</u>. To cross-reference a third plural subject in a tenseless transitive clause, the third singular Set A affix <u>x</u>-/<u>r</u>- is prefixed to the stem in accordance with the verbal agreement statements in (9) and (10), and <u>eb</u> is suffixed. (In fact, as (31) shows, <u>eb</u> is suffixed to the Set B form.) <u>E'</u> cannot be used, nor can <u>e'x</u> or <u>e'r</u>. The fact that <u>eb</u> is used to cross-reference an Ergative NP provides additional evidence that eb is not a 3rd plural Set B form (see § 1.4.1), and that e'x/e'r are not 3rd plural Set A forms.

(31)a. **x** - bok -ak - in- **eb**
A3-call-asp- B1 - p
'that they call me' (Stewart,1980:66)

b.* **e'x** - bok -ak -in

(32)a. **R** -ochben -ak -**Ø**- **eb** nak t -e'- xic Coban.
A3-accompany-asp-B3- p when tns-p -go Coban
'They will accompany him when they go to Cobán.'

b.* **E'r** -ochben - ak nak t -e'-xic.

That is, if eb were strictly a Set B form, it should not be able to cross-reference an Ergative NP, as it does in (31a) and (32a). Furthermore, were eb a Set B verbal affix, sentences in which the subject is 3rd singular and DO is 3rd plural, should not be ambiguous with sentences in which the subject is 3rd plural and the DO is 3rd singular. But these sentences (out of context) are ambiguous.

(33) R - il -om -Ø -eb.
A3-see-perf-B3-p
'He has seen them.'/ 'They have seen him.'

Under each of the readings in (33), the transitive subject is cross-referenced for person by the Set A prefix r- and the DO is cross-referenced for person by the Set B null affix. The difference is that in the first reading -eb cross-references the number of the DO and in the second reading, it cross-references the number of the transitive subject. I assume that the B3 affix occurs before -eb because of examples like (31a) and because that is the expected position of a Set B affix in a tenseless clause (see §1.2.3). The ambiguity arises because B3 is null and because -eb is able to cross-reference 3rd plural DOs (see §1.6.4) and 3rd plural subjects in tenseless transitive clauses. Given a context, these clauses are not ambiguous.

(34) Nak ta -Ø -chal- k li hab r -il -ak -Ø - eb a'an
when tns-B3-come-asp the rain A3-see-asp -B3- p they

c'a'ru t - Ø -e'x -banu.
what tns-B3-p A3-do
'When the rain comes they'll see what they should do.'

Summing up: to cross-reference a 3rd plural Ergative NP in a tenseless clause, the 3rd singular Set A affix must prefix to the verb stem and eb must suffix. The morpheme which is traditionally analyzed by Mayan linguists as the 3rd plural Set A affix (e'x/e'r) may not be used. If eb is analyzed as a Set A marker there is no explanation for the fact that it can cross-reference the DO of a clause (and the intransitive subject, as in (29a)). If eb is analyzed as a Set B marker, three facts still remain to be explained. First, why it is that eb can cross-reference a transitive subject, second, why it is not possible to express a 3rd plural subject and 3rd plural DO in a tenseless transitive clause, and third, why sentences with a 3rd plural subject and 3rd singular DO are ambiguous with sentences that have a 3rd singular subject and 3rd plural DO. If however, eb is analyzed as a marker of number for subjects and DOs, the first problem disappears and in addition, there is an explanation for the ambiguity. There is also an explanation for the fact that there cannot be two 3rd plural arguments in a tenseless clause: eb can cross-reference only one.

1.6.3 Tensed Transitive Clauses: The Erg Relation

The verbal configuration discussed earlier for Set A and B affixes in tensed transitive clauses is <u>Tns-B-A-X</u>. To cross-reference the 3rd plural Ergative NP in tensed clauses <u>e'</u> must occur as a prefix and <u>eb</u> may not be used. As predicted by the Verbal Agreement statements in (9) and (10), the Set A affix is immediately prefixed to the verb stem and cross-references 3rd singular person.

(35)a. Qu -in- e' x- tenk'a.
tns-B1- p A3- help 'They helped me.'

b.* Qu-in - x - tenk'a -eb.
tns-B1-A3 - help -p ('They helped me.')

(36)a. T -at -e' r - il.
tns-B2- p A3- see 'They will see you.'

b.* T -at - r - il- eb.
tns-B2- A3-see- p ('They will see you.')

Table VIII summarizes the use of the 3rd plural number markers in tensed and tenseless clauses.

<u>Table VIII</u>: 3rd Plural Marking for the Erg Relation in Tensed and Tenseless Transitive Clauses.

	tensed	tenseless
e'	prefix	*
eb	*	suffix

This result is analogous to the 3rd plural marking for Unergs (§ 1.6.1). That is, in both Tables VII and VIII, <u>e'</u> may only occur as a prefix in tensed clauses, and <u>eb</u> may only occur as a suffix in tenseless clauses. 3rd plural Ergs and Unergs are distinguished in that the Set A (person) affix must prefix to the verb stem in tensed and tenseless transitive clauses, as predicted independently by the rules for Verbal Agreement.

1.6.4 Tensed and Tenseless Transitive Clauses: The DO Relation

E'/eb may cross-reference a 3rd plural DO. The distribution of these affixes are complicated by the fact that their presence is conditioned by phonological and morphological rules in tensed clauses. In tenseless clauses, on the other hand, their distribution is quite straightforward: Eb must suffix. E' may not be used.

(37)a. Cu - il -om -eb.
A1- see -perf-p 'I have seen them.'

b.* Cu -il -om -e'.

c.* E'- cu- il -om.

d.* Eb- cu -il -om.

In tensed clauses, eb may prefix or suffix. The condition which determines the position of eb in a tensed transitive clause is given in (38).

(38) Condition on 3rd Plural DO Marking:
In a tensed transitive clause, if the subject is 3rd person and the DO is 3rd person plural (and the 3rd plural DO is cross-referenced), then eb must suffix, otherwise eb may prefix or suffix.

For example, in (39) and (40) below, the subject is non-3rd person and eb cross-references the plural DO as a prefix or as a suffix.

(39)a. X - **eb** - in-ch'aj.
tns-p - A1- wash 'I washed them.'

b. X - in - ch'aj - **eb**.
tns-A1 - wash -p 'I washed them.'

(40)a. X - **eb** - ka -ch'aj.
tns- p - A1p-wash 'We washed them.'

b. X -ka- ch'aj - **eb**.
tns-A1p-wash - p 'We washed them.'

It is important to note that a grammar that treats e' and eb as Set B forms will require an explanation for the fact that only the 3rd plural form eb may suffix in the pattern Tns-A-X-B, while first and second forms cannot. Thus, while (39) and (40) exemplify the fact that eb may prefix or suffix given the condition in (38), (41) exemplifies the fact that 1st and 2nd person Absolutive forms cannot.[14]

(41)a.* X- in -ch'aj- **at**.
tns-A1-wash - B2 ('I washed you.')

b.* X - a - ch'aj - **o**.
tns-A2- wash -B1p ('You washed us.')

c.* X -ka - ch'aj - **ex**.
tns-A1p-wash -B2p ('We washed you (plural).')

Finally, as shown in (42), in clauses with a 3rd person subject, eb must suffix, as predicted by (38).

(42)a. Qui- x - saq'u- **eb**.
tns- A3- hit - p 'He hit them.'

b.* Qu - **eb** - x- sac'.
tns- p - A3 -hit ('He hit them.)

c.* Qu- **e'** -x- sac'.
tns-p -A3- hit ('He hit them.') but:'They hit him.'

Note that this same generalization holds for vowel initial verb stems.

(43)a. Qui -r -il - **eb** .
tns-A3-see- p 'He saw them.'

b.* Qu- **eb** - r - il.
tns-p -A3- see ('He saw them.')

c.* Qu- e' -r -il.
tns-p -A3 -see ('He saw them.') but:'They saw him.'

(42) and (43) are relevant for three reasons. First, (42a) and (43a) are not ambiguous. If _eb_ is suffixed in a _tensed_ transitive clause, it _must_ cross-reference the DO. Second, neither _eb_ nor _e'_ may occur in the Set B prefix position to cross-reference the plural DO. Third, both (42c) and (43c) are grammatical with a plural subject and singular DO reading. If _e'_ were unambiguously a Set B form (as claimed by Pinkerton 1976b and others), it would not be capable of inducing a plural Ergative interpretation. For this reason, _eb_ must suffix if the subject is 3rd singular.

In addition to the morphological condition (38), there is also a phonological condition which interacts with the use of _eb_ versus _e'_ in a tensed transitive clause. As shown below, in tensed transitive clauses both _eb_ and _e'_ may prefix to cross-reference the final DO. However, _e'_ may only occur before consonants.

(44)a. Nequ -eb-_a_cu- il.
tns - p -$\bar{A}$2 -see 'You see them.' (E&C,Gr:247)

b.* Nequ- e'- _a_cu- il. ('You see them.')

```
but: c. Nequ- e'- cu - il.
        tns-  p - A1 -see     'I see them.'
```

Eb is not restricted in this way, as (45) exemplifies.

```
(45)  T  - eb - ka - take   sa'  be.
      tns- p - A1p -follow  on   road
      'We'll follow them on the road.'             (E&C,Gr:248)
```

Other examples of tensed clauses with 3rd plural DOs follow:

```
(46)a.  Ch- eb -acu- ocsi  sa'  cab.
        tns-p - A2- enter  in   house
        'You may let them in the house.'           (E&C,Gr:248)

    b.  X - e' -cu- ocsi  sa'  cab.
        tns-p  -A1- enter in  house
        'I let them in the house.'                 (E&C,Gr:248)

    c.  Inc'a' chic na - Ø -cu-aj   nequ-e'-cu-il  r -u.
        not   again tns- B3-A1-want tns- p-A1-see their-face
        'I don't want to see their faces again.'  (E&C,KK.6)

    d.  X - eb - in-tenk'a.
        tns-p - A1 -help     'I helped them.'     (E&C,Gr:247)

    e.  Junelic nequ-e' - ka- c'oxla.
        always  tns- p - A1p- think
        'We always think/worry about them.'        (E&C,Gr:245)
```

The phonological rule which determines the use of eb versus e' in (44)-(46) is motivated on independent grounds. Roughly, there are two environments in which a bilabial implosive is devoiced: 1) in final position, and 2) before voiceless obstruents. For example, in the NP in (47a) below, the b of eb is voiced.[15]

```
(47)a.  eb  laj  tul
        p   ncl  sorceror    'the sorcerors'
        phonetically: [ ɛɓ lax tu:l̥ ]
```

But, in (47b), the b of eb is voiceless.

```
    b.  eb  ka- tz'i'
        p   A1p-dog          'our dogs'
        phonetically: [ ɛp  qa c'iʔ ]
```

This rule may be expressed as (48), and can be ordered with respect to (49) which applies optionally.

(48) ɓ ⟶ [-voice] / ___ { -voice
+obstruent }

/ ___ #

(49) p ⟶ [ʔ] / ___ [+ cons]

As a consequence of (48), eb ---> ep before voiceless obstruents (e.g. the 1st person Set A affixes), and ep ---> e' optionally before consonants, as a result of (49): thus accounting for the overlap of e' and eb with 1st person transitive subjects (as in (44c), and (45)). Notably, (48) does not apply before vowels, therefore, eb and not e' will always occur in tensed transitive clauses with 1st person singular subjects cross-referenced by the Set A affix in, and 2nd person subjects cross-referenced by a, acu, e, or er. This evidence provides the justification for the linkage of eb and e' as allomorphs.

Table IX summarizes the use of the 3rd plural DO markers in tensed and tenseless transitive clauses.

Table IX: 3rd Plural Marking for the DO Relation in Tensed and Tenseless Transitive Clauses.

	tensed	tenseless
e'	prefix	*
eb	prefix/ suffix	suffix

E' may prefix in tensed clauses when the phonological conditions of (48) and (49) are met. E' may never suffix. Eb may be prefixed or suffixed in tensed clauses, as predicted by (38). In tenseless clauses, eb must suffix.[16]

1.6.5 Summary

Number agreement, unlike Set A and B person agreement, is not always marked and it is subject to several conditions (morphological and phonological). However, three things are clear. First, if a 3rd plural nominal is cross-referenced (in a verbal or nominal expression), it must be cross-referenced with e'/eb. Second, Tables VII, VIII, and IX share the basic morphological generalization that eb must suffix in tenseless predications (when cross-referencing the Erg, Unerg, and the DO). Third, e' must occur as a prefix in tensed predications (when cross-referencing the Erg, Unerg, and DO, if phonological conditions are met). These facts make it difficult to argue that e' and eb are Set B affixes, and clearly point to a number distinction. If one were to argue that e' and eb are Set B affixes, despite the fact that they cross-reference Ergatives, the explanation would be quite complex, for there is no practical way to distinguish and predict their occurence. Based on morphology one could argue that there is a morphological distinction that eb be used in tenseless clauses, and e' in tensed, but such an analysis fails to predict that eb can cross-reference the final DO in tensed clauses. Based on grammatical relation, there is no argument because e' cross-references both Absolutives and Ergatives, and eb cross-references both Absolutives and Ergatives. Phonologically, there is also no argument. Notice, for example, that only in tensed transitive clauses is the phonological conditioning operative. That is, while e' may not occur before vowels when cross-referencing the DO of a tensed clause, it can, and must, occur before vowels in a tensed intransitive clause, as in:

(50)a. X - e' -(h)ilanc.
tns-p - rest 'They rested.'

b. Qu- e' -alina.
tns-p -run 'They ran away.'

c. Inc'a' nequ- e' -abin chi cü -u .
not tns- p -listen at my- face
'They don't listen to me.'

(51)a.* X - eb -(h)ilanc.

b.* Qu- eb - alina.

c.* Inc'a' nequ-eb-abin chi cü-u.

Hence, it is a combination of these three factors (i.e. grammatical relation, phonology, and morphology) which govern the use of e'/eb. The use of these allomorphs is broken down by (nuclear term) grammatical relation in (52).

(52) Distribution of e'/eb:

a. In tenseless clauses eb is determined by the nominal that heads a final Unerg arc (ixk-eb 'they are women'). In tensed clauses e' is used (x-e'-alina 'they ran').

b. In tenseless clauses eb is determined by the nominal that heads a final Erg arc (r-il-om-eb 'they have seen him'). In tensed clauses e' is used (x -in-e'x-tenk'a 'they helped me').

c. In tenseless clauses eb is determined by the nominal that heads a final DO arc (cu-il-om-eb 'I have seen them'). In tensed clauses e' may not be used if the Set A affix is vowel initial (* x-e'-acu-il 'you saw them', x-e'-cu-il 'I saw them'), elsewhere eb is used (x-eb-acu-il 'you saw them', x-acu-il-eb 'you saw them', x-eb-ka-tenk'a 'we helped them').

The principles for number agreement and number affix position are stated in (53) and (54).

(53) Number Agreement:
If e'/eb appears it must cross-reference a third plural nominal.

(54) Number Affix Position:[17]
The affix which is determined by the plural nominal is prefixed to the stem if the stem has a T/A/M prefix (cf § 1.3.1); otherwise, it is suffixed to the stem.

Number agreement is subject to the following constraint:

(55) Condition on 3rd plural DO Marking:
In a tensed transitive clause, if the subject is 3rd person and the DO is 3rd person plural (and the 3rd plural DO is cross-referenced), then eb must suffix, otherwise eb may prefix or suffix.

The statements in (53) and (54) interact with the phonological rules in (48) and (49). These phonological rules account for the occurence of e' as a marker of a DO in a tensed transitive clause, as already mentioned. However, these rules provide another explanation. They account for the occurence of e'x and e'r (i.e. eb + x $\longrightarrow$ e'x , and eb + r $\longrightarrow$ e'r), which had been previously analyzed as Ergative 3rd plural morphemes. That is, if eb occurs before the 3rd person Set A affix x/r, the environment for (48) is met and the rule must apply. (Recall the ungrammaticality of the phrases in (42b) and (43b).) The strong claim that is being made here is that e'/eb is an independent plural morpheme. The sequence r ... eb, or x...eb which is used to cross-reference 3rd plural Ergative NPs in tenseless transitive clauses (§ 1.6.2) and 3rd plural possessors of a relational noun (§ 1.4.1) is not a 'discontinuous' morpheme: r/x cross-reference person and are Set A markers. The Set A markers have two functions: they cross-reference the nominal heading the final Erg arc (see (9)), and they cross-reference the possessor in a possessive construction (see (24)). Eb cross-references number and is not a Set A marker, or a Set B marker. When eb is prefixed in tensed transitive clauses, the phonological rules in (48) and (49) will apply if the condition is met. While it may be the case that, in present day K'ekchi, e'x and e'r have been reanalyzed to signify an Ergative 3rd plural morpheme, the claim that is being made is that e'x and e'r are bimorphemic (p + A3).

Chapter 1 Footnotes

1. Abbreviations which appear in the K'ekchi sentence gloss are given in the List of Abbreviations. References to the examples are either in the form (author, year: page), (author, reference: page) or (author, reference. sentence number). Abbreviations which appear in the references to the examples include: B- Ava Berinstein, E&C- Francis Eachus and Ruth Carlson, F- Ray Freeze, H- Esteban Haeserijn, S- Guillermo Sedat, D- dictionary, G- Guia, and Gr- grammar. Unmarked examples are based on my fieldwork. Other examples are based on eighteen unpublished stories that I collected. These stories are cited by story number. Thus, the example corresponding to (B,S2.8) occurs in the eighth sentence of the second story.

The stories cited in the E&C references may be found in Eachus and Carlson (1971), however some of the K'ekchi texts are unpublished. The abbreviations for the E&C story references include C - How the Coconut Got its Marks, GG - The Ghost and the Guitar, J - The Jasmine Flower, KK - According to our Ancestors, MSS - The Marriage of the Sun and the Moon, O - Planting Quequesque, P - The Woodpecker, PGC - A Pilgrimage to the God Chajul, V - The Traveler, VGM - A Visit with the God of the Mountain, XH - The Phantom of the River.

The abbreviations corresponding to the story references found in Freeze (1976b) are LJ - Lazy John, and YB - The Two Young Bachelors.

2. The distinction between immediate preverbal (focus) position and clause initial (topic) position is made explicit in Chapter 3.

3. Pinkerton (1976b) suggests that OVS is not a permissible word order. Our conclusions concerning word order differ. There are text examples of OVS word order which suggest not only that it is permissible, but also that there are two sources for it: one in which the DO is Topic and another in which it is Focus.

4. See footnote 2.

5. Since the third singular Absolutive form is null (Ø), the only time ambiguity may result from Pro-Drop is if both the Subject and the Direct Object are third singular NPs and one, or both drop. There is no ambiguity if the clause is detransitivized, or contextualized within a discourse.

6. Table 1 is distinct from the 'traditional' representation of the Set A and B markers by previous researchers in Mayan (Kaufman 1976a), and specifically K'ekchi (Pinkerton 1976b, Stewart 1980, Haeserijn 1966), who analyze *e'/eb* as 3rd plural Set B forms and *e'x* and *e'r* as 3rd plural Set A forms. This representation of the Set A and B forms is given in Chart 1, below.

Chart 1: Set A and B Verbal Forms ('traditional' schema)

	Set A		Set B
	___/C	___/V	
s. 1	in	cu/incu	in
2	*a*	*a*cu	at
3	x	r	Ø
p. 1	ka	k	*o*
2	*e*	*e*r	ex
3	e'x	e'r	{ e' / eb }

Three peculiarities should be pointed out with respect to this chart:

1. The phonological similarity that holds between the third singular forms and the third plural Set A forms does *not* hold between the first singular and first plural forms, or the second singular and second plural forms.

2. The morpheme *e'* marks third plural in all sets (i.e. in Set A and B).

3. There are two third plural Set B affixes: *e'* and *eb* which appear to be in complementary distribution.

I have argued elsewhere (Berinstein 1981) that *e'/eb* is an independent plural morpheme and that *e'x* and *e'r* are bimorphemic.

7. The Set B affix occurs as a prefix only in clauses with an overt tense or aspect prefix. (The T/A prefixes are discussed in § 1.3.) Historically, the Set B markers were clitics which occurred in second position. Hence, they ended up *after* stems which had no tense prefix and *before* stems which did have a tense prefix. For this reason, the Set B affix is described as a 'suffix' to the tense marker (by Mayanists) and thus the unusual terminology.

8. If e'x and e'r are Set A forms, as is suggested by proponents of Chart 1 (see footnote 6) then they should be able to prefix to possessed nouns to cross-reference the plural possessor as other Set A affixes do; however, they cannot (* e'r-ak 'their pig'). Therefore, proponents of Chart 1 must posit a distinct representation for Set A verbal and nominal forms. The representation that has been proposed is given in Chart 2, below.

Chart 2: Set A Nominal Forms ('traditional' schema)

		____/C	____/V
s.	1	in	cu/incu
	2	a	acu
	3	x	r
p.	1	ka	k
	2	e	er
	3	x...eb	r...eb

In addition to the unnecessary redundancy between Charts 1 and 2, several facts remain unexplained. First, if e' and eb are Set B verbal forms, as indicated in Chart 1, why does eb occur as a discontinuous morpheme with a Set A affix in Chart 2? I.e. why does eb cross-reference 3rd plural possessors of a noun? Second, if e'x and e'r are Set A affixes, why can't they prefix to the possessed noun to cross-reference the 3rd plural possessor? Furthermore, as discussed in § 1.6.2, to cross-reference the 3rd plural Ergative NP in a tenseless transitive clause, r-/x- must prefix to the verb stem and eb must suffix. This raises two more questions; namely, why does eb cross-reference a 3rd plural Ergative NP if it is a Set B verbal form, and why can't e'x or e'r be used?

These problems arise because e' and eb are analyzed as Set B forms in Chart 1 and eb is also analyzed as a Set A form in Chart 2. These problems do not arise in my analysis since e'/eb is analyzed as an independent plural marker which may cross-reference third plural terms and non-terms.

9. One glance at Table III reveals the many phonological rules that are relevant to the morphological description of the tense/aspect prefixes. For example, the form of the prefix, given as n(a(c))- in (12a), is subject to a vowel harmony rule that is conditioned by the adjacent vowel. Basically, the quality of the vowel in the tense prefix is conditioned by the quality of the vowel in the Set B affix, unless Set B is third singular (Ø) in which case the prefix vowel is conditioned by the vowel in the Set A affix. The particular details of this phonological rule, or any other, i.e. the rule that determines the presence/absence of the

velar consonant associated with the prefix in (12a), or the vowel assimilation associated with the final vowel of the prefixes given in (12c, d, e, f) are not given here and have no bearing on the analyses presented in later sections.

10. There is an exception to the aspect marking principle: the irregular verb xic 'go' is suppletive in the past tense (co 'went') and -k cannot indicate incompletive aspect in the 'future' t(v)- or 'potential' ch(v)- tense/aspects. Thus, to say 'you will go' the form is t-at-xic, and the predicted form t-at-xik is ungrammatical. Another irregularity associated with this stem is that xic allows -ak to suffix in the subjunctive, as: xic-ak-at and ch-at-xic-ak. As far as I know, this is the only intransitive stem that allows a T/A/M prefix and -ak suffixation.

11. It is well known that in K'ekchi, as in most Mayan languages, there is a rule of h-deletion. For example, in the Coban dialect of K'ekchi, one hypothesized source of vowel length is due to intervocalic h-deletion in CVhVC roots. Thus, Coban bec 'walk' with h-loss, contrasts with Cahabon **behec** 'walk' without h-loss. Whether the h is analyzed as the final consonant of the stem in verbs like bicha(h) 'sing' (in 19), or as the initial consonant of the T/A suffix -(h)ak is not relevant to the generalization because regardless of the segmentation, if -k were an allomorph of -ak, we would expect a realization of h when -k is suffixed to finally intransitive stems that are 'seemingly vowel final'. But as exemplified in (16a) the form of the verb is **tatalinak** not: * **tatalinahak** , and as exemplified in (17a), the form of the verb is **chatalinak** , not: * **chatalinahak** .

12. The final vowel of the preposition chi assimilates to the adjacent vowel. This will occur with all Set A affixes which are vowel initial. For example: chi + in --> chin, chi + a --> cha, chi + e --> che.

13. 1-chômeurs and 3-chômeurs are also expressed in a relational noun. In fact, with one exception- 2-chômeurs- all non-nuclear R-signs are presented as possessors of a relational noun.

14. Pinkerton (1976b:55) claims that there are three possible orders for the affixation of the person pronouns to the verb stem.

> "Each of the three columns to the right of the gloss list the affixed morphemes (tense, subject, object) and the verb in a certain order. The variation Flora exhibited during elicitation is given. The page, then, reads as follows: "

GLOSS	tns-obj-subj-vb	tns-subj-vb-obj	tns-obj-subj-vb-obj
I washed you.	šatinč'ax	*šinč'axat	*šatinč'axat
I washed you (pl).	šesinč'ax	*šinč'axes	*šešinč'axes
I washed them.	šeb'inč'ax	šinč'axep	*šeb'inč'axep
You washed me.	šina:č'ax	*ša:č'axin	*šina:č'axin
You washed us.	šo:a:č'ax	*ša:č'axo:	*šina:č'axo:
You washed them.	šeb'a:c'ax	ša:č'axep	*šeb'a:č'axep
He/she washed me.	šinixč'ax	*šč'axin	*šinišč'axin
He/she washed you.	šatixč'ax	*šč'axat	*šatišč'axat
He/she washed us.	šo:šč'ax	*šč'axo:	*šo:šč'axo:
⋮	⋮	⋮	⋮

The asterisks in Pinkerton's pronominal paradigm above, are mine and indicate that I have not been able to duplicate these findings. As far as I know, there are no instances in which an Absolutive marker may prefix *and* suffix to a verb in K'ekchi (as in column 3), and an Absolutive form may *not* suffix to a verb stem that is affixed with a T/A/M prefix (as in column 2) (see § 1.3.1). The forms in column 1 are correct. It is unfortunate that other linguists have cited this data when describing the K'ekchi pronominal system (Stewart 1980:31).

An explanation for the fact that *eb* may suffix in tensed transitive clauses, while Absolutive markers cannot, follows from an analysis of *eb* as an independent plural morpheme. It should be noted therefore, that the historical origin of *eb* as a numeral classifier (Robertson 1976), as well as plural agreement in other Mayan languages (specifically those languages which cross-reference 3rd plural referents with *eb*, as Jacaltec, Chuj, Kanjobal, and Tojolobal) further support the conclusion that *eb* be analyzed as an independent plural marker (for details see Berinstein 1981).

15. The fact that *eb* may occur as a pre NP quantifier, as in (1) below (or (47) in the text), argues again, that *eb* is an independent morpheme, and not a Set B form.

(1)a. li cuink 'the man'

b. eb li cuink 'the men'

This is another argument for the distinction between person and number agreement in K'ekchi (and Mayan).

It should be noted that in sentences like (2) below, *eb*

could be analyzed as either a pre NP quantifier, or as a verbal suffix. I have suggested elsewhere (Berinstein 1981) that eb was 'originally' a pre NP quantifier that was reanalyzed as a verbal suffix by virtue of its position and perhaps by analogy with Set B affixes which can occur 'after' stems that lack a T/A/M prefix.

(2) X - in- ch'aj eb li coc'al.
rec-A1- wash p the children
'I washed the children.'

16. One last point should be mentioned. Two 3rd plural referents cannot be marked in a tenseless intransitive clause (* r-il-om-eb-eb (A3-see-perf-p -p)), nor can two 3rd plural referents be marked in a tensed transitive clause (* qu-eb-e'x-tenk'a (Tns- p -p A3-help)). The underlying principle that accounts for this is that since there is only one plural marker (e'/eb), two plural referents can't be marked by it. In some sense this is correct. But, there is one exception: Two 3rd plural (nuclear term) referents may be cross-referenced in a tensed transitive clause if eb occurs either as a suffix, or as I have suggested, as a pre NP quantifier (see footnote 15). For example,

(1)a. T - e'x -cuy (-)eb li coc'al
fut-p A3-forgive p the children
'They'll forgive the children.' (B,S2.46)

These facts are consistent with the condition given in (38) which predicts that eb will suffix if the subject is 3rd person (cf examples (42) and (43)).

17. E'/eb may cross-reference terms (IOs) (see Berinstein 1984b) and nonterms (Ablatives and Benefactives) (see Berinstein 1981) in verbal and nominal expressions, in addition to cross-referencing final nuclear terms (Subjects and Direct Objects) in verbal expressions. I am claiming that the principle that predicts the affix position in all of these instances, is stated in (54). This is an additional argument for treating e'/eb as an independent plural marker and not as a Set B form. Since clearly, if e'/ eb were a Set B (or Set A) form there would be no explanation for the fact that it can cross-reference 3rd plural terms and 3rd plural nonterms.

Chapter 2

PASSIVE

2.0 Introduction

The purpose of this chapter is to describe Passive and to discuss the interaction of Passive with focus.[1]

In K'ekchi, the initial DO of a transitive clause may be the final Subject of an (intransitive) Passive clause. Passive verbs are marked either by the suffix -e' or by final vowel lengthening. The rules which determine passive marking will be given shortly. In passive clauses, the initial subject/final chômeur is optional and is marked by -ban, a relational noun stem (derived from the verb 'do' banunc). The Set A pronominal affixes are prefixed to the relational noun and cross-reference the demoted subject. Thus, 1 chômeurs function as possessors of a relational noun- the properties of which were described in Chapter 1, §1.4.1.

Some active-passive pairs are presented in (1)-(5) below. In examples (3b) and (4b) passive is marked by final vowel length, not a distinct suffix (as -e'). The gloss reflects this difference by using an equal (=) sign to indicate that the stem is a passive one.

```
1)a.  X - eb-a - sac'  r- iq'uin li  pec.
      tns-p -A2-hit   A3 -with   the rock
      'You hit them with the rock.'

  b.  Ha'aneb  x - e' -saq'u- e'   r-iq'uin li pec ( a-ban).
      they     tns- p - hit  -pass  A3-with  the rock A2-by
      'They were hit with the rock (by you).'

2)a.  Qui- Ø -x- q'ue  li maton   r -e   lix Mar.
      tns-B3 -A3-give the present A3-Dat ncl Mar
      'He gave the present to Mary.'
```

b. Li matan **qui- Ø -q'ue- e'** r- e lix Mar x-ban li
the present tns-B3-give -pass A3-Dat ncl Mar A3-by the

cuink.
man
'The present was given to Mary by the man.'

3)a. Ti -Ø - x -puba.
tns-B3-A3 -shoot 'Someone will shoot him.'

b. Qui- Ø- r-abi li cuink a'an nak **ta- Ø-puba -k** .
tns-B3-A3-hear the man that that tns-B3-shoot=pass-asp
'That man heard that he would be shot.' (E&C,J.129)

4)a. Ti -Ø- x- camsi.
tns-B3-A3-kill 'Someone will kill her.'

b. Cui **ta-Ø- camsi -k** pero ta -Ø-yo'la- k cui'chic
if tns-B3- kill=pass-asp but tns-B3-born-asp again

porque cuan- Ø li ch'ina jasmin aran r -e lix yu'am.
because exist-B3 the little jasmine there A3-Dat her life
'If she is killed, she will be born again beacuse there is the little jasmine there for her life.' (E&C,J.165)

5)a. T - Ø -in- lok' li caxlan (lain).
tns-B3-A1- buy the chicken I
'I will buy the chicken.'

b. **Ta- Ø - lok'- e'- k** li caxlan (in-ban).
tns-B3- buy -pass asp the chicken A1-by
'The chicken will be bought (by me).'

The properties of this construction which must be accounted for are:

i) form of verb stem: The verb is suffixed with e' in (1b), (2b), and (5b) and it is not in (1a), (2a), or (5a). The final vowel is lengthened in (3b), and (4b) and it is not in (3a) or (4a).

ii) verbal agreement: The verb is affixed with a Set A and a Set B form in (2a)-(5a), but the verb is affixed with only a Set B form in (2b)-(5b).

iii) number agreement: The plural marker is determined by the nominal that heads a final 2-arc in (1a), but by the nominal that heads a final 1-arc in (1b).

iv) aspect: There is an aspectual suffix -k on the verb in the future t(v)- tense in (3b), (4b), and (5b), but there is no such suffix in (3a), (4a), or (5a).

v) case: The 'agent' is presented as an oblique (i.e. as possessor of a relational noun) in (1b), (2b), and (5b), but with no marking in (1a), (2a), and (5a).

Relational Grammar offers two concepts that provide the key to understanding this construction and its properties: a) the notion of advancement and b) the chômeur relation. These two, taken together, provide an understanding of this construction. Other necessary elements of the proposal are the definitions of 'transitive stratum', 'intransitive stratum', 'ergative', and 'asolutive', which were discussed in the Preface (§ 0.4.2).

In an advancement, a nominal bearing a GR at the c_i level, bears a GR that is higher on the relational hierarchy (1 > 2 > 3 > non-terms) at the c_{i+1} level. The universal characterization of passive by Perlmutter and Postal (1977) is said to contain the following sub-network:

6)

That is, a nominal heading a 2-arc in the c_i stratum (where the c_i stratum is a transitive stratum), heads a 1-arc in the c_{i+1} stratum. This is also referred to as a revaluation. A revaluation is any instance where some nominal heads a GR_x-arc in one stratum and a GR_y-arc in the next. If the GR_y-arc is higher on the relational hierarchy, the revaluation is said to be an advancement. If the GR_y-arc is lower on the relational hierarchy, the revaluation is said to be a demotion. The two strata that contain a revaluation are called the departure stratum and the arrival stratum, respectively.

Another principle of clause structure that is central to RG is the Stratal Uniqueness Law. This principle claims that no stratum can contain two arcs labelled with the same term R-sign. This law is stated formally in (7) and interacts with the Chômeur Condition, presented in (8).

7) Stratal Uniqueness Law:
Let '$Term_x$' be a variable over the class of Term R-signs, that is, '1', '2', or '3'. Then: If arcs A and B are both members of the c_kth stratum (b) and A and B are both $Term_x$ arcs, then A=B.

8) Chômeur Condition:
If some nominal a, bears a given term relation in stratum c_k, and some other nominal b, bears the same term relation in the following stratum c_{k+1}, then a bears the Chô relation in c_{k+1}.

Given the Stratal Uniqueness Law together with the Chômeur Condition, we can predict that the nominal that heads the initial 1-arc of a transitive clause will head a final Chô-arc in the corresponding Passive clause. This is exemplified in the RNs in (9a,b) below which are associated with the active and passive clauses in (5a,b).

9)a.

lok'   li caxlan   lain
buy   the chicken   I

b.

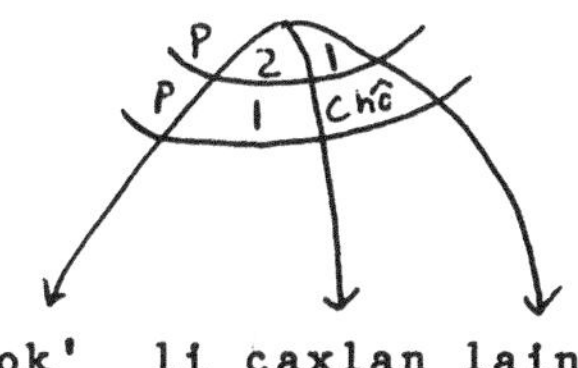

lok'   li caxlan   lain
buy   the chicken   I

The RN in (9a) represents the active transitive clause in (5a), and the RN in (9b) represents the passive clause in (5b). They are distinct in that the RN associated with (5a) is a single clause structure which has a final <u>transitive</u> stratum, while the RN associated with (5b) is a multi-level structure which has a final <u>intransitive</u> stratum. As predicted by the Chômeur Condition, <u>lain</u> must head a final Chô-arc. Were <u>lain</u> to head a final 1-arc, it would be in violation of Stratal Uniqueness.

I will now show how a passive analysis accounts for the morphological and grammatical properties of the construction outlined in (i)-(v) above. In § 2.1 arguments will be given for the final intransitivity of a passive clause. In § 2.2 it is argued that the initial DO of a transitive clause is subject of a corresponding passive. In § 2.3 it is argued that the initial subject of a transitive clause is final chômeur of a corresponding passive.

2.1 Evidence for Final Intransitivity

The rules for verbal agreement, passive marking, and aspect provide evidence for the final intransitivity of a passive clause.

2.1.1 Verbal Agreement

The point of this section is to show that a passive analysis of the b) sentences in (1)-(5) will provide an explanation for the differences in agreement exemplified in the active-passive pairs.

As previously discussed (Chapter 1, § 1.2), the verb must agree with the final subject and DO, if there is one. The subject of a transitive clause is cross-referenced by a Set A (ergative) marker, and the subject of an intransitive clause and the DO of a transitive clause is cross-referenced by a Set B (absolutive) marker. These rules are repeated below:

(10) <u>Verbal Agreement</u>:

(i) A nominal heading a final Erg arc determines Erg agreement in the verb.

(ii) A nominal heading a final Abs arc determines Abs agreement in the verb.

Like other intransitive clauses, the passive verbs take only one set of agreement affixes: the absolutive Set B. The lack of a Set A affix attests to the final intransitivity of these clauses. This follows from a rule of passive which advances a DO to subject. The resulting verb, lacking a DO, is intransitive and cross-references the final subject with a Set B affix.

2.1.2 Passive Marking

In this section, I propose a rule for passive marking which will account for the differences in form of verb stem between the active and passive pairs in the a) and b) sentences in (1)-(5).

The rule for passive morphology is complicated by the fact that there are two passive reflexes: the suffix -<u>e'</u>, and final vowel length. The verb takes -<u>e'</u> if it is a base CV(C) monosyllabic stem. If the verb is not monosyllabic, the final vowel is lengthened. This rule is stated in (11).

(11) <u>Passive Marking</u>:
If a nominal <u>a</u> heads an initial 2-arc with tail b and coordinate c_k (where c_k is a transitive stratum) and a non-initial 1-arc with tail b and coordinate c_{k+1}, then if the verb of b is monosyllabic, <u>e'</u> is suffixed, and if the verb of b is not monosyllabic, the final vowel of the stem is lengthened.

That -<u>e'</u> is suffixed to the verb in (1b), (2b), and (5b), but is not suffixed in (1a), (2a), or (5a), and that the final vowel is lengthened in (3b) and (4b), but is not in (3a) and (4a) follows from the Passive Marking rule in (11). That is, the (a) sentences in (1)-(5) do not involve a transition of 2 to 1 from a transitive stratum, whereas the (b) sentences do.

2.1.3 Aspect

In this section, I propose a rule of Intransitive/aspect marking which accounts for the fact that only the (b) sentences, and not the (a) sentences, are marked for incompletive aspect.

In K'ekchi, clauses with final intransitive strata must be marked for incompletive aspect if the verb is affixed with either a t(v)- 'future' or ch(v)- 'subjunctive/imperative' T/A/M prefix (see Chapter 1, §1.3).

12)a. Mare t - o - t'ane' - k.
maybe fut-B1p-fall -asp
'Maybe we will fall.'[2] (E&C,P.18)

b.* Mare t - o - t'ane'.

13)a. Ch -in -hilan - k sa' cu-ochoch.
A/M-B1- rest -asp in my-house
'That I may rest in my house.'[3] (E&C,Gr.149)

b.* Ch -in -hilan sa' cu-ochoch.

Clauses with final transitive strata are not marked for incompletive aspect when the verb is affixed with t(v)- or ch(v)- T/A/M prefixes.

14)a.* T - at-in- ch'ila - k.
fut-B2-A1- scold -asp
('I will scold you.')

b.* T - o - x - camsi - k.
fut-B1p-A3- kill - asp
('He will kill us.')

c.* T - Ø -in -c'am - k chak li si'.
fut-B3-A1- bring-asp dir the firewood
('I will bring the firewood.')

d.* Ta - Ø -ka- col - k.
fut-B3- A1p-save-asp
('We will save him.')

e.* Ch -at- r -osobtesi - k li yucua'.
A/M-B2-A3- bless -asp the father
('May the father bless you.')

The transitive clauses in (14a)-(14e) are ungrammatical with the aspectual suffix, but the (corresponding) passive clauses in (15a)-(15e) require it. This supports our hypothesis that -k marks incompletive aspect in finally intransitive clauses and that passive clauses are finally intransitive.

15)a. **T** - at - ch'ila - **k.**
fut-B2- scold =pass-asp
'You will be scolded.'

b. T - o - camsi - k.
fut-B1p-kill= pass-asp
'We will be killed.'

c. Ta -c'am - e' - k chak x-ban jun li cu-amigo
fut-bring-pass-asp dir A3-by one the my-friend

chi cu-il -bal cuulaj.
prep A1-see-nom tomorrow (E&C,Gr.283)
'She will be brought by my friend to see me tomorrow.'

d. T - Ø -in- yal cui'chic li coc' pim a'in re
fut-B3-A1-try again the small bush this in order

r -il - bal ma ta - Ø - col -e' - k.
A3-see-nom if tns-B3 -save-pass-asp (B,S1.6:90)
'I will try this small bush again to see if he will be saved.'

e. Ch -at -osobtesi - k x-ban li yucua'.
fut-B2- bless =pass-asp A3-by the father
'May you be blessed by the father.'

In finally intransitive clauses in other tense/aspects (as n(v)(C)- 'present/habitual', x- 'recent past', c-/qu(v)- 'remote past', or m(v)- 'negative'), the suffix -c must occur if it is preceded by a vowel.[4] For example:

16)a. Noc - o - alina c.
p - B1p- run 'We run.' (E&C,Gr.26)

b. X - o - alina c.
rec-B1p-run 'We ran.' (E&C,Gr.3)

c. C - o - atina c. 'We spoke.' (E&C,Gr.21)
pst-B1p-speak

d. M - at-c'oxla c chi k-ix.
neg A/M -B2-worry on-our-back
'Don't (you) worry about us.' (E&C,Gr.179)

If the verb stem ends in a nasal or liquid, -c is optional; again, as long as the clause is finally intransitive, as:

17)a. X - Ø - chal(c).
rec-B3- arrive 'He arrived.'

b. Na - Ø - cuar(c).
p -B3- sleep 'He sleeps.'

c. Qu -in- hilan.
pst-B1- rest 'I rested.'

c'. Qu - in - hilan c. 'I rested.'[5]

If the clause is finally transitive -c may not suffix to the verb, as exemplified in (18).

18)a.* Qui -Ø -k - elk'a - c.
pst-B3-A1p-steal - asp
('We stole it.')

b.* Qu -in - r- osobtesi - c li yucua'.
pst-B1- A3- bless -asp the father
('The father blessed me.')

Even though -c may not suffix to the transitive verb in (18), -c must suffix to the passive verb in (19). This follows from a passive analysis and a rule that only permits -c to occur in finally intransitive clauses.

19)a. Inc'a' na- Ø - x -nau nak li kana' Sakq'uim
not p -B3-A3-know that the miss Sakq'uim

qui - Ø - elk'a c x-ban li maus laj Quismes.
pst -B3- steal =pass-asp A3-by the evil ncl Quismes
'He didn't know that Miss Sakq'uim was stolen by the evil Quismes.' (B,S7.33)

b. Qu - in -osobtesi - c x-ban li yucua'.
pst- B1 -bless= pass-asp A3-by the father
'I was blessed by the father.'

As mentioned earlier, -c is only obligatory if preceded by a vowel. It should be noted, therefore, that -c does not suffix to passive verbs marked with -e' [eʔ].[6]

20)a.* X - in - ch'aj - e' - c.
rec-B1 - wash -pass-asp ('I was washed.')

b. X -in - ch'aj- e'.
rec-B1 - wash -pass 'I was washed.'

The aspectual evidence has provided two arguments for the final intransitivity of passive clauses. First, it was shown that the incompletive aspect marker -k must suffix to intransitive verbs if the verb is affixed with either t(v)- 'future' or ch(v)- 'optative' prefixes, and that -k may not suffix to transitive verbs. Like other intransitive verbs, -k must suffix to passive verbs (with -e' or final vowel lengthening) if the verb is prefixed with either t(v)- or ch(v)-. Second, it was shown that -c may suffix to intransitive verbs in non-future tense/aspects if the stem is vowel-final, and that -c may not suffix to transitive verbs. Like other intransitive verbs, -c must suffix to passive verbs that are marked by final vowel length in non-future tense/ aspects.

Subject to conditions which are not understood, -c may suffix to finally intransitive stems when tenseless. For instance, -c must suffix to all finally intransitive infinitives (whether or not it is preceded by a vowel or a consonant). Given this, it is more appropriate to analyze -c as marker of 'final intransitivity' which marks non-incompletive aspect by default. For this reason, -k, but not -c, is treated as an aspectual suffix in the intransitive/aspect marking rule presented in (22).[7]

(22) Intransitive/Aspect Marking:
If the final stratum is intransitive -k is suffixed to the verb stem in incompletive aspect, otherwise -c may suffix to the stem.

In addition to the rule in (22), the grammar will require a phonological rule that conditions the optionality of the -c suffix when preceded by a consonant in a 'tensed' clause.

The rule in (22) provides an explanation for the fact that in the active-passive pairs in (3)-(5) only the (b) sentences allow an aspectual suffix and the (a) sentences do not. This follows from the fact that the final stratum of the (b) sentences is intransitive while the final stratum of the (a) sentences is not. Central to this explanation is my claim that the (b) sentences involve an advancement of DO to Subject; consequently, the final stratum is intransitive.

2.2 Initial DO is Final Subject

2.2.1 Number Agreement

The most crucial evidence for the advancement of DO to subject are the agreement facts. As predicted by the verbal agreement rules (see § 2.1.1), the final 1 of an intransitive stratum determines Absolutive Set B agreement in the verb. By itself this is not evidence, since a final DO also determines Set B agreement. However, in the third person plural the affixes which cross-reference a final Unerg and a final DO differ and only the affix which cross-references a final Unerg can be used in passive clauses. It is argued that the difference in the form of the plural marker- e' versus eb - in active and passive clauses, as in (1a,b), follows from an analysis in which an initial DO advances to subject.

The distribution of e' and eb in tensed and tenseless transitive and intransitive clauses, and the rules for number agreement and number affix position were discussed in Chapter 1 (§ 1.6) and are repeated below for convenience.

(25) Distribution of e'/eb:

a. In tenseless clauses eb is determined by the nominal that heads a final Unerg arc (ixk-eb 'they are women'). In tensed clauses e' is used (x-e'-alina 'they ran').

b. In tenseless clauses _eb_ is determined by the nominal that heads a final Erg arc (_r-il-om-eb_ 'they have seen him'). In tensed clauses _e'_ is used (_x -in-e'x-tenk'a_ 'they helped me').

c. In tenseless clauses _eb_ is determined by the nominal that heads a final DO arc (cu-il-om-eb 'I have seen them'). In tensed clauses _e'_ may not be used if the Set A affix is vowel initial (* _x-e'-acu-il_ 'you saw them', _x-e'-cu-il_ 'I saw them'), elsewhere _eb_ is used (_x-eb-acu-il_ 'you saw them', _x-acu-il-eb_ 'you saw them', _x-eb-ka-tenk'a_ 'we helped them').

The principles for number agreement and affix position are stated in (26) and (27).

(26) _Number Agreement:_
If _e'_/_eb_ appears it must cross-reference a third plural nominal.

(27) _Number Affix Position:_
The affix which is determined by the plural nominal is prefixed to the stem if the stem has a T/A/M prefix; otherwise, it is suffixed to the stem.

In Passive clauses, number agreement is determined by a nominal that heads a final Unerg arc and _not_ a final 2-arc. As exemplified in (1a), _eb_ must cross-reference the DO of the transitive clause and _e'_ cannot be used. This follows from (25c). In contrast, _e'_ must cross-reference the subject of the passive clause in (1b) and _eb_ cannot be used. This follows from (25a). Thus, a passive analysis together with the principles of number agreement in (26) and (27) provide an explanation for the use of _eb_ versus _e'_ in active and passive clauses.[8]

2.3 Initial Subject is Final Chômeur

2.3.1 Verbal Agreement

The nominal corresponding to the 'agent' controls verbal agreement in the (a) sentences of (1)-(5), but it does not control agreement in the (b) sentences.

A passive analysis and the Chômeur Condition provide an explanation for this fact: The 'agent' is the initial 1 and final 1 in the (a) sentences. It controls agreement because agreement is with the final subject of the clause. The 'agent' is the initial 1 and final chômeur of the (b) sentences. It does not control agreement because chômeurs do not trigger agreement.

2.3.2 Case

In (28a) below, the nominal corresponding to the 'agent' of the clause is an unmarked NP. By this, it is meant that it bears no case markers, is not introduced by a preposition, and is not a possessor of a relational noun. In (28b), the nominal corresponding to the 'agent' of the clause is presented as possessor of the relational noun -ban. The difference in nominal case of the agent phrase in (28a,b) follows from a passive analysis and the case marking principle given in (29).

28)a. Ti- Ø - x - yoc' li che' laj Lu' .
tns-B3-A3- cut the tree ncl Lu'
'Pedro will cut the tree.'

b. Li che' t<u>a</u> - Ø - yoc' - e' x-ban laj Lu' .
the tree tns-B3 - cut - pass A3- by ncl Lu'
'The tree will be cut by Pedro.'

29) <u>Case Marking</u>: [9]
(i) Final nuclear terms are unmarked.

(ii) All other grammatical relations are presented as possessors of a relational noun.

That the nominal corresponding to the agent phrase in (28a) is unmarked follows from the fact that it is a final 1 and final nuclear terms are unmarked, as stated in (29i). That the nominal corresponding to the agent phrase in (28b) is presented as an oblique follows from the fact that it is a final chômeur and non-nuclear terms are presented as possessors of a relational noun, as stated in (29ii).

2.3.3 Topic/Focus

In this section, additional evidence that the initial 1 is a final chômeur is presented.

There are topics and foci in K'ekchi that both occur before the verb. This will be discussed in Chapter 3. What will be established here is that passive subjects may occur in a preposed position while 1-chômeurs cannot. I argue that this follows from a general constraint that prohibits chômeur extraction in K'ekchi.

First notice that the final 1 and the final chômeur may occur in post verbal position, as in:

30)a. X - e'- saq'u - e' in-ban.
tns-p - hit -pass A1-by
'They were hit by me.'

b. X - e' - saq'u - e' ha'aneb.
tns-p - hit -pass they
'They were hit.'

Only the final 1, however, may occur in preverbal position:

31)a.* **In-ban** x - e'- saq'u- e'.
A1-by tns-p - hit -pass
('By me they were hit.')

b. **Ha'aneb** x - e' -saq'u- e'.
they tns-p - hit -pass
'They were hit.'

The constraint proposed to predict the ungrammaticality of clauses like (31a) is presented in (32).

32) Chômeur Constraint:
A chômeur cannot head an overlay arc.

Since Top, Foc, and Rel are overlay relations and all appear in a preverbal position, (32) predicts the inability of chômeur extraction, in general.

As just mentioned, both the topic position and the focus position are preverbal, so without a context, if only one NP is preposed, it is often difficult to tell whether it is Topic or Focus. It turns out that passive clauses are frequently S-V because the subject is being focused. Some examples follow.

33) Yaljun nak li so'so'l qui- Ø-chap-e' cui'chic
suddenly the buzzard tns-B3-grab-pass again

chi x -jolom. (B,S1.57)
on his-head
'Suddenly, the buzzard was grabbed again on his head.'

34) **A'an** raj qui- Ø -chap-e' x- ban li so'sol ut
he prt tns-B3- grab-pass A3-by the buzzard and

qui- Ø - nuk' - e'. (B,S1.70)
tns-B3-swallow-pass
'He (the snake) was grabbed by the buzzard and was swallowed.'

In (33) and (34) above, the passive subjects li so'sol and a'an are focused and appear in the immediate preverbal focus position. Since topic position is S-initial, topic and focus are easily distinguished when two NPs are preposed. In (35a) below, the locative phrase occurs in S-initial position as Topic and the subject occurs in immediate preverbal position as Focus. Nuclear term extraction, as evidenced in (33) and (34), is unmarked.

35)a. [Sa' li cayil] [li ak] x - Ø -lok' -e' x-ban
in the market the pigs tns-B3-buy-pass A3-by
LOC TOPIC FOCUS

li ixk.
the woman
'In the market, the pigs were bought by the woman.'

Notice, however, that the subject chômeur may not occur in the preverbal position (as Topic or Focus). This is predicted by the Chômeur Constraint (32), and exemplified in (36).

36)a.* Sa' li cayil **x-ban li ixk** x - Ø-lok'-e'
in the market A3-by the woman tns-B3-buy-pass

li ak.
the pigs
('In the market, by the woman the pigs were bought.')

b.* **X-ban li ixk** x -Ø -lok'-e' li ak.
A3-by the woman tns-B3-buy-pass the pigs
('By the woman, the pigs were stolen.')

c.* **Li ixk** x - Ø -lok' - e' li ak **x- ban** .
the woman tns-B3-buy -pass the pigs A3-by (her)
('The pigs were bought by the woman.')

The reason the agent can't extract in (36) is because it heads a chô-arc, not because it is presented syntactically as a possessor of a relational noun, since other nonterms which are presented as possessors of a relational noun can extract and focus, as will be shown below.

In possessive constructions, a focused possessor may extract from the head noun. This is exemplified in (37).

In response to the question: 'Are all the children sick?'

37) Macua chixjunileb. **Li ch'ina xka'al** toj maji' na-Ø-
not all p the small girl not yet tns-B3-

ticla **li x-tik** .
begin the her-fever
'Not all of them. The smallest girl, her fever hasn't yet begun.' (E&C,Gr:197)

(37) can be compared to (38), where the possessor, li ch'ina xka'al, follows the head noun.

38) Toj maji' na-Ø -ticla **li x -tik li ch'ina xka'al** .
not yet tns-B3-begin the her-fever the small girl
'The smallest girl's fever hasn't yet begun.'

As in other possessive constructions, focused nonterm possessors may extract from the head (relational) noun. In (39) li kacua' Xucaneb is the focused Ablative possessor. The ablative relational noun stem is u (see Chapter 1 § 1.4.1).

39) **Li kacua' Xucaneb qu-Ø -e'x -elka li x -rabin**
the señor Xucaneb tns-B3-pA3-steal the his-daughter

chi r - u .
from-A3-Abl (B,S7.61)
'They stole Mr. Xucaneb's daughter from him.'

In contrast, the possessor of the 'agentive' relational noun stem -ban may not extract. Compare (36c) to (39). I argue that the reason li ixk in (36c) can not focus is because it is a 1-chômeur, and as predicted by (32), a chômeur may not head an overlay arc.

2.4 Summary

The properties of active and passive sentences were described. It was argued that an analysis of passive as an advancement of an initial DO to subject, together with the notion of chômeur and the Chômeur Condition could provide an explanation for the differences in verbal morphology, aspect marking, and verbal agreement in the active and passive pairs. Crucial to this analysis is the fact that active and passive sentences differ in 'transitivity'; the final stratum of the active being transitive and the final stratum of the passive being intransitive.

The number agreement principles (26) and (27) provided independent evidence that the initial 2 is a final 1, and the nominal case principle (29) provided independent evidence that the initial 1 is a 1-chômeur.

In addition, it was shown that frequent S-V word order in passive clauses is due to subject focus. In contrast, it was shown that the 'agent' in passive clauses was unable to focus. This followed from the constraint in (32) that 'a chômeur cannot head an overlay arc' and provided further evidence for a rule of passive and the Chômeur Condition.

Chapter 2 Footnotes

1. This analysis excludes the passive participle construction in K'ekchi since it does not involve an advancement of DO to Subject. The form of a passive participle is: trans. Vb + -bil + Set B. Since there is no T/A/M prefix, the Set B affix occurs as a suffix. Some examples follow.

1) Sac' - bil - at.
hit - part- B2 'You are hit.'

2) Li lok' -bil -Ø abono na-Ø -x -tenk'a ajcui'
the buy -part-B3 manure pr-B3-A3-help also
'The purchased manure also helps' (E&C,ACC:7)

Passive participles may indicate a condition or state as in (1) and they may also function attributively, as the adjectival NP in (2) exemplifies.

2. There is a phonological rule that applies to the sequence [vʔq] to produce [vqʔ]. Sometimes verbs, as in (12a), will be written as tot'anek' to reflect this change. However, it should be noted that the aspect marker itself is k [q], not: k' [qʔ]. Informally, this rule is:

V ʔ C # --> V C ʔ # where C = [q]

3. The vowel length in (13a) is the result of a regular phonological rule that lengthens vowels before final consonant clusters. This is the same rule that produces vowel length in such words as: cuink 'man'. This may be expressed informally as:

V --> VV / ___ [CC] #

4. The vowel (v) in the T/A/M prefixes is conditioned by phonological rules that are not relevant to this discussion.

5. See footnote 2.

6. Recall also (Chapter 1, § 1.3.2), that -c must suffix to adjective and noun stems that are vowel final, but may not suffix to adjective and noun stems that are consonant final. For example,

1) tix - o
old- B1p 'We are old.'

2) chunchu - c - o
seat -asp -B1p 'We are seated.'

7. In the past, Freund (1976) and Stewart (1980) have analyzed -c as a "non-future tense/aspect suffix". Freund, however, notes that -c is often absent in situations where it might be expected and present in others, when it is not expected. He concludes by saying that "it is not entirely clear how these classes should be defined" (Freund, 1976: 29). Rather than analyzing -c as an aspectual suffix, I am suggesting that -c be analyzed as an 'intransitive marker'.

It is interesting to note that in Quiche there is an intransitive marker -(i)c which is suffixed to intransitive stems if they are in clause final position. Mondloch (1978: 27) describes the suffix as an intransitive termination marker which "does not appear to mean anything. It simply means that the verb is at the end of the clause." -C is suffixed to intransitive stems ending in a vowel (like K'ekchi), and ic is suffixed to stems ending in a consonant. For example:

1)a. C - at - be - c.
tns-B2- go -termination 'You go.'

b. C - at - bin - ic.
tns-B2- walk-termination 'You walk.'

8. In passive clauses, the subject is frequently preposed. It is interesting to note that consistent with the properties of a final 1, the subject of a passive clause may occur in the expected sentence-final subject position, as in (1) and (2) below.

1) Qui - Ø - puba - a - c li cuink a'an .
tns- B3 -shoot-pass- asp the man that
'That man was shot.' (E&C,J.136)

2) Qui -Ø -x-yeh nak chi- Ø- mol -e' -c li quic' .
tns-B3-A3-say that tns-B3-gather-pass-asp the blood
'He said,"Let the blood be gathered."'

This is not an argument for a passive analysis because if the nominal were a final DO, it would occur in a postverbal position, as well. It is worthwhile noting because, as will be discussed in later chapters, there are two conditions in K'ekchi that restrict subject extraction and/or the position of a final 1. The final 1 of a passive clause is not subject to these restrictions.

9. The case marking principle will have to be revised when constructions involving 2-chômeurs are considered.

Chapter 3

K'EKCHI RESTRICTIONS ON FINAL ERGS: EVIDENCE FOR CLAUSE-INTERNAL MULTIATTACHMENT

3.0 Introduction

The properties of K'ekchi nuclear term extraction will be discussed. It will be shown that nominals heading a final Erg arc differ from nominals heading a final Abs arc in their ability to extract: A nominal heading a final Abs arc may freely topicalize, focus, question, and relativize. A nominal heading a final Erg arc may freely topicalize, but it may be focused, questioned, or relativized only in clauses with reflexive morphology.

In Relational Grammar, Topic, Foc, Q, and Rel are all overlay relations (Perlmutter and Postal 1983a:86). For the description of K'ekchi it is necessary to define a subclass of overlay relations which include only Foc, Q, and Rel. This subclass will be referred to collectively as nominals which bear a <u>narrow overlay</u> relation. I will (sometimes) refer to this subclass of relations as 'extractions', and to the nominal that bears the narrow overlay relation as the 'extractee'. The constraint which governs ergative extraction is:

<u>Constraint I</u>:
If a nominal heads a final Erg arc in a clause c, and it also heads a narrow overlay arc, it must head an Abs arc.

Notice that I involves no reference to level. If a final Erg heads an Abs arc - at any syntactic level - it may bear the Q, Foc, or Rel relation. Thus, if an initial Erg is a final Abs, it may bear the Q, Foc, or Rel relation (as in 2-3 Retreat clauses, Chapter 4), and if a final Erg heads an Abs arc at some non-final level, it too, by the above condition, will be able to focus, question, or relativize. In this chapter, it is argued that a nominal heading a final Erg arc may be focused, questioned or relativized in a reflexive clause. This follows from an analysis that posits clause-internal multiattachment (MA) in reflexive clauses (Perlmutter and Postal 1984, Rosen 1981). In the multiattachment analysis, which will be motivated below, one nominal heads an Erg arc <u>and</u> an Abs arc in the initial level of structure. At the final level of structure it heads only an Erg arc. Since the nominal which heads a final Erg arc also heads an Abs arc in the initial level of clause structure, it may bear a narrow overlay relation in a reflexive clause. Ergative extraction thus provides evidence for clause-internal multiattachment in K'ekchi.

A grammar that does not represent grammatical relations at multiple levels of structure will not be able to capture this generalization about K'ekchi extraction.

This paper is organized as follows: § 3.1 presents the basic properties of extraction. § 3.2 discusses a restriction on Ergative extraction. In § 3.3 arguments for clause-internal multiattachment are presented. It is argued that the condition on nuclear term extraction follows from an analysis that posits clause-internal MA in reflexive and retroherent unaccusative clauses. It is also argued that a grammar <u>without</u> the notion of MA will not be able to capture this generalization.

3.1 K'ekchi Extraction

For what follows it is important to be able to distinguish nominals which head Topic arcs from nominals which head Foc arcs. This section will discuss the diagnostics for distinguishing topics from foci. Some of the properties which characterize foci are also relevant to those nominals which bear the Q or Rel relation.

3.1.1 Topic versus Focus Position

If a nominal bears a narrow overlay relation (Q, Foc, or Rel), it must occur in immediate <u>preverbal</u> position. If a nominal bears the Topic relation, it must occur in <u>clause-initial</u> position. Given that the neutral word order is verb initial (V-(O)-S)), this distinction is often camouflaged by the fact that if only one NP precedes the verb it will be both preverbal and clause-initial in surface structure.

The basic order of elements stated on surface GRs is given in (1a). Topic and focus position relative to other elements is given in (1b) and (1c), respectively.

(1)a. V (2 chô) (3) (2) (3 chô) (Obl*) (1 chô*) 1 (*)

b. # Topic (X) V Y

c. Focus V Y

The * after (Obl) and (1 chô) in (1a) above, and after the subject relation in parentheses (*) is to indicate that the position of an oblique (locative, benefactive, instrument), or of a 1- chômeur is not fixed with respect to the final subject. Parentheses indicate optionality.

3.1.2 Instrumental and Locative Extraction

The importance of the distinction between clause-initial and (immediate) preverbal position will be exemplified in clauses with locative and instrumental topics and foci. It is shown that nominals heading a Topic arc must occur in clause initial position, while nominals heading a Foc arc must occur in preverbal position.

Instrumental and locative foci condition the presence of the postverbal clitic _cui'_. Instrumental and locative topics do not (Berinstein 1978). Crucially, _cui'_ appears only in clauses in which the extracted oblique (instrument or locative) occurs in immediate _preverbal_ position, not _clause-initial_ position.

Oblique topics are introduced by a preposition (as _chi_ 'with', or _sa'_ 'at, on, in'), or a relational noun (as _-iq'uin_ 'with').

In (2) below the instrumental and locative NPs occur in clause-initial position as Topic. This extraction is not marked by cui'.

(2)a. **R - iq'uin che' na- Ø- x- sac' li x- co'.**
A3-with stick tns-B3-A3-hit the his-daughter
'With a stick, he beat his daughter.' (E&C,Gr.161)

b. **R- iquin ch'ich' t -Ø -a -set' li pach'aya'.**
A3-with machete tns-B3-A2-cut the grass
'With a machete, you cut the grass.' (E&C,Gr.161)

c. **Chi c'uc'um nequ-e'-tz'ibac li najter cuink.**
with pens tns- p- write the old men
'With pens, the old men/ancients write.' (H,D.351)

d. **Sa' li q'uiche' na-Ø-chal li ha' ut li ru che'.**
from the forest tns-B3-come the water and the fruits
'From the forest comes the water and the fruits.'

e. **Sa' q'uiche' cuan-Ø len-Ø aj elk'.**
in mountains exist-B3 say-B3 ncl thieves
'In the mountains, they say there are guerillas.'
(Sp.'En la montaña hay guerrillos dicen.') (H,G.60)

In contrast, if the instrumental or locative NP is focused, its extraction must be marked by cui'. The absence of cui' is ungrammatical, as noted in (3b), (4b), and (5b).

(3)a. Aran tinq'ue retal ma **a'an** na-Ø -x -col
there I will give notice if that tns-B3-A3-defend

cui' r -ib li so'sol.
cui' him-self the buzzard
'There I will observe if that (the bush) is what the buzzard defends himself with.' (B,S1.78)

b.* Aran tinq'ue retal ma **a'an** na-Ø-x-col r-ib li so'sol.

(4)a. **Li q'uiche'** (li) x -Ø-yoq'u-e' cui' li che'.
the forest that tns-B3-cut-pass cui' the trees
'It was in the forest that the tree was cut.'

b.* **Li q'uiche'** (li) x -Ø-yoq'u-e' li che.'

(5)a. **Chaki ch'och'** li cuanqu-eb **cui'** .
dry land that exist-p cui'
'It was dry land that they were on.' (E&C,C.2)

b.* **Chaki ch'och'** li cuanqu-eb.

Extraction of the instrument or locative NP as Q (as in (6)), or Rel (as in (7)) also requires the presence of cui'. The rule that determines cui' is given in (8).[1]

(6)a. C'a'ru t- Ø -a -tz'ek **cui'** l - a- mul ?
what tns-B3-A2-empty cui' the-A2-garbage
'What are you going to empty your garbage in?'

b. C'a'ru x -Ø -e'x -yoc' **cui'** ?
what tns-B3-p A3-cut cui'
'What did they cut it with?'

c. C'a' ta ru ti- Ø -x- col **cui'** r-ib?
what possibly tns-B3-A3-defend cui' him-self
'What could he possibly defend himself with?'
(E&C,J.148)

d. C'a'ru t -at- c'anjela -k **cui'** ?
what tns-B2-work -asp cui'
'What are you going to work with?' (H,D:115)

In (7) the instrumental or locative NP bears the Rel relation. In these examples the head noun precedes the relative clause which is optionally introduced by li, the definite article. As in the examples in (3)- (6) above, cui' obligatorily marks the extraction.

(7)a. K'es li ch'ich' li x -Ø-in-yoc' **cui'** li cu-ok.
sharp the machete that tns-B3-A1-cut cui' the my-foot
'The machete was sharp that I cut my foot with.'
(E&C,Gr:162)

b. Qu- e'-cüulac li tz'i' sa' li tzul bar
tns-p- arrive the dog to the mountain where

qu-e'-takla -c **cui'**.
tns-p-send=pass-enc cui' (B,S7.15)
'The dogs went to the mountain where they were sent.'

```
c.  X-mac    a'an  nak   cuan-Ø    li  bar   na -Ø -el
    A3-fault that that  exist-B3 the where tns-B3-come

cui'   li  x-ya'al  li  coco.
cui'   the its-juice the coconut                    (E&C,C.10)
'Because of that, that is where the coconut juice comes
out.

d.  Anakcuan ta- Ø -ka -rak'  li  plet   li    cuanc-o
    now      tns-B3-A1p-finish the fight that  exist-B1p

cui'  chan-  li  cuink  r- e   li capitan.
cui'  said-B3 the man    A3-Dat the captain
'"Now we will finish the fight that we are in," said the
man to the captain.'                              (E&C,J.143)
```

(8) Cui' Placement:[2]
If a nominal heads an initial Instrument or Loc arc in a clause c and that nominal also heads a narrow overlay (Q, Foc, or Rel) arc, then cui' must occur in postverbal position in clause c.

The rule for cui' placement captures an important generalization for K'ekchi syntax (and Mayan, see footnote 1). Specifically, there is independent evidence for the notion 'narrow overlay' which will be motivated further in subsequent sections.

The positional difference between topic and focus will now be exemplified in clauses with two fronted NPs. It will be argued that 1) the position of a nominal heading a narrow overlay arc is immediate preverbal, and 2) the position of a nominal heading a Topic arc is clause-initial.

In (9a) and (9b) the subject topic occurs in clause-initial position. The oblique instrumental occurs in preverbal focus position. The presence of cui' signals that the instrument is focus. (9a) and (9b) differ in their final transitivity. (9a) is a transitive clause. Verbal agreement is with the final subject laj Lu' and the direct object li che'. (9b) is a finally intransitive (passive) clause. The absolutive third singular Set B affix cross-references the final subject li che'.

(9)a. [Laj Lu'] [oxib chi ch'i ch'] x -Ø -x -yoc'
ncl Pedro three of machetes tns-B3-A3-cut
S-Topic Inst Focus

cui' li che'.
cui' the tree
'Pedro, with 3 machetes he cut the tree.'

b. [Li che'] [r- iq'uin li ch'i ch'] x -Ø-yoq'u-
the tree A3- with the machete tns-B3-cut-
S- Topic Inst. Focus

e' cui' .
pass cui'
'As for the tree, with the machete it was cut.'

If the order of the two preposed NP's were reversed, the corresponding sentences would be ungrammatical. This is because cui' marks instrument and locative foci, not subject foci, as exemplified in (10) below.

(10)a.* [oxib chi ch'ich'] [laj Lu'] x- Ø -x-yoc'
three of machetes ncl Lu' tns-B3-A3-cut

cui' li che'.
cui' the tree
('With 3 machetes, Pedro cut the tree.')

b.* [R-iq'uin li ch'ich'] [li che'] x- Ø -yoq'u-e'
A3-with the machete the tree tns-B3-cut- pass

cui' .
cui'
('With the machete, the tree was cut.')

Furthermore, cui' does not mark instrumental topics. For these two reasons, the sentences in (10a) and (10b) can not be interpreted as having either a Subject Focus, or an Instrument Topic.

Finally, observe the text example in (11). That cui' does not occur in this sentence follows from the fact that cui' does not mark Locative Topics (ut sa' ruc'alil lix quenk) or Subject Focus (c'ot caxlan).

(11) [Ut sa' r -uc'alil li x-quenk'] [c'ot caxlan]
and in their-bowls the their-beans manure chicken

chic cuan-Ø chi sa'.
again exist-B3 inside
'As for their bowls of beans, there was chicken manure inside.' (E&C,GG.10)

These facts further support the positional difference which often serves to distinguish topics from foci.

3.1.3 Distributional Properties of Topics

The distinction between topic and focus is not purely positional. As in other languages of the world, the topic is basically what 'the sentence is about' or 'the theme of the discourse' (Li and Thompson 1976).

3.1.3.1 The Conjunction ut

As a rule of thumb, topics may be distinguished from foci in that they are often introduced by the conjunction ut 'and' as illustrated in (12), below.

(12)a. [Ut li saj al] qui-Ø-x - yeh sa' x - ch'ol
and the young boy tns-B3-A3- say in his-heart

nak mamin t -Ø - in- cuy a'an.
that never tns-B3- A1- endure that (E&C,J.54)
"As for the young boy, he said to himself, 'Never, will I endure that.'"

b. [Ut li saj cuink, li al a'an, laj sic'ol
and the young man the boy that the seeker of

ichaj,] co'o-Ø cui'chic chi r- atinan-quil li rey.
grass go -B3 again to A3- talk -nom the king
'As for the young man, the boy that one, the hunter of grass, he went again to talk to the king.' (E&C,J.45)

c. [Ut li r- ixakil] qui-Ø -x - canab sa' jun li
and the his- wife tns-B3-A3-leave in one the

mu sa' x -mu li pim chi-r - e li caratera.
shadow in its-shadow the mt on-its-mouth the road
'As for his wife, he left her in a shadow, in the shadow of the mountain beside the road.' (E&C,J.94)

In (12a) the topic is a final Erg, in (12b) the topic is a final Unerg, and in (12c) the topic is a final DO.

3.1.4 Distributional Properties of Foci

Foci are generally contrastive or emphatic. The distributional properties of foci are detailed in Sections 3.1.4.1 -3.1.4.4 in an effort to establish some language-particular diagnostics for foci in K'ekchi.

3.1.4.1 Negation

The contrastive properties of foci are evidenced under negation. This will be illustrated with the discontinuous negative form moco..ta.[3]

(13)a. [moco li cuink ta] na- Ø -alina a'ban li al.
neg the man neg tns-B3- run but the boy
'It's not the man who runs, but the boy.'

b. [moco li cuink ta] x- Ø-in-sac' a'ban li ixk.
tns-B3-A1-hit but the woman
'It's not the man that I hit, but the woman.'

c. [moco che' ta] x- in- x- sac' cui'.
stick tns-B1-A3- hit cui'
'It wasn't a stick that he hit me with.'

d.* [moco che' ta] x - in- x - sac'

In (13a)- (13c) the nounphrase circumfixed by moco...ta is the focus of the clause. As evidenced in (13d), if the instrument heads a Foc arc (or more generally, if the instrument heads a narrow overlay arc), cui' must occur as a postverbal clitic. Extraction of nuclear term foci is unmarked, as exemplified in (13a, b).

3.1.4.2 The Emphatic Particle ha'

The emphatic particle ha' may introduce the focused NP. This is exemplified in (14) below.

(14)a. Ha' li cuink x -Ø - t'ane'.
emph the man tns-B3- fall
'That's the man who fell.'

b. Ha' li ic x - Ø - in- lok'.
emph the chile tns-B3- A1- buy
'That's the chile I bought.'

c. Ha' li ch'ich' n -in- c'anjelac cui'.
emph the machete tns-B1 work cui'
'That's the machete I work with.'

d.* Ha' li ch'ich' n -in-c'anjelac.

In (14a-c) the focused NP has a contrastive value. It is introduced by the emphatic particle ha' and occurs in preverbal position. As evidenced in (14d), if the instrument is focused, cui' must occur.

3.1.4.3 Use of the Demonstrative

A demonstrative pronoun a'in 'this', a'an 'that', a'ineb 'these', or a'aneb 'those' may co-occur with the focused NP. The demonstrative may be preposed or postposed. If the demonstrative is postposed, it may be used in conjunction with ha' as: ha' NP a'an.

(15)a. Entonces r-iq'uin a'in, li ixk a'an
then A3- with this the woman that

qui-Ø -ch'aj-o'.
tns-B3-diff- inch (E&C,T.39)
'Then after this, that woman became difficult.'

b. Ha' li jun a'in t -Ø -incu-aj.
emph the one this tns-B3- A1 -want
'This is the one I want.' (E&C,Gr.118)

c. Li mesleb a'in x- Ø -in-mes cui'
the broom this tns-B3-A1-sweep cui'

x -sa' li cabl.
its-inside the house
'This is the broom I will sweep the house with.'

d.* Li mesleb a'in x -Ø - in-mes x -sa'
the broom this tns-B3-A1-sweep its-inside

li cabl.
the house
('This is the broom I will sweep the house with.')

If the NP in preverbal position co-occurs with a demonstrative pronoun, it will have the contrastive properties typical of foci. (15d) is ungrammatical because if the instrument is Focus, cui' is obligatory.

3.1.4.4 The Particle <u>pe'</u>

The "insistence" particle <u>pe'</u> (as it is named by Haeserijn 1979:254) may be used in conjunction with a focused NP for emphasis. <u>Pe'</u> must occur in clause-second position. Therefore, it may occur postposed to the focused NP, as in (16a), or in conjunction with the emphatic particle <u>ha'</u>, as in (16b).

(16)a. L<u>a</u>at pe' t - at-cam- k.
you pe' tns- B2-die-asp
'You are the one that will die.'

b. Ha' pe' l<u>a</u>at t - at-cam- k.
emph pe' you tns- B2-die-asp
'You are the one that will die.'

3.2 A Restriction on Ergative Extraction

In § 3.1 we isolated five diagnostics for foci. Using those diagnostics as a criteria for focus, it will be argued in this section that a nominal heading a final Erg arc and a Foc arc may not 1) occur in preverbal position, 2) be circumfixed by <u>moco</u>...<u>ta</u>, or co-occur with 3) the emphatic particle <u>ha'</u>, 4) a demonstrative pronoun, or 5) the insistence particle <u>pe'</u>, unless it is the subject of a reflexive clause. Otherwise put: a final Erg can bear the Foc relation only in a reflexive clause.

3.2.1 Reflexive Clauses

Reflexive clauses in K'ekchi are finally transitive. Two pieces of evidence confirm this: the verbal agreement rule and the aspect rule.

3.2.1.1 Verbal Agreement

The predicate agrees with its subject and its direct object, if there is one. Thus, the defining morphological property of a transitive stem is the presence of a Set A and a Set B affix, while the defining morphological property of an intransitive stem is the lack of a Set A affix. The predicates in (18a-c) agree with the final Subject and DO of the clause and are cross-referenced by the Set A and Set B affixes, as determined by the rules for person agreement in (17) below.

(17) Person Agreement:
  a. A nominal heading a final Erg arc determines Erg agreement in the verb.

  b. A nominal heading a final Abs arc determines Abs agreement in the verb.

(18)a. Qui- Ø -x- sutk'esi r -ib chok' tz'unun.
tns-B3-A3- change A3-self as hummingbird
'He turned himself into a hummingbird.'
(E&C,MSS.14)

  b. M - Ø -a -q'ue acu-ib sa' ch'a'ajquilal
neg-B3-A2-put A2-self in difficulty
'Don't put yourself in danger.' (E&C,Gr:183)

  c. Ma x - Ø - r -il r -ib laj Lu' sa' lem?
Q tns-B3-A3-see A3-self ncl Lu' in mirror
'Did Pedro see himself in the mirror?'

The verbal morphology of the reflexive clauses in (18a-18c) supports the claim that these clauses are finally transitive. It should be noted that agreement with the DO in a reflexive clause must be cross-referenced by the third singular Set B affix. This is because the reflexive noun -ib is syntactically possessed by a pronoun which is coreferential with the subject. As in other possessive clauses (see Chapter 1), verbal agreement is controlled by the head noun, not the possessor. For example,

```
(19)a.  Qui - Ø -cu-il   l-  a -punit.
        tns- B3- A1-see the A2-hat
        'I saw your hat.'

    b.*  C - at-cu-il  l - a -punit.
         tns-B2-A1-see
         ('I saw your hat.')
```

3.2.1.2 Aspect

As discussed in Chapter 2, aspect marking is conditioned by final (in)transitivity in K'ekchi. Specifically, the incompletive aspectual affix -k must suffix to the predicate of a finally intransitive clause, if the predicate is affixed with either the t(v)- future, or ch(v)- optative T/A/M prefixes.

```
(20)a.  Ch -in-hilan- k    sa' cu-ochoch.
        opt-B1-rest -asp   in  my-house
        'that I may rest in my house'        (E&C,GR:149)

    b.  Ta -Ø-lok'-e' - k   li caxlan   x-ban li  ixk.
        fut-B3-buy-pass-asp the chicken A3-by the woman
        'The chicken will be bought by the woman.'

    c.  T - o - cuar - k
        fut-B1p-sleep-asp
        'We are going to sleep.'
```

The sentences in (20) are finally intransitive. The presence of the -k suffix is obligatory. -C may be suffixed in other tense/aspects if the clause is finally intransitive but, neither -c nor -k may be suffixed if the clause is finally transitive. The principle that determines -c and -k affixation is given in (21).

(21) Intransitive/Aspect Marking:
If the final stratum is intransitive -k is suffixed to the verb stem in incompletive aspect, otherwise -c may suffix to the stem.

As is evidenced in (22), -k may not suffix to the verb stem in a reflexive clause in the incompletive aspect.

(22)* T - Ø -acu- il - k acu-ib sa' lem.
fut-B3-A2 -see -asp A2-self in mirror
('You will see yourself in the mirror.')

Summing up: two morphological facts attest to the final transitivity of reflexive clauses. First, the verb bears the (Ergative) Set A affix, as exemplified in (18a-c). Second, the verb can not bear the incompletive suffix -k which must occur on finally intransitive stems if the stem is affixed with the future tense t(v)- prefix, as in (22).

The evidence which distinguishes Ergative extraction from Absolutive extraction will now be presented.

3.2.2 Ergative Versus Absolutive Extraction

First, it will be shown that an Erg NP may not occur in the focus position, as defined in (1c). Compare sentences (9a) and (9b), repeated below, to (23a) and (23b).

(9)a. [Laj Lu'] [oxib chi ch'i ch'] x -Ø -x -yoc'
ncl Pedro three of machetes tns-B3-A3-cut
S-Topic Inst Focus

cui' li che'.
cui' the tree
'Pedro, with 3 machetes he cut the tree.'

```
b. [ Li  che' ] [ r- iq'uin li ch'i ch'] x  -Ø -yoq'u-e'
     the tree      A3- with the machete   tns-B3-cut -pass
      S- Topic          Inst Focus

   cui'.
   cui'
   'As for the tree, with the machete it was cut.'
```

(9a) is a finally transitive clause. (9b) is a finally intransitive (passive) clause. The subject topics of (9a) and (9b) occur in clause initial position. As evidenced earlier ((12a-c)), a nominal heading a final Erg or a final Abs arc may bear the Topic relation.

In both (9a) and (9b) the instrument is Focus of the clause. As such, it occurs in preverbal position and its extraction is marked by the presence of cui'.

In (23) below, the subject occurs in preverbal focus position, and the oblique topic occurs in clause-initial position. Cui' does not occur since cui' marks the extraction of instrument and locative foci, not topics.

```
(23)a. [ R- iq'uin laso ]  [ li caxon ] ta -Ø -cubsi    -k
         A3- with   rope     the box    tns-B3-lower=pass-asp
          Inst  Topic        S- Focus

   sa'  li  jul.
   in   the hole                                   (E&C,Gr:290)
   'With rope, the coffin will be lowered into the hole.'

(23)b.*  [ R- iq'uin laso ]  [ lain ] t  -Ø - in -cubsi
           A3- with   rope       I      tns-B3- A1 -lower
           Inst  Topic         S-Focus

   li caxon.
   the box
   ('With rope, I will lower the coffin.')
```

(23a) and (23b) differ in their final transitivity. (23a) is a finally intransitive (passive) clause. The final subject li caxon is cross referenced with the third singular Set B affix. (23b) is a finally transitive clause. The final subject lain is cross referenced with the first singular Set A affix, and the direct object li caxon is cross referenced with the third singular Set B affix.

In (23a) the Unerg NP is Focus. In (23b) the Erg NP cannot be Focus. The ungrammaticality of (23b) is not due to the preposing of the instrument phrase, since instruments may be topics in transitive and intransitive clauses; rather, the ungrammaticality of (23b) is due to the preverbal position of the Ergative NP.

(24) R-iq'uin laso t - Ø- in-cubsi li caxon (lain).
A3- with rope tns-B3- A1-lower the box I
'With rope, I will lower the coffin.'

As (24) shows, lain may occur in subject final position, and its presence is optional. This is the first indication that nuclear terms are not alike with respect to topic and focus. Specifically, Absolutives may be Topic or Focus. Ergatives may head a Topic arc, but as will be shown below, require a special environment to head a Foc arc.

3.2.2.1 Yes-No Qustions

There are Yes-No questions on a focused structure. For example, in (25a) the DO tikcual ban occurs in its 'normal' object position. This can be compared to (25b) where the DO occurs in the focus position.

(25)a. Ma x -Ø -a - q'ue cu- e **tikcual ban** ?
Q tns-B3-A2- give A1-Dat hot medicine
'Did you give hot medicine to me?'

b. Ma **tikcual ban** li x - Ø -a -q'ue cu-e ?
Q hot medicine that tns-B3-A2-give A1-Dat
'Was it hot medicine that you gave to me?' (H,G.81)

If the focused NP heads a final Erg-arc, the sentence is ungrammatical. As exemplified in (26), laat may occur in its normal subject final position (26a), but it cannot occur in the focus position (26b).

(26)a. Ma x - Ø -a -q'ue cu- e tikcual ban **laat** ?
Q tns-B3- A2-give A1-Dat hot medicine you
'Did you give hot medicine to me?'

b.* Ma **laat** li x -Ø -a -q'ue cu- e tikcual ban?
Q you that tns-B3-A2-qive A1-Dat hot medicine
'Was it you that gave hot medicine to me?'

(26b) is ungrammatical because the Erg NP may occur in focus position only in a reflexive clause, as in (27).

(27) Ma **laat** x - Ø- a -q'ue acu-ib sa' servicio?
Q you tns-B3- A2-give A2 -self to service
'Did you join the army?' (lit. 'Was it you that gave yourself to service?')

The constraint in (28) will tentatively distinguish Erg focus from Absolutive focus.

(28) Erg Extraction Constraint:(to be revised)
A final Erg may focus only if it is coreferential with the DO.

3.2.2.2 Moco...ta

The contrastive properties of Absolutive and oblique foci were evidenced under negation in § 3.1.1.2. In this section we will consider Erg foci.

(29)a. [moco li cuink ta] na- Ø -alina a'ban li al.
neg the man neg tns-B3- run but the boy
'It's not the man who runs, but the boy.'

b. [moco li cuink ta] x- Ø-in-sac' a'ban li ixk.
tns-B3-A1-hit but the woman
'It's not the man that I hit, but the woman.'

c.* [moco li cuink ta] x- in- x- sac' a'ban li ixk.
tns-B1-A3- hit but the woman
('It's not the man that hit me, but the woman.')

As evidenced in (29a) and (29b) final absolutives may be focused. (29c) is ungrammatical because a final Erg may not focus in this context. However, a final Erg may be circumfixed by moco ...ta and focus in a reflexive clause, as in (30).

(30) [moco li cuink ta] x - Ø -x -toch' r -ib
tns-B3-A3-hit him-self

ha' li ixk li x -Ø -x- toch' r - ib.
emph the woman that tns-B3-A3-hit her-self
'It's not the man who bumped himself, it's the woman who bumped herself.'

3.2.2.3 Ha'

The emphatic particle ha' may introduce the focused nominal (§ 3.1.4.2). However, as shown below, a final Erg may not be introduced by ha' unless it is the focused subject of a reflexive clause.

(31)a. Ha' li cuink x -Ø - t'ane'.
emph the man tns-B3- fall
'That's the man who fell.'

b. Ha' li ic x - Ø - in- lok'.
emph the chile tns-B3- A1- buy
'That's the chile I bought.'

c.* Ha' li cuink x - Ø- x -lok' li ic.
emph the man tns-B3-A3- buy the chile
('That's the man who bought the chile.')

d. Ha' eb li ch'ich' x- Ø -e'x-toch' r-ib-(eb).
emph p the metal tns-B3-pA3-hit A3-self-p
'Those are the cars that crashed.' (lit. bumped themselves/each other)

(32)a. Ha' li ixk (li) x- Ø- yabac.
emph the woman that tns-B3- cry
'That's the woman who cried.'

b. Ha' li ik a'an (li) x- Ø- x- c'am chak laj Lu'.
emph the cargo that that tns-B3-A3-bring dir ncl Lu'
'That's the cargo that Pedro brought.'

c.* Ha' laj Lu' (li) x- Ø -x -c'am chak li ik.
('Pedro is the one who brought the cargo.')

d. Ha' li calejenac (li) x - Ø- x -toch' r- ib sa'
emph the drunk that tns-B3-A3-hit A3-self on

li x- jolom.
the his-head
'That's the drunk who bumped himself on his head.'

In (31a), (31b), (32a), and (32b) the focused Absolutive NP is introduced by the emphatic particle ha'. (31c) and (32c) are ungrammatical because ha' may not introduce the Erg unless it is the final (focused) subject of a reflexive clause, as in (31d) and (32d).

3.2.2.4 Demonstratives

As noted in § 3.1.4.3, a demonstrative pronoun may co-occur with a focused nominal for emphasis. As shown below, a demonstrative may co-occur with a focused Ergative NP only if it is coreferential with the DO.

(33)a. A cuink a'in junelic na - Ø-tz'ulun arin Coban.
prt man this always tns-B3-come here Coban
'This man always comes to Cobán.' (E&C,P.5)

b. A'an jun li na'leb na-Ø -ka-nau lao sa'
that one the idea tns-B3-A1p-know we in

ka- yank - il arin sa' ka-tep, Alta Verapaz.
our-between-poss here in our-land Alta verapaz
'That is one story that we know in our community
amongst us) here in our land, Alta Verapaz.' (B,S1.94)

c.* (Ha') li tz'i' a'an x -in- x -tiu.
emph the dog that tns-B1-A3 -bite
('That's the dog that bit me.')

d. (Ha') li tz'i' a'an x -Ø -x-tiu r -ib.
tns-B3-A3-bite him-self
'That's the dog that bit himself.'

A final Absolutive may co-occur with the demonstrative pronoun to focus, as in (33a) and (33b). However, a final Erg (33c) may not, unless it is the subject of a reflexive clause (33d).

(34) below is an example from a text. In the first sentence the NP li capitan is established as the new subject topic (note the conjunction ut). Li capitan remains the subject for the next three clauses. As the 'same subject' in a chain of clauses, li capitan need not be overt until there is a change of topic or focus. The verb of the third clause camsi 'to kill' is preceded by the NP li cuink a'an which co-occurs with the demonstrative pronoun in focus position. Both arguments of the verb are third singular, as evidenced by the agreement. Is the preposed NP the new subject focus, or DO focus? As predicted by (28), the preposed NP li cuink a'an can only be DO focus.

(34). Ut li capitan qui-Ø -x-yeh nak inc'a' na- Ø-cu -aj,
and the captain tns-B3-A3-say that not tns-B3-A1-want

chan-Ø . Qui-Ø -xucuac li capitan porque na- Ø -x -nau
said-B3 tns-B3-afraid the captain because tns-B3-A3-know

nak li cuink a'an ac x- Ø -x -camsi ut qui-Ø -x-
that the man that already tns-B3-A3-kill and tns-B3-A3-

yo'obtesi cui'chic r -ib.
create again A3- self. (E&C,J.144-5)

"As for the captain, he told him that 'No, I don't want it (to fight).' The captain was afraid because he knew that he had already killed that man and he (that man) had come back to life again (lit. created himself again)."

As borne out by the prediction of (28), if a nuclear term occurs in preverbal position in a transitive clause, and the Subject and DO are not coreferential, then that nuclear term must be a focused DO.

3.2.2.5 Pe'

A focused Absolutive NP may co-occur with the 'insistence' particle pe' (and the emphatic particle ha') as in (35a) and (35b) below, but an Ergative NP may not co-occur with either of these particles unless it is the focused subject of a reflexive clause as in (35d)[4].

(35)a. **Ha' pe'** laat li yo -c -at chi x-camsin-quil-eb
emph pe' you that cont-asp-B2 prep A3-kill- nom -p

eb l -in halau, eb l -in q'uiche' ak. Laat **pe'** yo -c -at
p the-my tepez p the-my wild pigs you pe' cont-asp-B2

chi x- camsin-quil-eb l -in quej.
prep A3- kill -nom -p the-my deer

'You are the one who is (in the process of) killing my tepezcuintles and my wild pigs. You are the one who is killing my deer.' (B,S3.108-9)

(35)b. { laat pe' / ha' pe' laat   t- at-in-muk r-iq'uin-eb li
tns-B2-A1-bury A3- with-p the

xul cui' t - e'-cam-k .
animal if tns- p- die-asp
'You are the one I will bury with the animals, if they die.'

c.* { laat pe' / ha' pe' laat   t - in-a -col
tns - B1-A2-defend
('You are the one that will defend me.')

d. { laat pe' / ha' pe' laat   t -Ø -a -col acu -ib.
tns-B3-A2-defend your-self
'You are the one that will defend yourself.'

Briefly summing up, we have established five properties of foci. It was shown that Absolutive and Ergative foci differ with respect to these properties. I argued that the difference between Absolutive and Ergative foci followed from the constraint on Ergative extraction, tentatively stated as (28). A nominal heading a final Erg arc may head a Foc arc only if it is coreferential with the DO of the clause. As such, an ergative NP may occur in preverbal position only in a reflexive clause.

3.2.2.6 Q and Rel

We have seen that Absolutives may focus freely, but that Ergative focus is restricted to a reflexive clause. Absolutive and Ergative extractions differ in two other ways: 1) the questioning of an Erg is restricted to reflexive clauses, and 2) the relativization of an Erg is restricted to reflexive clauses. These two processes interact with the characterization of ergative extraction because nominals bearing the Q, Foc, or Rel relation must occur in the preverbal position. Constraints governing ergative extraction should therefore capture this generalization. This suggests the following more general revision of (28).

(36) Erg Extraction Constraint:(to be revised)
A final Erg may bear a narrow overlay relation only if it is coreferential with the DO.

In (37) below, the final Absolutive intransitive subject (37a), and DO (37b,c) are questioned. It is not possible to question the final Erg, unless it antecedes a reflexive.

(37)a. Ani x -Ø -t'ane'?
who tns-B3-fall 'Who fell down?'

b. Ani x -Ø -x- yoc'?
who tns-B3-A3-cut 'Who did he cut?'

c. Ani x - Ø-x -yoc' ha'an? 'Who did he cut?'
who tns-B3-A3-cut 3s pro (not:'Who cut him?')

d. Ani x -Ø-x -yoc' r -ib?
who tns-B3-A3-hit him-self 'Who cut himself?'

There is no difference in meaning between (37b) and (37c). The only way to express 'Who cut him?' is in a finally intransitive (Retreat) clause.(2-3 Retreat is discussed in Chapter 4.) Thus, as proposed in (36), a final Erg can be Q only if it is coreferential with the DO. Observe the questions in (38).

(38)a. C'a'ru nequ-Ø-e'r - aj li cu̲ink?
what tns-B3-pA3- want the man
'What do the men want?'

b. Ani nequ- Ø-e'r- aj li cu̲ink?
who
'Who do the men want?' (not:'Who wants the men?')

(38b) is not ambiguous. If the subject and DO are non-coreferential and a nuclear term is questioned, then Q must be the final Absolutive of the clause.

As seen in (37) and (38), an Abs NP may be questioned with *ani*, but an Erg NP has a special restriction. It may be questioned with *ani* only if it is coreferential with the DO, supporting the tentative constraint proposed in (36).

In (39) the final Unerg NP bears the Rel relation. In these examples the head noun precedes the relative clause which is optionally introduced by *li*, the definite article. As exemplified below, a wh-question word as *ani* 'who', or *c'a'ru* 'what' may also introduce the relative clause.

(39)a. [Na'bal] li nequ-e'-xic r - iq'uin aj ilonel
many that tns- p -go A3- with n.cl seer

nequ- e' -cam.
tns- p- -die
'Many of those that go to the shaman die.' (E&C,NBN.8)

b. Qui-Ø- oso' [li cuink] li qui-Ø -chal li plet.
tns-B3-finish the man that tns-B3-come the fight
'The man that came to the fight was finished off.'
(E&C,J.161)

c. Sa' c'alebal cuan-Ø [li ani] na-Ø -xic chi
in village exist-B3 the who tns-B3-go to

r - il - bal junak aj ilonel.
A3-see - nom a ncl seer (E&C,NBN.6)
'In the village there are those who go to see a shaman.'

d. Na- x -col -eb [ani] nequ-e'-tiqu-e' x-ban
tns-A3-save- p who tns- p-bite-pass A3-by

li c'ant'i.
the snake (B,S1.93)
'He saves those who are bitten by the snake.'

In (40) the final DO bears the Rel relation. Again, the relative clause is optionally introduced by li, this use of li is distinct from its use as a definite article which must precede the NP.

(40)a. Bar x -Ø- a-lok' [li mesleb] li x - Ø- cu-il
where tns-B3-A2-buy the broom that tns-B3-A1-see

sa' l -acu-ochoch ?
in the-A2 -house
'Where did you buy the broom that I saw in your house?'

b. Ma chabil-Ø [li chin] x - Ø - in-takla acu-e ?
Q good -B3 the orange tns-B3- A1-send A2-Dat
'Are the oranges good that I sent to you?'(E&C,Gr:77)

c. T -Ø - e'x-q'ue retal bar na -Ø- x-tau chak laj
tns-B3-pA3-give notice where tns-B3-A3-find dir ncl

yac [li c'a'ru] na- Ø- x -tz'aca.
fox the what tns-B3-A3- eat
'They would watch where the fox goes to find his food (lit. the what he eats).' (B,S7.62)

d. X - Ø - x -cam [li ixk] li x - Ø -r -il li
tns-B3-A3- die the woman that tns-B3-A3-see the

cuink.
man
'The woman that the man saw died.' (not: 'The woman that saw the man died.')

Since there is no special marking associated with the movement or deletion of nuclear term NPs in K'ekchi, one might wonder whether (40d) is ambiguous. It is not. (40d) can only be understood as a clause in which the DO is Rel, not a clause in which the Erg is Rel.

However, a nominal which heads a final Erg arc may be Rel as predicted by (36), and exemplified in (41), if it is coreferential with the DO.[5]

(41) X - Ø -x- cam [li ixk] li x - Ø -x -toch' r -ib.
tns-B3-A3-die the woman that tns-B3-A3-hit A3-self
'The woman that bumped herself died.'

We have seen that nuclear term nominals heading final Abs arcs may bear a narrow overlay relation. However, nominals heading final Erg arcs are restricted in a particular way. They may only bear a narrow overlay relation if they antecede a reflexive. At this point it is not clear why the subject of a reflexive clause is exceptional, or what, if anything, it has in common with intransitive subjects and DOs. In this sense the constraint in (36) fails to capture a generalization about K'ekchi extraction. Namely, that a (nuclear term) nominal must head an <u>Abs arc</u> to bear a narrow overlay relation. The revised ergative extraction constraint is given in (42) and follows from an analysis that posits clause-internal multiattachment in K'ekchi reflexive clauses.[6]

(42) <u>Ergative Extraction Constraint:</u>
If a nominal heads a final Erg arc in a clause c and it also heads a narrow overlay arc, it must head an Abs arc.

Arguments for this analysis are presented in the next section.

3.3 Evidence for Clause-Internal Multiattachment

Following recent RG proposals (Aissen 1982, Johnson and Postal 1980, Perlmutter to appear, Perlmutter and Postal 1984, Postal 1981, Rosen 1981), coreference will be represented by multiattachment (MA). The relational networks of reflexive structures (but not all reflexive structures, see Rosen 1981) involve a stratum in which a single nominal heads two neighboring arcs.

Some RG definitions:
Two arcs are <u>neighbors</u> iff they have the same tail.
Two arcs <u>overlap</u> iff they have the same head node, and
two arcs are <u>parallel</u> iff they are neighbors <u>and</u> overlap.

In (43a) the 1-arc and the 2-arc are neighbors. In (43b) <u>a</u> heads two overlapping arcs, and in (43c) <u>a</u> heads two parallel arcs.

(43)a. b. c.

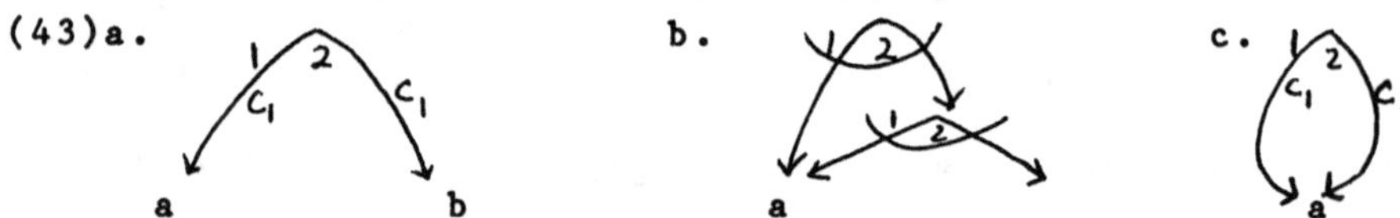

The MA hypothesis (within a single clause) is basically that there exist structures where one nominal bears two (or more) grammatical relations in the same stratum, as in:

(44)a. Mary likes herself. b.

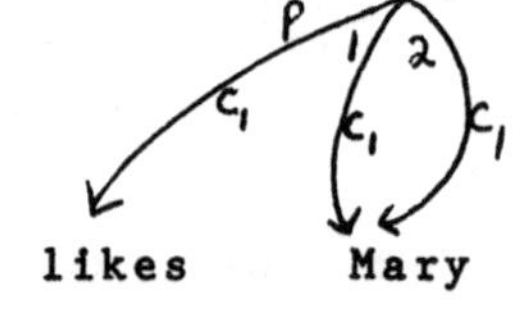

In (44b), <u>Mary</u> heads a 1-arc and a 2-arc in the same stratum. These arcs are parallel. Perlmutter and Postal (1984) suggest that the notion of MA can characterize the notion of coreference. Reflexive constructions would involve clause-internal MA and equi constructions would involve cross-clausal MA (defined below). For example, in (44) above, Mary would be correctly understood as both the initial 1 and the initial 2 of the clause.

The definition of cross-clausal MA and clause-internal MA is given in (45).

(45) Multiattachment:

a. Cross-clausal (or 'general') MA: Two or more overlapping arcs with distinct tails are headed by the same nominal.

b. Clause-internal (or 'reflexive') MA: Two or more parallel arcs sharing a coordinate are headed by the same nominal.

Two properties distinguish 'reflexive' MA from 'general' MA. First, in reflexive MA the arcs have the same tail. In general MA the arcs have distinct tails. Second, in reflexive MA the arcs must share a coordinate i.e. they must be in the same stratum. General MA, on the other hand, is not restricted to the same stratum. Discussion of general MA constructions (equi and ascensions) is presented in Chapter 6.

Given the definition of clause-internal MA (45b), we can now distinguish the subnetworks of the Passive and reflexive RNs in (46) and (47) below.

(46) Reflexive sub RN

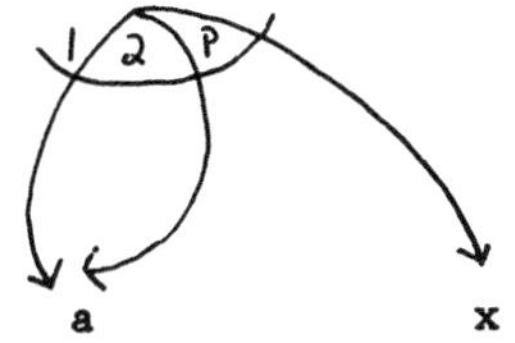

(47) Passive sub RN

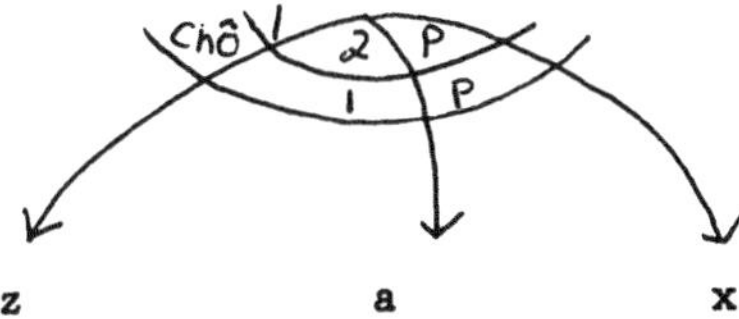

The structure in (46) is distinct from a passive RN. In particular, there is no advancee arc. In the Passive sub RN _a_ heads a 2-arc at the initial level and a 1-arc at the final level. In the reflexive RN _a_ heads a 1-arc and a 2-arc at the initial level. In the reflexive RN, and not in the Passive RN, _a_ bears two grammatical relations in the _same stratum_. I will refer to this stratum as a 1 (coreferential) 2 MA stratum, abbreviated: 1:2.[7] Given the definition in (45b), (46) involves multiattachment and (47) doesn't. Unlike Italian, in K'ekchi every instance of clause-internal (nuclear term) coreference must involve MA. However, not every clause-internal MA involves coreference.

It has been assumed (Perlmutter and Postal 1984) that all MAs which involve coreference must be resolved in a well formed RN. Or more precisely:

(48) A nominal may not head two parallel arcs labelled with a central R-sign at final level.[8]

Therefore, if reflexivization is represented syntactically by MA, as it is in (44), then the MA must be resolved in such a way that no nominal heads more than one arc with the same tail in the final stratum.

Perlmutter's (to appear) proposal (based on joint work with Postal) for the resolution of multiattachment is that RNs with (clause-internal) MA have arcs headed by pronouns whose function is to 'absorb' all but one of the grammatical relations borne by the multiattached nominal. Further, the grammatical relation in the MA stratum that gets 'absorbed/replaced' is the one that is the lower on the relational hierarchy (1> 2> 3> Obl) of R-signs. For example, the final stratum corresponding to the RN in (44b) would contain a 2-arc headed by a pronoun, as in:

(49)

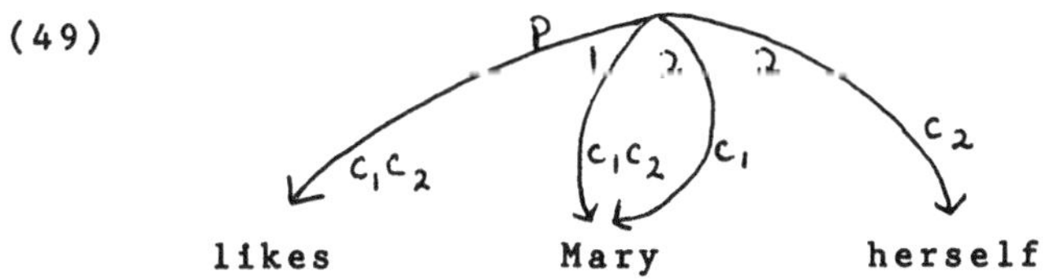

The pronoun is realized as the reflexive <u>herself</u> in (49) because it meets the conditions for reflexive pronouns in English. In the final stratum <u>herself</u> bears one of the same R-signs as one of the two (initially) doubly attached arcs. In this way, the MA in the initial stratum is resolved and the condition in (48) is met. This proposal for MA resolution is referred to as 'pronoun birth'.

Not all multiattachments require pronoun birth. A multiattachment can be resolved by <u>cancelling</u> one of the doubly attached arcs without pronoun birth. This proposal for the resolution of MA is due to Rosen (1981). She argues convincingly that 1:2 and 1:3 MA strata in Italian are resolved by cancelling the object arc.

Similarly, Gerdts (1983) argues that reflexive clauses in Halkomelem (Salish) are initially transitive involving a

1:2 MA. Multiattachment is resolved by cancelling the 2-arc, resulting in an intransitive final stratum.

Cancellation has also been attested in the Mayan language, Tzotzil. Aissen (1982) provides evidence for an initial 1:3 multiattachment which is resolved by cancelling the 3-arc.

Two forms of resolution have been discussed: pronoun birth and cancellation. If, for example, a language has a 1:2 MA stratum, resolution may involve either 2 birth or 2 cancellation. Corresponding to these two resolutions are finally transitive and intransitive reflexive clauses, respectively.

Now let us return to K'ekchi ergative extractions and the constraint proposed in (42) to govern them. It was shown that final Absolutives freely focus, question, and relativize. In contrast, Ergative NPs focus, question, and relativize only in reflexive clauses. (42) claims that a final Erg must head an Abs arc to be Q, Foc, or Rel. I argue that Ergatives may bear narrow overlay relations in reflexive clauses because they head an Abs arc in an initial 1:2 MA stratum. Unlike Italian and Halkomelem, K'ekchi reflexive clauses are finally <u>transitive</u>. The initial 1:2 MA is resolved by <u>2 birth</u>. For example, the RN associated with (33d), repeated below as (50), is (51).

(50) Li tz'i' a'an x - Ø -x-tiu r-ib
the dog that tns-B3-A3-bite A3-self
'That's the dog that bit himself.'

(51)

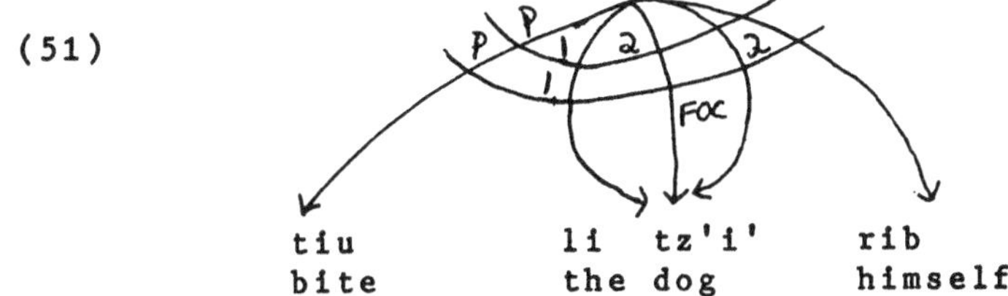

The nominal that heads the final Erg arc may focus in (50) because it heads an Abs arc. The 2 arc of the initial 1:2 MA satisfies this condition, stated in (42) and repeated below for convenience.

(42) Ergative Extraction Constraint:
If a nominal heads a final Erg arc in a clause c and it also heads a narrow overlay arc, it must head an Abs arc.

The constraint proposed to govern ergative extraction (42) assumes the notion of multiattachment. This proposal, henceforth the MA hypothesis, will be compared to a grammar without the notion of MA, henceforth the NOMA hypothesis (no MA). It is argued that the notion of MA is required to capture the generalization of nuclear term extraction in K'ekchi. These arguments provide evidence that linguistic theory must countenance the notion of multiattachment.

3.3.1 A Condition on Ergative Extraction

The first argument is based on the condition for ergative extraction. It is argued that there is independent evidence for MA in the representation of coreference. Under the

MA hypothesis the syntactic condition that governs ergative extraction is given in (42). Under the NOMA hypothesis the semantic condition that governs ergative extraction is given in (36). These are renumbered as (52) and (53), respectively.

(52) <u>MA Condition on Ergative Extraction</u>:
If a nominal heads a final Erg arc in a clause c and it also heads a narrow overlay arc, it must head an Abs arc.

(53) <u>NOMA Condition on Ergative Extraction</u>:
A nominal heading a final Erg arc can head a narrow overlay arc only if it is coreferential with the DO.

In order to account for the distribution of nuclear term extractees in K'ekchi, we pose two questions: 1) Is there a property that subjects of intransitive clauses, DOs, and subjects of reflexive (transitive) clauses share? and 2) Why are subjects of non-reflexive (transitive) clauses distinct from the class of nominals in (1)?

Under the MA grammar there is a generalization that unites the class of nuclear term extractees and accounts for their distribution: A nuclear term extractee must head an Abs arc. The class of nominals in (1) head Abs arcs, while the class of nominals in (2) do not. Assuming the notion of MA, subjects of reflexive clauses pattern like the class of nominals in (1) because they head Abs arcs, i.e. the 2-arc in the initial 1:2 MA stratum satisfies this condition.[9]

Under the NOMA grammar there is not a generalization that unites the class of nuclear term extractees. If (53) is the only condition on RNs involving narrow overlay relations, than an Erg can bear a narrow overlay relation only if it is the subject of a reflexive clause. The NOMA grammar cannot provide an explanation of what it is that subjects of intransitive clauses, DOs, and subjects of reflexive clauses share, or why it is that reflexive clauses are exceptional.

The MA grammar allows an overt statement characterizing the distributional properties of nuclear term extractees. The NOMA grammar does not. This is the first argument for preferring a MA grammar to a NOMA grammar.[10]

3.3.1.1 MA versus NOMA: Addenda

As noted earlier (§3.2.1), reflexive morphology and possessive constructions are structurally similar in at least three ways. First, the reflexive noun -<u>ib</u> is obligatorily possessed and agrees in person with its possessor. As in other possessive constructions, pronominal possessors are omitted.

```
(54)a.  cu-ochoch
        A1-house            'my house'

    b.  cu-ib
        A1-self             'myself'

    c.  li   x -na'
        the A3-mother       'his mother'

    d.  r - ib
        A3-self             'himself'

    e.  li   x -rabin   laj Lu'
        the A3-daughter ncl Lu'        'Pedro's daughter'
```

Second, in both reflexive and possessive clauses, number agreement (with the possessor) in the third plural is optional. (The rules governing person and number agreement follow from the Nominal Agreement rules stated in Chapter 1, §1.4). If eb is suffixed to the possessed noun, the possessor must be plural. If eb is not suffixed, the possessor may or may not be plural.

(55)a. r- ib
A3-self 'himself/herself/themselves'

b. x- coc'al
A3-children 'his/her children/their children'

c. r -ib - eb
A3-self-p 'themselves'

d. x -coc'al -eb
A3-children-p 'their children'

Finally, as in other possessive constructions, verbal agreement is with the head noun, not the possessor.

(56)a. X - Ø -a -toch' acu-ib.
tns-B3-A2-hit A2-self
'You bumped yourself.'

b. X - Ø -a -lok' l - in -punit.
tns-B3-A2-buy the- A1 -hat
'You bought my hat.'

Given these three structural similarities between reflexives and possessives, a proponent of a no MA grammar might propose the following alternate to the NOMA condition on Ergative extraction in (53):

(57) <u>NOMA II</u>:
A nominal heading a final Erg arc can head a narrow overlay arc only if it is coreferential with the Possr DO.

This alternate NOMA proposal can be quickly dismissed in favor of the MA condition, repeated below.

(52) <u>MA Condition on Ergative Extraction</u>
If a nominal heads a final Erg arc in a clause c and it also heads a narrow overlay arc, it must head an Abs arc.

The English equivalents of the sentences in (58a) and (58b) below have analogous syntactic structures in the NOMA II grammar, but not in the MA grammar. The initial and final GRs posited under each analysis are illustrated in the relational networks in (59) and (60).

(58)a. Pedro$_i$ painted his$_i$ house.

b. Pedro painted himself.

RNs for (58a) and (58b)

(59) <u>NOMA II</u>

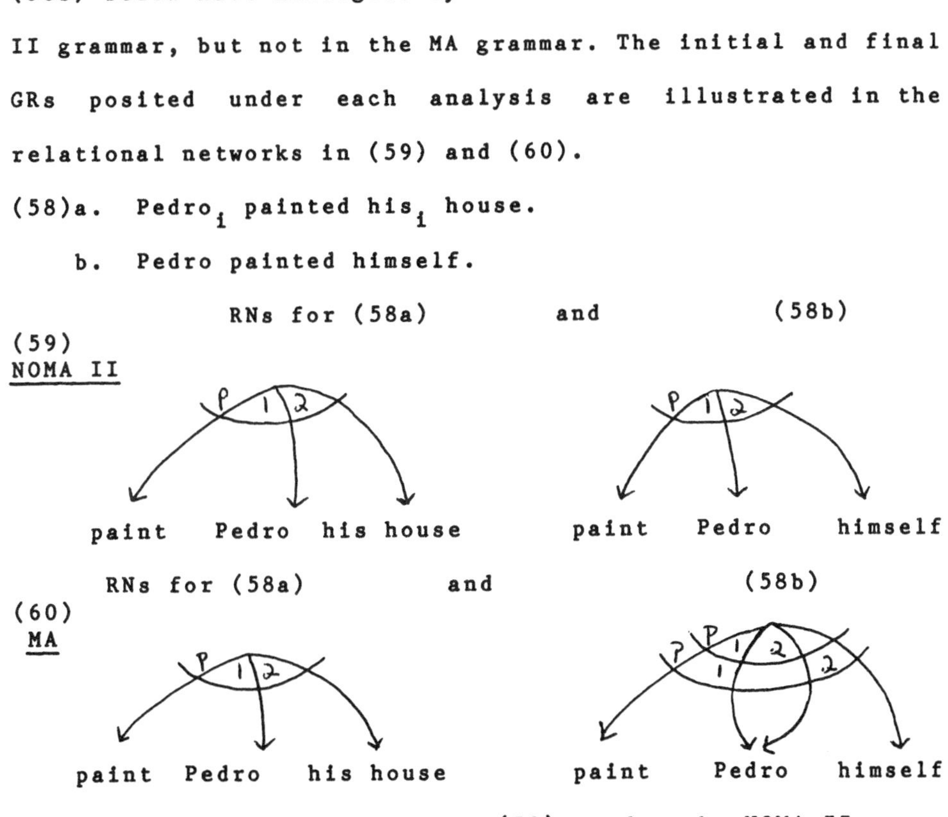

As evidenced by the RNs in (59), under the NOMA II grammar 'Pedro' is initial and final Erg in sentences (58a) and

(58b). Furthermore, the NPs 'his house' and 'himself' are both initial and final DOs in sentences (58a) and (58b).

As evidenced by the RNs in (60), under the MA grammar 'Pedro' is initial and final Erg, and 'his house' is initial and final DO in (58a). In (58b) 'Pedro' is a final Erg, but is multiattached in the initial stratum, heading a 1-arc and a 2-arc. 'Himself' is a final DO, but does not bear a GR at the initial level.

The question that will distinguish between the adequacy of Constraints (57) and (52) is whether or not the nominal heading the final Erg arc in sentences like (58a) can be Q, Foc, or Rel.

Under the NOMA II grammar, (57) predicts that the nominal heading the final Erg arc can extract if it is coreferential with the Possr DO. Thus, the NOMA II grammar predicts that Ergative extraction in (58a) will follow from the same principle that allows Ergative extraction in reflexive clauses. On the other hand, under the MA grammar, (52) claims that the nominal that heads the final Erg arc can bear the Q, Foc, or Rel relation if it heads an Abs arc. Since the nominal that heads the final Erg arc in (58a) does <u>not</u> head an Abs arc, the MA grammar predicts that Erg extraction in such a clause will be ungrammatical. This is the case, as evidenced in (61a-d) below.

(61)a.* Ha' li cuink x -Ø -x -sac' li x -ka'al.
emph the man tns- B3-A3-hit the his-daughter
('That's the man$_i$ that hit his$_i$ daughter.')

(61)b.* Ha' laj c'ayinel (li) na - Ø - x -c'ay li r - ak.
emph the vendor who tns-B3- A3-sell the his-pigs
('That's the vendor$_i$ who sells his$_i$ pigs.')

c.* Ha' lain (li) x -Ø -in-bes li incu-ismal.
emph I who tns-B3-A1-cut the my-hair
('I'm the one who cut my hair/gave myself a hair-cut.')

d.* Ha' laj banonel (li) qui-Ø -x -col li x- na'.
emph the doctor who tns-B3-A3-save the his-mother
('That's the doctor$_i$ who saved his$_i$ mother.')

The expressions in (61a-d) may only be expressed in a detransitivized (Retreat) clause. Otherwise put: the extractee must head an Abs arc, as predicted by the MA grammar. Were there an initial 1:2 MA, resolution would necesitate 2 Birth. However, this is not possible, as indicated in (62).

(62)a.* Ha' li cuink x- Ø -x-sac' li r- ib x-ka'al
emph the man tns-B3-A3-hit the his-self his-daughter
('That's the man who hit his own daughter.')

b.* " " " x- Ø -x- sac' r-ib li x-ka'al.

c.* " " " x- Ø -x- sac' li x-ka'al r-ib .

Under the MA grammar the ungrammaticality of the sentences in (61) follows from the fact that the final (focused) subject does not head an Abs arc at any level.

Under the NOMA II grammar there is no explanation for the ungrammaticality of the sentences in (61). In fact, it claims that the structure of these clauses is the same as the structure of the clauses in (31d), (32d), (33d), and (35d). Thus, the final subject should be able to focus, since it is coreferential with the Possr DO.

I conclude that the condition in (57) is untenable for K'ekchi and that the proper generalization is captured in (52) under the MA grammar.

3.3.2 A Condition on Inanimate Nominals

The second argument that will distinguish a no multiattachment grammar from a multiattachment grammar depends on a condition on inanimate nominals.

An inanimate nominal can head a final Abs arc. In (63), (64), (65), and (66) the inanimate nominal heads a final Unerg arc.

(63) Li ik' na- Ø -ec'an sa' x- yank li xak.
the wind tns-B3-rustles in its-between the leaves
'The wind rustles between the leaves.' (E&C,CQ.4)

(64) Qui- Ø - sa li ha'.
tns-B3-evaporate the water
'The water evaporated.' (H,D:291)

(65) Li chok nequ-e'-nume' chi r - u choxa.
the clouds tns- p -pass on its-face sky
'The clouds pass by in front of the sky.'

(66) X - Ø -c'am - e' chak li ha'.
tns-B3-carry-pass die the water
'The water was brought.'

And in (67) and (68) the inanimate nominal heads a final DO arc.

(67) X - Ø -in-c'am chak li ha'.
tns-B3-A1-carry dir the water
'I brought the water.'

(68) Moco yal ta usilal a'an qui-Ø -x-ba̲nu.
neg true neg favor that tns-B3-A3-do
'That wasn't a true favor that he did.' (B,S6.64)

However, an inanimate NP may not always head a final nuclear term arc. For instance, there are passive clauses in which the inanimate NP heads a Chô-arc, but there are no corresponding active clauses in which the inanimate NP heads a final Erg arc. The tentative constraint proposed to account for this fact is stated as:

(69) An inanimate nominal cannot head a final Erg arc.

Some active-passive pairs are given in (70)-(72). The (a) examples are passive clauses. A passive 1-chômeur is introduced by the relational noun -ban. In the (b) examples it is shown that the inanimate NP may not be a final Erg.

in response to the question: 'How are your children?'
(70)a. Cau - eb ca'ajcui' li mas ca'chin x- Ø -tau -e'
strong-p but the most small tns-B3-find-pass

chic **x-ban** ojb .
again A3- by cough (H,Gr:140)
'They are strong, but the smallest one has been found again by the cough/has caught a cold again.'

b.* Cau- eb ca'ajcui' li mas ca'chin x - Ø- x -tau
tns-B3-A3-find

(li) ojb .
the cough
('They are strong, but the smallest one, the cough caught her.')

(71)a. Lix ka'al a'an li qui-Ø- puba -c **x- ban**
ncl girl that who tns-B3-shot=pass-enc A3- by

li cak .
the lightning (E&C,MSS.97)
'That's the girl who was shot/hit by lightning.'

b.* Lix ka'al a'an li qui-Ø -x-puba **li cak** .
tns-B3-A3-shoot the lightning
('That's the girl that the lightning shot/hit.')

(72)a. Qui-Ø -c'at-e' **x-ban li cak** li x-jolom.
tns-B3-burn-pass A3-by the lightning the his-head
'His head was burned by the lightning.' (B,S7.87)

b.* Qui-Ø -x- c'at li x -jolom **li cak** .
tns-B3-A3-burn the his-head the lightning
('The lightning burned his head.')

The passive RN associated with (72a) is given in (73) and the RN for the corresponding transitive clause (72b) is given in (74).

(73)

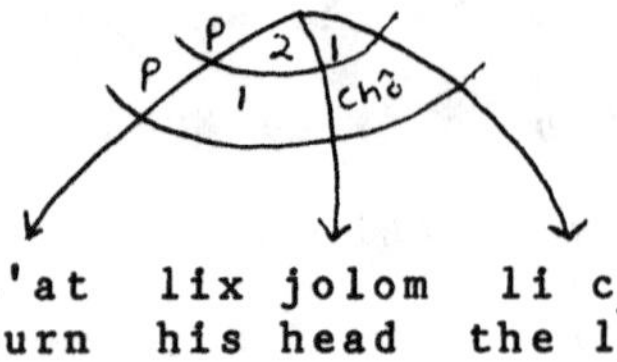

P P 2 1 1 Chô

c'at lix jolom li cak
burn his head the lightning

(74)*

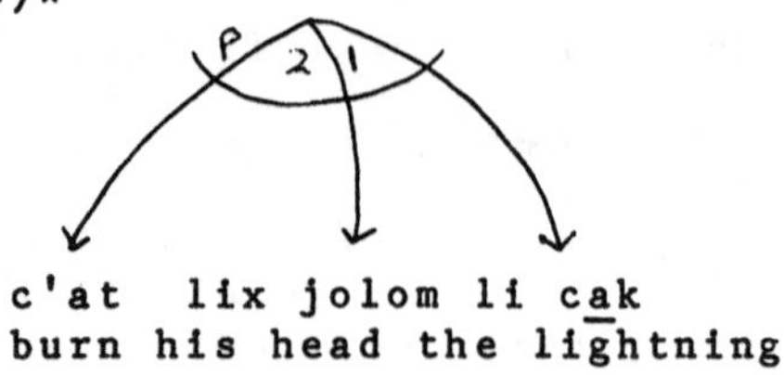

P 2 1

c'at lix jolom li cak
burn his head the lightning

In accordance with the prediction in (69), the (b) sentences in (70)-(72) are ungrammatical.[12,13]

Superficially, it appears to be the case that an inanimate NP cannot head a final Erg arc. However, as shown in (75)-(77) an inanimate NP can head a final Erg arc if it is subject of a 'reflexive' clause. These sentences are all finally transitive. The reflexive object controls third singular Set B agreement. The inanimate NP controls Set A agreement.

(75) X - Ø-e'x -toch' r - ib **li ch'ich'.**
tns-B3-pA3-hit A3-self the metal
'The cars collided/hit each other.' (H,D.328)
(Sp. 'Los carros se rozan.')

(76) Nequ-Ø -e'x-tiu r-ib **li po ut li sak'e.**
tns-B3-p A3-eat A3-self the moon and the sun
'The moon and the sun eclipse/eat themselves.'
(Sp.'la luna y el sol se comen mutuamente') (H,D.325)

(77) **Li ninki xox** na- Ø -x- bon r-ib
the big spot tns-B3-A3-spread A3-self
'Smallpox spreads itself/is contagious.'
(Sp. translation offered by consultant:'La viruella se contagiosa.') (E&C,NX.15)

Under the MA grammar, the condition in (78) accounts for the ungrammaticality of the (b) sentences in (70)-(72) and for the grammaticality of the sentences in (75)-(77).

(78) MA Condition on Inanimate Ergs:
If an inanimate nominal heads a final Erg arc, it must head an Abs arc.[14]

Assuming the notion of MA, the final Erg in these sentences does not head an Abs arc in the transitive counterpart of the passive clauses in (70b)-(72b), but does head an Abs arc in a 1:2 MA stratum in the 'reflexive' clauses. (The structure of the sentences in (75)-(77) will be discussed in the next section.)

Under the NOMA grammar, the proposed condition for inanimate Ergs is stated in (79).

(79) NOMA Condition on Inanimate Ergs: (to be revised)
An inanimate nominal may head a final Erg arc only if it is coreferential with the DO.

In the MA grammar there is a generalization that unites the class of nuclear term inanimate nominals and accounts for their distribution: A nuclear term inanimate nominal must head an Abs arc.

In the NOMA grammar there is not a generalization that unites the class of nuclear term inanimate nominals and there is no principle that accounts for their distribution. Finally, there is no explanation for why reflexive clauses are exceptional. The condition on inanimate nominals provides an argument in favor of the MA hypothesis.

3.3.2.1 Retroherent Unaccusative Clauses

We must explain why the clauses in (75)-(77) have reflexive morphology. That is, if we compare a sentence like (77) 'smallpox is contagious' to a sentence like 'that's the dog that bit himself' (50), only in the latter case is there a potential for distinct reference. Yet, both sentences in K'ekchi are finally transitive and have reflexive morphology.

Under the MA grammar, the Unaccusative Hypothesis together with the notion of multiattachment provide an explanation for these facts. Under the NOMA grammar an ad hoc constraint on reflexivization is required.

The Unaccusative Hypothesis (Perlmutter 1978) claims that there exist initial strata having a 2 and no 1. The advancement of the 2 to 1 from an <u>unaccusative</u> stratum is known as unaccusative advancement. This is exemplified in the RN in (80).[15]

(80)

(81) is a typology of the plain and retro(herent) 2-1 advancements (Perlmutter and Postal 1984) that occur in the world's languages.

(81) Typology of Plain and Retro 2-1 advancements[16]

Plain Passive	Retro Passive
Plain Unaccusative	Retro Unaccusative
Plain Imp(ersonal) Passive	Retro Imp(ersonal) Passive
Plain Imp Unaccusative	Retro Imp Unaccusative

For example, passive is the advancement of 2-1 from a transitive stratum. Alongside plain passive is retroherent passive. This too, is the advancement of 2-1 from a transitive stratum, but the advancee retains the 2 relation in the arrival stratum, as in:

(82)a. plain passive

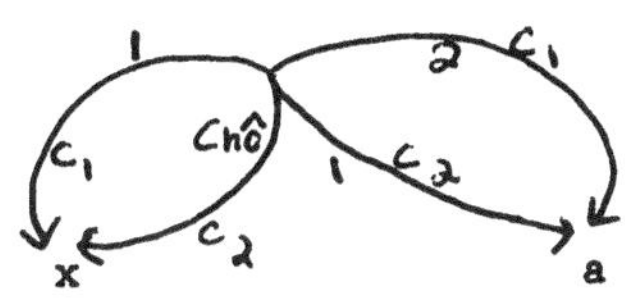

b. retroherent passive

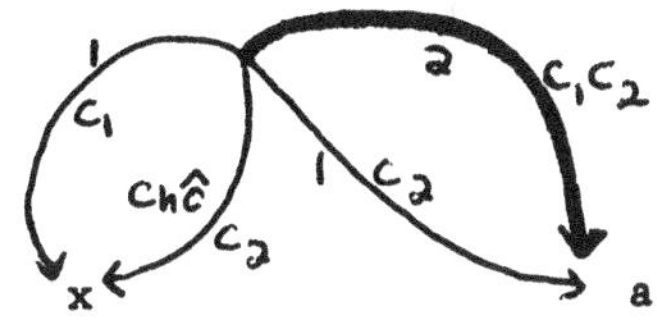

In (82a) the nominal _a_ heads two parallel arcs- the 1-arc and the 2-arc- in different strata. In (82b) the nominal _a_ heads two parallel arcs in the same stratum, thus accounting for the reflexive morphology associated with constructions of this type. Distinct from reflexive structures discussed so far, the 1:2 MA stratum in retroherent advancements is _non-initial_. Furthermore, retroherent MA does not involve coreference.

Unaccusative advancement is the advancement of 2-1 from an unaccusative stratum, as in (80). And alongside plain unaccusative advancement is <u>retroherent</u> <u>unaccusative</u>. This is the advancement of 2-1 from an unaccusative stratum, but the advancee retains the 2 relation in the arrival stratum. An example from Italian (Rosen 1981) is exemplary.

(83)a. La catena si è rotta.
'The chain broke.'

b.

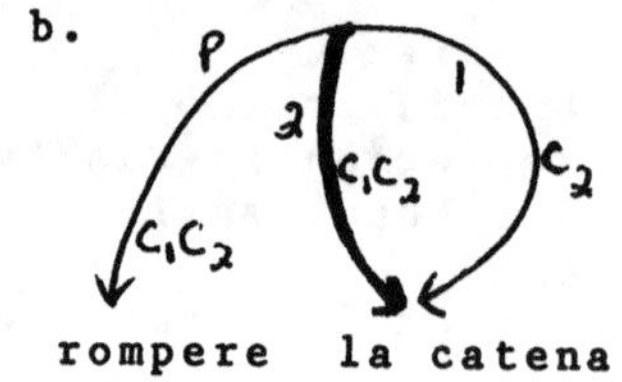

The subnetwork of (83b) is associated with (83a). Both Perlmutter (to appear) and Rosen (1981) provide several arguments for the initial unaccusativity of these clauses. Notice that the verb carries with it the reflexive clitic <u>si</u>. Reflexive morphology is not associated with plain unaccusative, as evidenced in (84a) below.

(84)a. La nave è affondata.
'The ship sank.'

b.

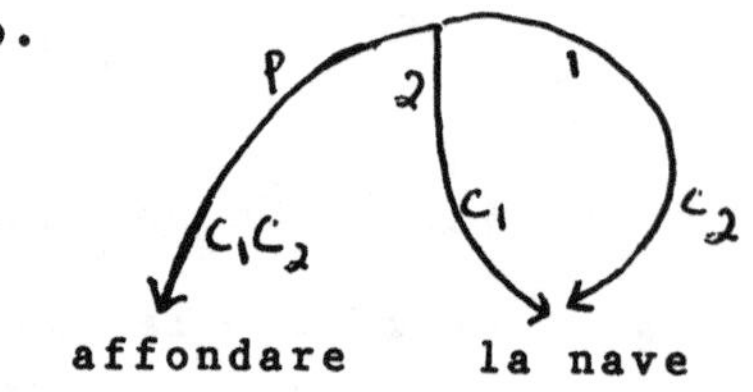

While retroherent advancement clauses have reflexive morphology, they genuinely lack the semantics of a reflexive clause. The retroherent unaccusative clauses in Italian (83) involve multiattachment, but do not involve coreference. This same observation is relevant to K'ekchi and will help provide an account of the reflexive morphology in (75)-(77). In particular, the structure associated with (77) is represented in the relational network in (85).

(85)

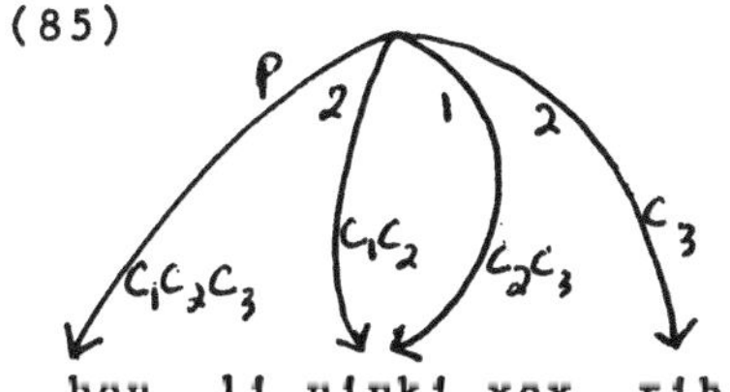

or in the stratal diagram:

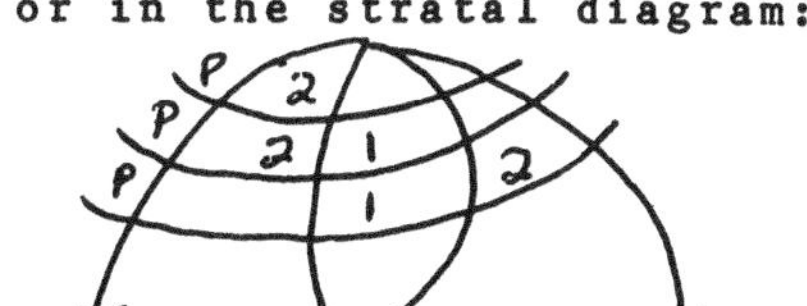

In (85) there is an initial unaccusative stratum. The 2 advances to 1 by retroherent unaccusative advancement. At the c_2 level there is a 1:2 MA stratum. As in the resolution of other MA strata, MA is resolved by 2 birth and the birth arc assumes the lower of the R-signs in the MA stratum. Thus, the reflexive noun rib heads a final 2 birth arc.

According to the MA grammar, an inanimate nominal may head a final Erg arc in sentences (75)-(77) because it heads an Abs arc in a non-initial 1:2 MA stratum. The constraint proposed in (78) captures this generalization.

According to the NOMA grammar, the condition in (79) claims that an inanimate NP can head a final Erg arc only if it is coreferential to the DO. Crucially, in retroherent unaccusative clauses the final 1 and 2 are not coreferential. To account for the sentences in (75)-(77) under this approach, an ad hoc constraint on reflexivization would be required. Given a definition of 'reflexivization' as in (86) below, the NOMA condition on inanimate Ergs can be reformulated as (87).

(86) <u>NOMA Condition on Reflexivization</u>:
A clause <u>c</u> is a 'reflexive' clause if -<u>ib</u> heads a final 2-arc in clause <u>c</u>.

(87) <u>NOMA Condition on Inanimate Ergs</u>: (revised version)
An inanimate nominal can head a final Erg arc only if it is subject of a 'reflexive' clause.

Under the NOMA grammar two statements (86) and (87) are required to account for the distribution of ergative inanimate nominals. Under the MA grammar only one statement (78) is required. This provides an argument against the NOMA grammar and for the MA grammar.

3.3.3 Inanimate Extraction

It might be argued that the inanimate nominals in sentences like (75)-(77) are not final Ergs. In this section I argue that these inanimate nominals are subject to the Ergative Extraction Constraint, discussed earlier (§ 3.3.1), thus providing additional evidence for the final transitivity of retroherent unaccusative clauses in K'ekchi.

As is shown in (88) and (89a) below, an inanimate nominal heading a final Erg arc can bear a narrow overlay relation. However, as (89b) exemplifies, an inanimate nominal cannot always bear a narrow overlay relation.

(88) Li n_i_nki xox a'an jun yajel na- Ø- x-bon
the big spot that one sickness tns-B3-A3-spread

r- ib.
A3-self (E&C,NX.26)
'That smallpox is a sickness that spreads itself/is contagious.'

(89)a. Ha' eb li ch'_i_ch' x- Ø -e'x-toch' r- ib.
emph p the metal tns-B3-pA3-hit A3-self
'Those are the cars that hit/crashed into each other.'

b.* Ha' eb li ch'_i_ch' x - Ø -e'x -toch' li k'a.
the bridge
('Those are the cars that hit/crashed into the bridge.')

I argue that the ungrammaticality of (89b) follows from both the Condition on Inanimate Ergs (78) and the Condition on Ergative Extraction (52), as stated under the MA grammar. What these conditions have in common is that both require that the NP in question ha' eb li ch'ich' head an Abs arc. That (89b) is ungrammatical provides additional evidence for the final transitivity of retroherent unaccusative clauses because if the clause were finally intransitive, the inanimate nominal would head an Abs arc and thus be able to extract. The inanimate nominals in (88) and (89a) may extract and bear a narrow overlay relation because they head an Abs arc in a non-initial 1:2 MA stratum. Thus, under the MA grammar the condition on inanimate Erg extraction is completely characterized by one generalization (52), the same constraint that governs ergative extraction elsewhere in the language.

The characterization of ergative extraction under the NOMA grammar does not predict the grammaticality of (88) and (89a). The NOMA extraction constraint (53) states that a nominal heading a final Erg arc may bear a narrow overlay relation only if it is coreferential to the DO. In retroherent unaccusative clauses the final 1 and 2 are not coreferential. Therefore, the revised version of the NOMA extraction constraint given in (90) below, plus the constraint on reflexivization given in (86) (repeated below), will be required to explain this construction.

(90) <u>NOMA Condition on Ergative Extraction</u>:
A nominal heading a final Erg arc can head a narrow overlay arc only if it is subject of a 'reflexive' clause.

(86) <u>NOMA Condition on Reflexivization</u>:
A clause *c* is a 'reflexive' clause if -*ib* heads a final 2-arc in clause *c*.

The NOMA grammar uses the condition on reflexivization in two ways: first, to account for reflexive clauses which involve coreference (i.e. initial 1:2 MAs), and second, to account for retroherent clauses which do not involve coreference (i.e. non-initial 1:2 MAs). However, there is no explanation for why ergatives cannot extract in 'non-reflexive' clauses, or for why inanimate nominals cannot head a Erg-arc in 'non-reflexive' clauses.

Under the MA grammar, multiattachment together with the unaccusative hypothesis provides an account for the reflexive morphology _without_ coreference. The inanimate nominal argument provides additional evidence for multiattachment and coreference as independent notions. As exemplified by retroherent unaccusative clauses, not all instances of MA involve coreference. It was shown that the key to understanding the reflexive morphology in (75)-(77) and (88)-(89) followed from the claim that these clauses involve a non-initial 1:2 MA stratum. In addition, evidence for the final transitivity of retroherent unaccusative clauses followed from the fact that the inanimate nominal was subject to the same extraction constraint as other final Ergs.[17]

It was also argued that given the notion of MA, _two_ generalizations about K'ekchi syntax could be made explicit. _First_, ergative extractees must head an Abs arc. _Second_, ergative inanimate nominals must head an Abs arc. A grammar without the notion of MA (i.e. the NOMA) was unable to state either of these generalizations explicitly and in addition, required an ad hoc constraint on reflexivization (86).

3.3.4 A Condition on Cross-Clausal Multiattachment

In Chapter 6, cross-clausal MAs will be discussed in detail. However, one aspect of the cross-clausal MA argument presented in Chapter 6 is relevant to the present discussion and provides an additional argument for preferring a MA grammar to a NOMA grammar. This argument depends also on an analysis of 2-3 Retreat clauses and a constraint proposed to govern them (as discussed in Chapter 4).

In 2-3 Retreat clauses, an initial DO is final IO. There are two consequences of this demotion; first, there is final intransitivity, and second, the final subject of a Retreat clause (in K'ekchi) must extract and bear a narrow overlay relation. The constraint that guarantees this is:

(91) Retreat Subject Constraint:
If the initial DO is the final IO of a clause c, then the nominal heading the final subject arc of clause c must also head a narrow overlay arc.

The Retreat clause corresponding to the transitive clause in (92a) is given in (92b). The morphological reflex of Retreat is -o. The subject must extract and bear a narrow overlay relation. In (92b), lix Rosa, the final 1 of the retreat clause, heads a Foc-arc. (92c) is ungrammatical besause the final 1 of the Retreat clause occurs in its neutral sentence-final position.

(92)a. Ti- Ø -x -lok' li tib lix Rosa .
fut-B3-A3-buy the meat ncl Rosa
'Rosa will buy the meat.'

b. Lix Rosa ta -Ø -lok'-o -k r -e li tib.
ncl Rosa fut-B3-buy- R-asp A3-Dat the meat
'It's Rosa who will buy the meat.'

c.* Ta - Ø - lok'-o - k r-e li tib lix Rosa .
fut- B3- help-R-asp A3-Dat the meat ncl Rosa
('Rosa will buy the meat.')

As argued in Chapter 6, there are complex clauses with Retreat infinitival complements. The subject of the Retreat infinitive is multiattached to the controller (1, or 2) in the main clause and it is the controlling nominal in the main clause that must extract and bear a narrow overlay relation.

Infinitival complements heading a nonterm arc are introduced by the preposition _chi_. The infinitive is not cross-referenced for person agreement or tense. The form of the infinitive is Vb + _c_. The (retreat) revaluation marker is suffixed to the verb stem. In (93a) below, we know that _lix Rosa_ is the final 1 in the upstairs clause because of the form of the complement.

(93)a. Lix Rosa _ta_ -Ø-xic chi lok'oc r -e li tib.
ncl Rosa fut-B3-go prep buy=Rinf A3-Dat the meat.
'It's Rosa who will go to buy the meat.'

b.* T_a_ -Ø -xic chi lok'oc r-e li tib.

c.* T_a_ -Ø -xic chi lok'oc lix Rosa r-e li tib.

d.* T_a_ -Ø-xic chi lok'oc r-e li tib lix Rosa.

The RN associated with (93a) is given in (94). The coreference between victim and controller is represented through MA. However, in (93a) the victim is the final 1 of a Retreat clause. The constraint in (91) claims that the final 1 of a Retreat clause must head a narrow overlay arc. Given the notion of MA, _lix Rosa_ heads the final 1-arc of the retreat clause and therefore, according to (91), it must also head a narrow overlay arc. (93b,c,d) are ungrammatical because the nominal heading the final 1 arc in the Retreat clause doesn't head a narrow overlay arc. This provides strong evidence for the notion of cross-clausal MA since it is the <u>controller</u> of the retreat infinitive (in the main clause) that must extract and head the narrow overlay arc.

(94)

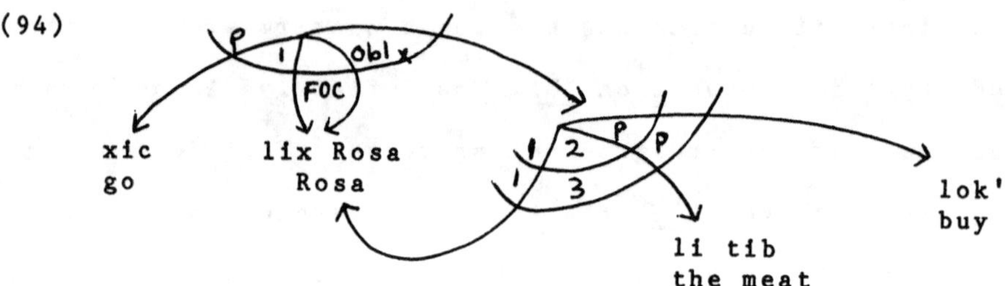

If the controller of the Retreat infinitive heads a final Erg arc, it too, by the above condition (91), should have to bear a narrow overlay relation. This prediction is borne out.[18]

(95) Ani ta - Ø -r -aj lok'oc r -e li tib?
who fut-B3-A3-want buy=Rinf A3-Dat the meat
'Who wants to buy the meat?'

The RN associated with (95) is given in (96). <u>Ani</u> heads a final Erg arc and a Q arc. Under the MA grammar, extraction of <u>ani</u> is sanctioned because <u>ani</u> heads an Abs arc: the 1-arc in the Retreat complement satisfies this condition. Furthermore, under the MA grammar, this phenomenon is explained without any additional apparatus. It follows straightforwardly from the Ergative Extraction Constraint (52) and the Retreat Subject Constraint (91)- both independently required.

(96)

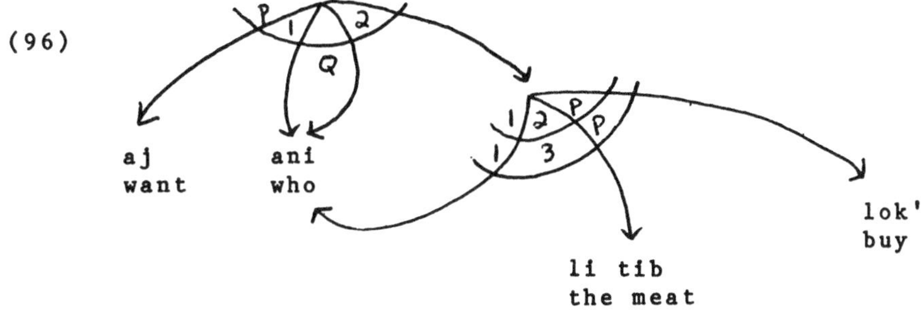

Under the NOMA grammar, the Ergative Extraction Constraint (90) does not account for the grammaticality of sentences like (95). Instead, the NOMA grammar will be unneccessarily complicated and the revised constraint will have to be stated as a disjunction.

(97) <u>NOMA Condition on Ergative Extraction</u>: [19]
A nominal heading a final Erg arc can head a narrow overlay arc if it is subject of a 'reflexive' clause or if it is coreferential with a nominal that heads an Abs arc.

In addition to the condition in (97), the NOMA grammar will require the condition on reflexivization (86), repeated below.

(86) <u>NOMA Condition on Reflexivization</u>:
A clause c is a 'reflexive' clause if -<u>ib</u> heads a final 2-arc in clause c.

Finally, under the NOMA grammar, the Retreat Subject Constraint as it is stated in (91) will not be sufficient. Crucially, since there is no multiattachment, (91) only accounts for subject extraction of the final 1 in simple clauses. It does not account for the extraction of <u>lix Rosa</u> in sentences like (92b), or for the extraction of <u>ani</u> in sentences like (95). Therefore, it too, must be stated as a disjunction.

(98) NOMA Retreat Subject Constraint:
If the initial DO is the final IO of clause c, then the nominal heading the final subject arc of clause c, or the controlling nominal that is coreferential with the final subject of clause c must also head a narrow overlay arc.

Under the MA grammar the constraint on ergative extractees in a) reflexive clauses, b) retroherent unaccusative clauses, and c) cross-clausal (retreat complement) clauses is completely characterized by one generalization. Under the NOMA grammar there is no generalization. In order to account for the distribution of ergative extractees without MA, both the Retreat Subject Constraint and the Ergative Extraction Constraint must be stated as disjunctions, plus an ad hoc condition on relflexivization is required. This is strong evidence against the NOMA grammar and for the MA grammar.

3.3.5 Summary

In order to account for the distribution of ergative extractees and ergative inanimate nominals, two grammars were compared: a grammar with the notion of MA and a grammar without it. The formulations under each grammar are listed below.

MA Grammar	NOMA Grammar
Condition on Erg Extraction	Condition on Erg Extraction
If a nominal heads a final Erg arc in a clause c and it also heads a narrow overlay arc, it must head an Abs arc.	A nominal heading a final Erg arc can head a narrow overlay arc if it is subject of a 'reflexive' clause or if it is coreferential with a nominal that heads an Abs arc.

MA Grammar	NOMA Grammar
Condition on Inanimate Ergs If an inanimate nominal heads a final Erg arc, it must head an Abs arc.	Condition on Inanimate Ergs An inanimate nominal may head a final Erg arc only if it is subject of a 'reflexive' clause.
Retreat Subject Constraint If the initial DO is the final IO of clause c, then the nominal heading the final subject arc of clause c must also head a narrow overlay arc.	Retreat Subject Constraint If the initial DO is the final IO of clause c, then the nominal heading the final subject arc of clause c, or the controlling nominal that is coreferential with the final subject of clause c must also head a narrow overlay arc.
	Condition on Reflexivization A clause c is a 'reflexive' clause if -ib heads a final 2-arc in clause c.

These formulations are required in order to account for 1) ergative extractions (§3.3.1), 2) inanimate ergatives (§3.3.2), 3) inanimate ergative extractions (§3.3.3), and 4) ergative cross-clausal extractions (§3.3.4) under each of the grammars.

The MA grammar provides an elegant solution and is able to capture the generalization governing ergative extraction and ergative inanimate nominals. The NOMA grammar is unable to state the generalization explicitly, requires two disjunctive conditions, and an ad hoc condition on reflexivization. On the basis of this evidence, I reject the NOMA grammar and accept the MA grammar. Conditions on MA are stated in the next section.

3.3.6 Conditions on Clause-Internal MA

In K'ekchi, only 1:2 MAs are allowed. The RN in (101) is associated with the sentence in (99a) and it is not well-formed. This RN is ruled out by (100) because there is a 1:Ben MA stratum.

(99)a.* Lix Mar qui-Ø -x- boj li po'ot chok' r- e r-ib.
ncl Mar tns-B3-A3-sew the huipil for A3- Ben A3-self
('Mary sewed the huipil for herself.')

b.* Laj Xal qui-Ø-x-q'ue li utz'u'uj chi r -e r-ib.
ncl Xal tns-B3-A3-put the flowers on A3- Loc A3-self
('Baltazar put the flowers on top of himself.')

c.* Lain x- Ø -cu-elk' li tumin chi cu- u cu- ib.
I tns-B3-A1-steal the money from A1- Abl A1-self
('I stole the money from myself.')

d.* Lain t- Ø -in-c'am li ik in-ban cu-ib.
I tns-B3-A1-carry the cargo A1- Ag A1-self
('I will carry the cargo by myself.')

e.* Lix Mar qui-Ø- x-takla li hu r - e r -ib.
ncl Mar tns-B3-A3-send the letter A3- Dat A3-self
('Mary sent the letter to herself.')

(100) MA Condition:[20,21]
The only clause-internal MA that is well-formed is 1:2.

(101)*

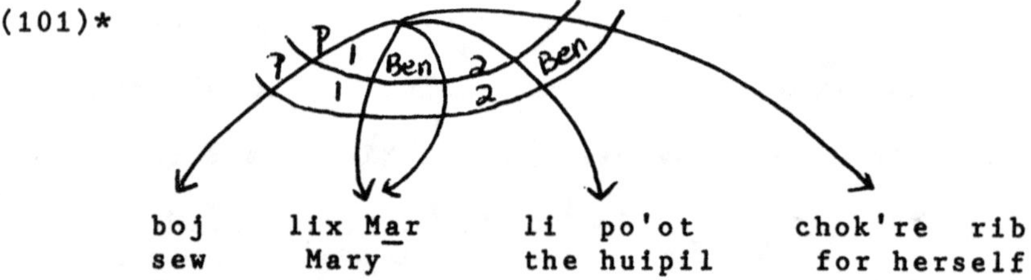

As discussed earlier, an arc headed by -ib must resolve a 1:2 MA. This condition on resolution is stated as (102).

(102) <u>Condition on Resolution</u>:
A 1:2 MA must be resolved by 2-birth.

Conditions on MA, as in (100) and (102) have a cross-linguistic value in that they provide a source of comparison with other languages where conditions on MA have also been stated, as in Italian (Rosen 1981). As MA constructions are attested in other languages, it is possible that conditions on MA, like (100), will be subject to line drawing. For example, in reflexive clauses where the antecedent is a final 1, the following MA strata have been attested:

Italian: 1:2, 1:3, 1:Ben, 1:Loc
Tzotzil: 1:2, 1:3
K'ekchi: 1:2

A framework, as RG, which incorporates the notion of MA will be able to make cross-linguistic predictions about reflexive and retroherent clauses and state them as generalizations. The K'ekchi conditions on MA, stated in non-language-specific terms, will contribute to an empirically supported theory of 'reflexives'.

Chapter 3 Footnotes

1. In the Nahuala dialect of Quiche, extraction of the Locative as Q, Foc, or Rel is also marked by the postverbal insertion of the particle wih; the Quichean cognate of K'ekchi cui'. And like K'ekchi, if the Locative is extracted as Topic, wih does not occur.

As argued by Norman (1978), Instruments may head a Foc arc, in which case wih marks the extraction. However, Instruments must advance to DO in order to head a Q or Rel arc. The advancement of instrument-2 is marked by the verbal suffix b'e. Instrumental extraction in a b'e clause is not marked by wih since wih marks the extraction of questioned or relativized (final) instruments, not (final) DOs.

2. Cui' may optionally cliticize to the locative bar 'where' as in:

(1)a. Bar cui' qui-Ø -x -muk li ixim li ixk ?
where cui' tns-B3-A3-hide the corn the woman
'Where did the woman hide the corn?'

b. Bar qui-Ø-x- muk cui' li ixim li ixk ?
'Where did the woman hide the corn?'

3. Another negative form macua' 'it isn't' can also illustrate this point.

4. The syntax of the yo + nominalization construction is discussed in Chapter 6. Yo is a higher unaccusative predicate. In (35a) laat 'you' heads a final Abs arc and is cross-referenced by the second singular Set B affix. The Set B forms prefix to stems with an overt tense prefix, and suffix elsewhere, as in:

(1)a. Ixk - at.
woman-B2
'You are a woman.'

b. X - at -t'ane'.
tns-B2 -fall
'You fell down.'

Since yo does not occur with a tense prefix, the Set B form at is suffixed in (35a).

5. There is one exception to this. Some speakers allow an Erg to bear the Rel relation in a restricted environment. For those speakers who allow this, an additional constraint with the following effect would be required:

I. A final Erg may head a Rel arc in a clause c if it is 3rd person and the final 2 of clause c is not 3rd person.

6. There are however, grammatical counterparts to (23b), (26b), (29c), (31c) (32c), (33c) and (35c). Crucially in these grammatical sentences, the focused nominal which heads the initial Erg arc heads a final Abs arc in a detransitivized Retreat clause. Discussion of 2-3 Retreat is postponed until Chapter 4.

7. I have introduced a convention for the representation of multiattachment. A 1-(coreferential) 2 is 1:2, similarly, a 1-(coreferential) 3 is 1:3, a 1-(coreferential) Benefactive is 1:Ben, and so on.

8. It is not clear that (48) is a linguistic universal. (48) is the underlying assumption that led Perlmutter (to appear) and Perlmutter and Postal (1984) to their proposal of 'pronoun birth', which will be discussed below.

9. The generalization captured by the MA grammar can also be stated as:

If a nominal heads a nuclear term arc in a clause c and it also heads a narrow overlay arc, it must head an Abs arc.

In an earlier version of this paper (Berinstein 1984a) the extraction constraint was stated in this way.

10. I am assuming that the overt statement of generalizations is an argument for a grammar.

11. In footnote 5 it was noted that some speakers allow a final Erg to bear the Rel relation in a restricted environment. Therefore, the constraint proposed in footnote 5 would be required for those speakers under both the NOMA and COMA grammars and hence cancels itself out as an argument for or against either of these hypotheses.

12. The only way to express the (b) sentences in (70)-(72) is to detransitivize them. Retreat is also possible. Crucially, the inanimate NP heads an initial Erg arc and a final Abs arc in a Retreat clause. As in the active-passive pairs, the corresponding active transitive counterpart of the Retreat clause is ungrammatical. This follows from the tentative constraint proposed in (69).

13. In Jacaltec, as in K'ekchi, an inanimate nominal may not normally head a final Erg arc. Craig (1977) reports the following intransitive clauses (1a), (2a), with no active transitive counterpart.

(1)a. Xpehi te' pulta yu cake.
close cl/the door by wind
'The door was closed by wind.'

b.* Speba cake te' pulta.
close wind cl/the door
('The wind closed the door.')

(2)a. Chin xiw yu sc'ejalholo.
I am scared by dark
'I am scared by dark.'

b.* Chin xibte sc'ejalholo.
me it scares dark
('The dark scares me.')

The inanimate nominal in (1a) and (2a) occurs as the oblique possessor of the instrumental relational noun stem -u; it may not occur as the final Erg, even though the verbs in these clauses may be finally transitive, as evidenced in (3), below.

(3)a. Speba naj te' pulta.
close cl/he cl/the door
'He closed the door.'

b. Chin haxibte an.
me you scare 1p
'You scare me.'

14. Notice that the MA condition on inanimate nominals (78) also predicts that the subject of a Retreat clause can be an inanimate nominal even though the corresponding subject in the active clause cannot (see footnote 12).

15. There is a growing literature on unaccusative advancement and the unaccusative hypothesis (Perlmutter 1978). Some of the languages that have been argued to have initially unaccusative clauses include Albanian (Hubbard 1980), Choctaw (Davies 1981), Lakhota (Williamson 1979), Turkish (Özkaragöz 1980), Georgian (Harris 1981), Italian (Rosen 1981), and Halkomelem (Gerdts 1981).

16. The term 'retroherent' was introduced by Rosen (1981) as a cover term for constructions which were previously described as 'reflexive passive', 'reflexive unaccusative', and 'reflexive impersonal passive' in Perlmutter (1978).

17. The analysis for retroherent unaccusative advancement proposed for K'ekchi differs from retroherent unaccusative clauses discussed by others (see footnote 16). In K'ekchi the initial level is unaccusative, however, the final level is <u>transitive</u>. In the languages discussed earlier, the final level of the retro clause was <u>intransitive</u>. This raises an interesting issue about the notion of 'cancellation' and 'birth'. For instance, we have seen that there are initially transitive clauses which involve a 1:2 MA and 2-cancellation. In this case, the final stratum is intransitive (as in French and Halkomelem reflexives). There are also initially transitive clauses which involve a 1:2 MA and 2 birth. In this case, the final stratum is transitive (as in K'ekchi reflexives). Thus, the resolution of an <u>initial</u> 1:2 MA stratum by cancellation results in final intransitivity, while resolution by birth results in final transitivity.

I am claiming that an analogous situation occurs in retroherent unaccusative clauses. If the <u>non-initial</u> 1:2 MA is resolved by cancellation, the result is a finally intransitive clause (as in Italian retroherent unaccusative clauses). If the 1:2 MA is resolved by birth, the result is a finally transitive clause (as in K'ekchi retroherent unaccusative clauses).

The point is that irrespective of the initial (in)transitivity of the clause, if a 1:2 MA stratum (initial or non-initial) is resolved by cancellation, the final level will be intransitive, and if it's resolved by birth the final level will be transitive.

18. If the (infinitival) complement heads a final 2-arc, it is not introduced by the preposition <u>chi</u>.

19. The formulation of the Ergative Extraction Constraint under the MA grammar (52) and the formulation of it under the NOMA grammar (97) account for all of the data I have. They also make the following additional predictions:

(1) A nominal heading a final Erg arc can bear a narrow overlay relation in sentences like: 'Who wants to leave?' because it would head an Abs arc in the downstairs clause, and

(2) A nominal heading a final Erg arc cannot bear a narrow overlay relation in sentences like: 'Who wants to hit John?' where John heads a final 2-arc, because it would not head an Abs arc at any level.

This data however, is not crucial to the argument.

20. Assuming the notion of MA together with the Oblique Law provides an explanation for the ungrammaticality of sentences involving 1:Obl MAs (see Berinstein 1984a). However, in K'ekchi, sentences involving 1:3 MAs are also ungrammatical and these would not be ruled out by the Oblique Law, hence (100).

21. Since a grammar without MA will also require an additional statement to rule out non-nuclear term reflexives, as in (99), the formulation of such a constraint will not provide an argument for or against a MA grammar.

Chapter 4

SUBJECT FOCUS AND 2-3 RETREAT

4.0 Introduction

The subject of this chapter is the demotion of direct object to indirect object in K'ekchi. The analysis presented here differs from past analyses which labeled this construction the 'agentive-antipassive' (a name first introduced to Mayanists by Thom Smith-Stark 1976a). The agentive-antipassive is now a cover term used by Mayanists to describe certain constructions in which the agent is focused, relativized, or questioned. The label, as such, reflects the function of this construction in Mayan but, is noncommittal about the mechanism for detransitivization. It is, however, slightly misleading since 2-3 Retreat and Antipassive are syntactically distinct constructions (Berinstein 1980, Davies 1984), as will be discussed in Chapter 5.

Syntactically, the (a) and (b) sentences below differ in that the initial direct object _li cuink_ 'the man' is a final indirect object in (1b) but is a final direct object in (1a). These sentences differ also in that (1a) is transitive (as reflected by the verbal agreement with the final subject and DO of the clause), while (1b) is intransitive. Finally, the (a) and (b) sentences below also differ in that the final subject _li c'anti'_ 'the snake' is focus in (1b) and is not in (1a).

(1)a. X- Ø -x -lop li cuink li c'anti'.
rec-B3-A3-bite the man the snake
'The snake bit the man.'

b. Li c'anti' x -Ø -lop-o -c r-e li cuink.
the snake rec-B3-bite-R-asp A3-Dat the man
'It was the snake that bit the man.'

In a Retreat clause, a nominal which is an initial direct object ('2') is a final indirect object ('3'). It is the claim of this paper that such a demotion has taken place in sentence (1b), but not in (1a). There are two consequences of this demotion; first, there is final intransitivity, and second, the final subject of a Retreat clause (in K'ekchi) must bear a narrow overlay (Q, Foc, or Rel) relation.

2-3 Retreat: If a nominal a is a 2 of clause b in stratum c_k, it may be a 3 of clause b in stratum c_{k+1}.

The following transition is permitted:

(2)

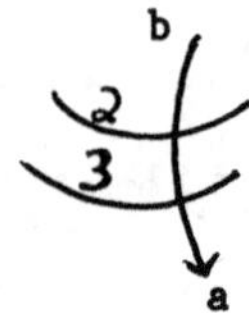

Four types of arguments are presented as evidence for the demotion analysis (2-3 Retreat). I show that in Retreat clauses 1) there is a final intransitive stratum (§4.1), 2) the initial Erg is a final Abs (§4.2), 3) the initial direct object is a final indirect object (§4.3), and 4) the initial indirect object is a final chômeur (§4.4).

Using the five diagnostics established for foci in Chapter 3, it will be shown that the final subject of a Retreat clause must bear a narrow overlay relation. The constraint that guarantees this is given in (3).

(3) If the initial DO is the final IO of a clause c, then the nominal heading the final subject arc of clause c must also head a narrow overlay arc.

Crucial to the 2-3 Retreat analysis is the claim that Retreat clauses involve two levels of structure: an initial level which is transitive and a final level which is intransitive. The relational network associated with (1a) is given in (4a). This clause has a single-level transitive structure. The relational network associated with (1b) is given in (4b). The initial DO of the clause <u>li cuink</u> 'the man' is the final IO, and as predicted by (3), the final subject of the Retreat clause is focused.

(4)a.

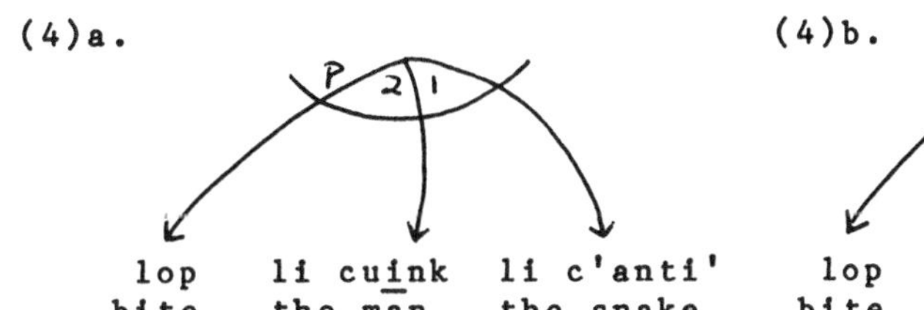

(4)b.

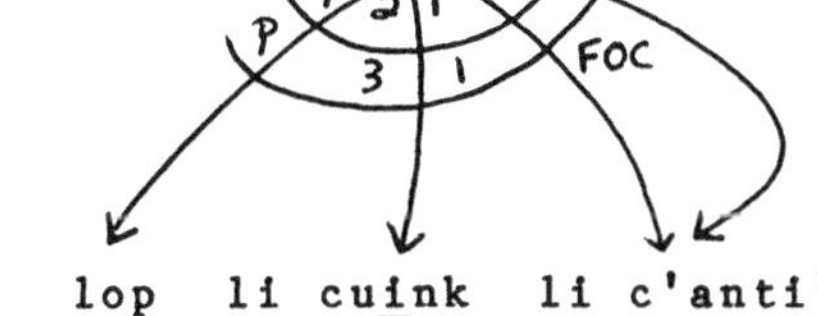

4.1 Arguments for 2-3 Retreat

Consider the sentence triplets in (5)-(8), below. The (a) sentences are active transitive clauses. The (b) sentences are intransitive Retreat clauses. The subject of the Retreat clause must be focused (i.e. occur in preverbal position), for this reason, the (c) sentences are ungrammatical.

(5)a. X - Ø -x- sac' li tz'i' li cuink.
rec-B3-A3- hit the dog the man
'The man hit the dog.'

(5)b. Li cuink x- Ø-sac'-o-c r-e li tz'i'.
the man rec-B3-hit-R-asp A3-Dat the dog
'It was the man who hit the dog.'

c.* X- Ø- sac'-o-c r-e li tz'i' li cuink.

(6)a. T -at-e'x-ch'aj laat.
fut-B2-pA3-wash you 'They will wash you.'

b. Heba'an t-e'-ch'aj-o-k acu-e
they fut-p-wash -R-asp A2 -Dat
'They are the ones who will wash you.'

c.* T- e'-ch'aj-o-k acu-e heba'an.

(7)a . T - at-cu-a'bi.
fut-B2-A1-listen 'I will listen to you.'

b. Lain t - in-a'bi -n- k acu-e.
I fut-B1-listen-R-asp A2 -Dat
'I'm the one who will listen to you.'

c.* T- in-a'bi -n-k acu-e (lain).

(8)a. T -in-x -tenk'a lix Rosa.
fut-B1-A3-help art Rosa 'Rosa will help me.'

b. Lix Rosa ta- Ø- tenk'a-n -k cu-e.
art Rosa fut-B3-help -R-asp A1-Dat
'Rosa is the one who will help me.'

c.* Ta -Ø-tenk'a -n-k cu-e lix Rosa.

There are several differences between the (a) and (b) sentences which must be explained: (1) verbal morphology: the (b) sentences have the suffix -o, or -n, whereas the (a) sentences have no such suffix. (2) verb agreement: in the (b) sentences there is one person marker which agrees with the final Subject, in the (a) sentences there are two person markers and agreement is with the final Subject and Direct Object. (3) aspect: the (b) sentences may have the intransitive suffix -c, or the incompletive aspect suffix -k, the

(a) sentences may not. (4) properties of DO: the DO is presented like a final IO (in a 'marked' possessive construction) in the (b) sentences, but is presented in the 'unmarked' case in the (a) sentences. (5) properties of subject: in the (b) sentences the final subject is in preverbal position and, as evidenced in the (c) sentences, it may not occur in its normal subject-final position. In contrast, in the (a) sentences the subject may occur in subject-final position or, it may be omitted.

The framework of Relational Grammar through the concept of demotion together with Focus can provide an explanation for these facts. Arguments for a 2-3 Retreat analysis follow.

4.1.1 Evidence for Final Intransitivity

The rules for 1) Retreat marking, 2) Verbal Agreement, 3) Aspect, and 4) Case will be given- all of which argue for the final intransitivity of the Retreat clause.

4.1.1.1 Retreat Marking

The rule that conditions Retreat morphology is presented in (9).

(9) Retreat Marking:[1]
If a nominal *a* heads an Erg arc with tail *b* and coordinate c_k, and an Abs arc with tail *b* and coordinate c_{k+1}, then the verb of clause *b* has the suffix -*o* (if the verb is monosyllabic) or the suffix -*n* (if the verb has two or more syllables).

In the (b) clauses in (5)-(8), the final subject heads an initial Erg arc and a final Abs arc, therefore Retreat morphology is required. Since Retreat marking can only occur in finally intransitive clauses, the presence of the -o, -n verbal reflex provides evidence for the final intransitivity of Retreat clauses.

4.1.1.2 Verbal Agreement

Verbal agreement is with the final Subject and Direct Object of the clause. Transitive verbs must have both a Set A (Ergative) and Set B (Absolutive) verbal affix. By this definition, if the verb is marked with only one affix, it can not be transitive. As exemplified in (5)-(8), the (a) sentences have both a Set A and a Set B affix, and these clauses are finally transitive. The (b) sentences have only a Set B affix. These clauses are finally intransitive. The verbal agreement rules which determine person agreement and the position of the Set A and B affixes are given in (10) and (11).

(10) Person Agreement:

a. A nominal heading a final Erg arc determines Erg agreement in the verb.

b. A nominal heading a final Abs arc determines Abs agreement in the verb.

(11) Set A and B Affix Positions:

a. The affix which is determined by the nominal that heads a final Erg arc is immediately prefixed to the stem.

b. The affix which is determined by the nominal that heads a final Abs arc is suffixed to the stem in tenseless clauses and prefixed in tensed clauses.

In Retreat clauses there is one verbal affix in agreement with the final Subject. This argues that (i) the clauses are finally intransitive, and (ii) that there are no final DOs in Retreat clauses. An analysis of 2-3 Retreat and the verbal agreement rules in (10) and (11) predicts precisely that. The reason the "logical object" does not control verbal agreement in a Retreat clause is because it is a final Indirect Object and Indirect Objects do not control verbal agreement.

4.1.1.3 Aspect

As discussed in Chapter 2 with respect to passive clauses, aspect marking is conditioned by final (in)transitivity. In clauses with t(v)- future, or ch(v)- optative T/A/M prefixes, the aspectual suffix -k is required if the final stratum is intransitive. In clauses with n(v)- present, x- recent past, c-/qu- remote past, or m(v)- negative T/A/M prefixes, the aspectual suffix -c may occur if the final stratum is intransitive. Neither -k nor -c may occur if the final stratum is transitive.

(12) Intransitive/Aspect Marking:
If the final stratum is intransitive -k is suffixed to the verb stem in incompletive aspect, otherwise -c may suffix to the stem.

The rule which conditions the optionality of the -c suffix is given in (13). If -c is in word final position and is immediately preceded by a nasal, or liquid, it may delete, as exemplified in (14)-(16).

(13) optional:

$$c \longrightarrow \emptyset \ / \ \begin{bmatrix} +son \\ +cons \end{bmatrix} \ \text{—} \ \#$$

(14)a. X - Ø-chal.
rec-B3-arrive 'He arrived.'

b. X - Ø-chalc. 'He arrived.'

(15)a. Na- Ø -cuar.
p -B3-sleep 'He sleeps.'

b. Na- Ø -cuarc. 'He sleeps.'

(16)a. Na- Ø - sutin cutan chi cü-u.
p- B3-make dizzy day in my-front
(Sp. 'Estoy mareado.' (lit. ' El dia da vueltas en frente de mi.')) 'I am dizzy.' (H.D:312)

b. Na- Ø -sutinc in-jolom x -mak x- sib -el
tns-B3-make dizzy my-head its-fault its-smoke-poss

a - raxbot. (Sp. 'Mi cabeza da vueltas por causa del
your-cigarette humo de tu cigarro.') (H.D:312)
'I am dizzy because of the smoke from your cigarette.'[2]

In contrast to -c, which is optional, -k is obligatory. Compare (17) below to (14) above, (18) below to (15) above, and (19) below to (16) above.

(17)a. Ta- Ø - chal - k.
fut-B3-arrive-asp 'He will arrive.'

b.* Ta- Ø - chal.

(18)a. Ta- Ø -cuar - k.
fut-B3-sleep-asp 'He will sleep.'

b.* Ta- Ø -cuar.

(19)a. Ta- Ø- sutin - k li ka-cua' chi r - u
fut-B3-go around-asp the our-lord in its-front

li santicles. (Sp. 'La imagen dará vueltas en frente de la
the church iglesia.') (H.D:312)

(19)b.* Ta- Ø -sutin li ka-cua' chi r-u li santicles.[3]

Regardless of the tense prefix, neither -c nor -k may occur in finally transitive clauses, as evidenced in (20).

(20)a.* T - at- e'x- ch'aj- k laat.
fut-B2-pA3 -wash -asp you ('They will wash you.')

b.* X - at- e'x- ch'aj- c laat.
rec-B2- pA3- wash-asp you ('They washed you.')

c.* T - in- x-tenk'a- k lix Rosa.
fut-B1-A3-help -asp ncl Rosa ('Rosa will help me.')

d.* X -in- x-tenk'a- c lix Rosa.
rec-B1-A3-help -asp ncl Rosa ('Rosa helped me.')

These phrases are grammatical if -c and -k are omitted. The grammatical counterpart of (20a) is given in (6a), and the grammatical counterpart of (20c) is given in (8a).

In Retreat clauses with T/A/M prefixes other than t(v)- or ch(v)-, -c is optionally conditioned by the rule in (13). Since there are two retreat suffixes -o, and -n, the aspect marking principle, given in (12), together with an analysis of 2-3 Retreat predicts that the -c suffix will be optional in those clauses with Retreat affix -n, but obligatory in those clauses with Retreat affix -o. This is the case. In (21), -c is optional. In (22), -c is obligatory.

(21)a. Li cuink a'an x- Ø -tz'iba-n- c r -e li hu.
the man that rec-B3-write- R-asp A3-Dat the letter
'That's the man who wrote the letter.'

b. Li cuink a'an x- Ø- tz'iba -n r-e li hu.
rec-B3-write -R
'That's the man who wrote the letter.'

(22)a. Li cuink a'an qui-Ø-lok'-o - c r- e li ch'ich'.
pst-B3-buy-r- asp A3-Dat the machete
'That's the man who bought the machete.'

b.* Li cuink a'an qui-Ø-lok'-o r-e li ch'ich'.
pst-B3-buy-R
('That's the man who bought the machete.')

In retreat clauses with t(v)-, or ch(v)- T/A/M prefixes, -k is obligatory (with both -o and -n retreat affixes). In (23a) below, ch(v)- is prefixed to the verb stem in a retreat clause. The absence of -k is ungrammatical, as evidenced in (23b).

(23)a. Li Dios chi-Ø -osobtesi- n - k r- e li ixk.
the God A/M-B3-bless - R- asp A3-Dat the woman
(Sp.'Que Dios bendiga a la señora.')
'May God bless the woman.' (E&C,Gr:149)

b.* Li Dios chi- Ø- osobtesi - n r-e li ixk.

In (23c) below, t(v)- is prefixed to the verb stem in a retreat clause. Again, as predicted by the aspect marking principle, -k is obligatory.

(23)c. L- in- yucua' ta-Ø- il - o- k k - e
the my -father fut-B3-see-R- asp A1p-Dat
'My father will see us.'

d.* L-in-yucua' ta -Ø- il- o k -e.
fut-B3-see-R

As shown in (17)-(19), in finally intransitive clauses if the stem is prefixed with ch(v)- or t(v)-, -k aspect is obligatory. In retreat clauses, if ch(v)- or t(v)- is prefixed to the stem, -k aspect is obligatory (23). In tense/aspects other than ch(v)- and t(v)-, the presence of -c is optionally conditioned by the rule in (13). C- must occur in retreat clauses with reflex -o, but is optional in retreat clauses with reflex -n. This was exemplified in (14) -(16), (21), and (22). Neither -c nor -k may occur in finally transitive clauses (20). These facts provide further evidence for the final intransitivity of retreat clauses (and for the syntactic difference between the (a) and (b) sentences in (5)-(8)).

4.1.1.4 Case

The case marking principle is given in (24). Subjects and Direct Objects are unmarked. Indirect Objects, and Obliques are expressed in a possessive construction as possessors of a relational noun (see Chapter 1).

(24) Case Marking:[4]
(i) Nuclear terms are unmarked.
(ii) All other grammatical relations are presented as possessors of a relational noun.

The rules governing person and number agreement in relational nouns follow from the nominal agreement principles in (25) and (26) below.

(25) Nominal Agreement:
(i) The possessor of a noun determines Set A agreement on the noun.

(ii) Third plural possessors of nouns optionally determine number agreement.

(26) Nominal Affix Positions:
(i) Set A affixes prefix to the possessed noun.

(ii) If number agreement is determined, eb must suffix to the possessed noun.

The 'logical object' of a retreat clause is presented as the possessor of the obligatorily possessed IO relational noun stem -e. This argues that the 'logical object' of a retreat clause is not a DO. Furthermore, it argues that it is an IO, since it is presented in the same form as other final IOs. For example, compare the form of the objects in (27) and (28). In (27) the initial IO is a final IO. In (28) the initial DO is a final IO. The fact that these objects share the same morphological shape and agreement pattern follows from an analysis of 2-3 Retreat together with the case marking and nominal agreement principles described above.

(27)a. Junelic na -Ø-a -q'ue cu-e li tumin.
always tns-B3-A2-give A1-Dat the money
'You always give money to me.'

b. C'am chak cu-e jun chic sec' in-cape.
bring dir A1-Dat one more cup my-coffee
'Bring another cup of coffee to me.' (E&C,Gr:109)

(28)a. Junelic laat nac-at-tenk'a-n cu-e .
always you tns-B2-help -R A1-Dat
'You always help me.'

b. Li x-yucua'-il li tzul x- Ø -cam-o-c cu-e .
the its-father-poss the mt tns-B3-take-R-asp A1-Dat
'The God of the mountain took me.' (E&C,MG.28)

In (27) and (28) the final IO is first person singular. The Set A first person singular affix cu- is prefixed to the IO relational noun stem -e. This follows from the statements in (25i) and (26i).

If the final IO is third person plural and number agreement is determined, then eb must suffix to the possessed noun, as claimed in (26ii). This is exemplified in (29) and (30). In (29), the initial IO is the final IO of a transitive clause. In (30), the initial DO is the final IO of a retreat clause.

```
(29)a. Lain  t  -Ø-in-yeh  r - e- eb li  coc'al .
        I    tns-B3-A1-tell A3-Dat- p the children
       'I will tell it to the children.'

    b. Ma  x- Ø - x -si  r- e -eb li  ixk   li  utz'u'uj?
       Q  rec-B3-A3-give A3-Dat-p the women the flowers
       'Did he give the flowers to the women?'

(30)a. A'an ajcui' c - ox- Ø -k'axtesi-n-c   r- e-eb .
       she  also  pst-dir-B3-deliver -R-asp A3-Dat-p
       (Sp. 'Ella misma los fue a entregar a ellos.')
       'She herself went to deliver them.'      (B.S7,44)

    b. A'aneb li  nequ-e'-c'ac'ale-n-c   r-e- eb li
        they  the  tns-p- guard  -R-asp A3-Dat-p the

 rok ha' .                                    (B.S2,37)
stream    'They are the ones who guard the streams.'
```

In both (29) and (30) the third person singular Set A affix r- is prefixed to the relational noun. This follows from the rules in (25i) and (26i). Since the final IO is plural and number is marked, eb must suffix to the relational noun stem. This follows from the rule in (26ii).

In sum, it has been argued that there is no final DO in a retreat clause. This follows from the case marking principles in (24) and provides evidence for the final intransitivity of retreat clauses. It has also been argued that the nominal agreement of the 'logical object' in retreat clauses, as in (28) and (30), is determined by the same nominal person and number agreement principles as are the IOs in transitive clauses, as in (27) and (29). Thus, a 2-3 Retreat analysis allows one to account for the case and nominal agreement facts in terms of final IO.

4.2 Initial Erg is final Abs

As already discussed (Chapter 3), there are transitive clauses that prohibit the focusing, questioning, or relativization of the final subject. Further, it was argued that the constraint that governs narrow overlay relations specifically restricts final Ergs. That is, a final Erg may only bear a narrow overlay relation if it heads an Abs arc. This constraint is stated in (31), below.

(31) Erg Extraction Constraint:
If a nominal heads a final Erg arc in a clause c and it also heads a narrow overlay (Q, Foc, or Rel) arc, it must head an Abs arc.

Thus in K'ekchi, even though both of the clauses in (32) are finally transitive, the subject can only be Foc (Q, or Rel) in the sentence associated with (32a), but not with the sentence associated with (32b).

(32)a. X -Ø -x- sac' r -ib li cuink.
tns-B3-A3-hit A3-self the man 'The man hit himself.'

b. X -in-x -sac' li cuink.
tns-B1-A3-hit the man 'The man hit me.'

In both (32a) and (32b) li cuink heads a final Erg arc, but at the initial level of structure li cuink heads an Erg arc and an Abs arc in (32a), and only an Erg arc in

(32b). Because the final Erg in (32a) heads an Abs arc (at some level of structure) it is able to bear a narrow overlay relation. On the other hand, in (32b) the final Erg does not head an Abs arc at any level, therefore it can not bear a narrow overlay relation. So how does one say 'That's the man who hit me!' or 'Who hit me?', or 'The man that hit me died.' in K'ekchi? The only way to say such sentences is in a retreat clause. In this sense, retreat is used for the questioning, focusing, or relativization of an initial Erg. That is, since the final subject of a retreat clause heads an Abs arc, it is able to focus, question, or relativize. For example,

(33)a. Ha' li cuink qui-Ø -sac'-o-c cu-e.
emph the man tns-B3-hit- R-asp A1-Dat
'That's the man who hit me.'

b.* Ha' li cuink qu-in-ix- sac'.
emph the man tns-B1-A3-hit
('That's the man who hit me.')

The RNs associated with (33a) and (33b) are given in (34a) and (34b), respectively. In both (34a) and (34b) ha' li cuink heads an initial Erg arc. In (34a) however, ha' li cuink heads a final Abs arc, while in (34b) it heads a final Erg arc.

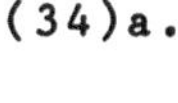
(34)a.

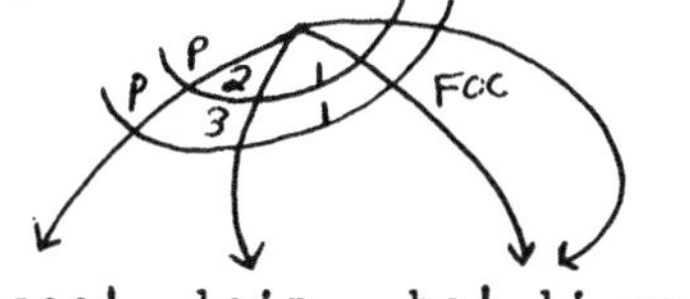

sac' lain ha' li cuink
hit me the man

(34)b.*

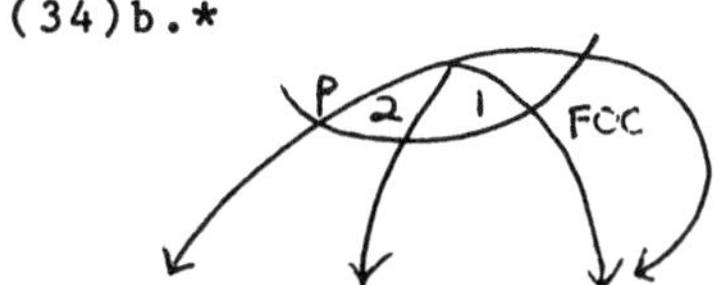

sac' lain ha' li cuink
hit me the man

As predicted by the Ergative Extraction Constraint, the final 1 of the transitive clause in (33b) cannot be focused. In contrast, the final 1 of the corresponding retreat clause in (33a) can be focused.

This observation provides an argument for the multilevel structure of a retreat clause. The final subject of a retreat clause can be Q, Foc, or Rel because it heads a <u>final Abs arc</u>. On the other hand, the final subject of the corresponding transitive clause cannot be Q, Foc, or Rel because it does not head an Abs arc.

4.2.1 Q and Rel

In this section, it will be shown that the final subject of a retreat clause, unlike the final subject of a transitive clause, can be questioned and relativized. This provides additional evidence for the final intransitivity of retreat clauses and supports the conclusion that the subject of a retreat clause heads an initial Erg arc and a final Abs arc.

The questioning of an Erg differs from the questioning of a DO in that retreat morphology is required for the former and disallowed for the latter.

(35)a. Ani x - Ø -x-sac' ?
who tns-B3-A3-hit 'Who did he hit?'

b. Ani x -Ø -sac'-o-c r-e ?
who tns-B3-hit-R-asp A3-Dat 'Who hit him?'

(36)a. C'a qui-Ø -x -b<u>a</u>nu li ixk ?
what tns-B3-A3-do the woman
'What did the woman do?' (E&C,XH.4)

b. Ani t<u>a</u>- Ø -p<u>a</u>b<u>a</u>-n- k r -e ?
who tns-B3-ask -R-asp A3-Dat
'Who will ask him?' (E&C,SM.9:23)

It is important to note the difference in the verbal morphology between the (a) and (b) sentences above. Crucially, in the (a) sentences, where an object is being questioned, the verb has <u>transitive</u> morphology. That is, the verb is cross-referenced with two person markers: the Set B third singular (<u>Ø</u>-) and the Set A third singular (<u>x</u>-) pronouns. On the other hand, in the (b) sentences, where an Erg is being questioned, the verb has <u>intransitive</u> morphology. That is, the subject agreement is Absolutive (<u>Ø</u>-) and the initial DO no longer controls verbal agreement; rather, it is presented in the form of a Dative relational noun <u>re</u>. Finally, the (b) sentences condition the presence of the retreat suffixes -<u>o</u> (as in (35b)) and -<u>n</u> (as in (36b)). The intransitive aspectual suffix also appears in the (b) sentences.

The rules established for Retreat Marking, Verbal Agreement, Aspect, and Case in Section 4.1 argue that the (a) sentences are finally transitive, and that the (b) sentences are finally intransitive. This supports our conclusion that the subject of a Retreat clause can be Q because it heads a (final) Abs arc (Erg Extraction Constraint). For this reason, the corresponding subject of the active transitive clause can not be questioned (focused, or relativized). The transitive analogue of the sentences in (35b) and (36b) are therefore ungrammatical, as evidenced in (37a) and (37b) respectively.

(37)a.* Ani x -Ø -x -sac' a'an?
who tns-B3-A3-hit 3s pro ('Who hit him?')

b.* Ani ti- Ø -x -paba a'an?
who tns-B3-A3-ask 3s pro ('Who will ask him?')

In (37), ani heads a final Erg arc and a narrow overlay arc but, does not head an Abs arc. The ungrammaticality of (37a,b) follows from the Ergative Extraction Constraint (31).

Particular to 2-3 Retreat in K'ekchi is the fact that the final subject of a Retreat clause must bear a narrow overlay relation. This constraint was stated in (3) and is repeated below as (38).

(38) Retreat Subject Constraint:
If the initial DO is the final IO of a clause c, then the nominal heading the final subject arc of clause c must also head a narrow overlay arc.

Further examples of Retreat clauses in which the final subject is Q are given in (39)-(47) below.

(39) Ani na- Ø-ch'aj-o-c r-e l - a -sec' ?
who tns-B3-wash-R-asp A3-Dat the-A2-cup
'Who washes your cup?' (E&C,Gr:114)

(40) Ani na- Ø -mich' -o -c r -e li pim sa' be ?
who tns-B3-uproot-R-asp A3-Dat the bush on road
'Who uproots the bushes on the road?' (E&C,Gr:114)

(41) Ani na -Ø -il -o-c k- e ?
who tns-B3-see-R-asp A1p-Dat
'Who takes care of us?' (E&C,Gr:149)

(42) Ani qui-Ø - yeh- o-c er-e ?
who tns-B3-tell-R-asp A2p-Dat
'Who told you (pl)?' (E&C,Gr:149)

(43) Ani anchal qui-Ø -yo'oba-n r -e a chabil na'leb ?
who Qu tns-B3-begin -R A3-Dat good custom
'Who began this fine tradition?' (H.D:39)

(44) Ani x - Ø -lok'-o-c r -e li r -ochoch nach'
who tns-B3- buy -R-asp A3-Dat the A3-house near

r - iq'uin li r - ochoch lix Rosa ?
its-side the her- house art Rosa
'Who bought the house next to Rosa's (house)?' (E&C,Gr:108)

(45) Ani x - Ø -q'ue-o-c r- e li ac'ach r- ubel li
who tns-B3-put -R-asp A3-Dat the turkey A3-under the

chacach ?
basket 'Who put the turkey under the basket?' (E&C,Gr:167)

(46) Ani ta -Ø -banu-n- k r -e lix nink'e ?
who tns-B3-do -R-asp A3-Dat the fiesta
'Who is going to celebrate the fiesta?' (E&C,Gr:299)

(47) Ani ta -Ø -ochbeni-n- k cu-e ?
who tns-B3-accomp -R-asp A1-Dat
'Who will accompany me?' (E&C,Gr:149)

The questions in (39)-(47) above cannot be expressed in a transitive clause because the final Erg must head an Abs arc if it is to bear the Q relation (see Chapter 3). Similarly, it will be shown below that the final Erg must head an Abs arc if it is to bear the Rel relation.

(48)a. X - Ø -x-cam li ixk li x- Ø -r-il li cuink.
tns-B3-A3-die the woman that tns-B3-A3-see the man
'The woman that the man saw died.'
(not: 'The woman that saw the man died.')

b. X-Ø-x-cam li ixk li x- Ø-il -o-c r- e li cuink.
tns-B3-see-R-asp A3-Dat the man
'The woman that saw the man died.

In (48a) the DO is Rel. The clause is unambiguous. The Erg can not be understood as Rel. The only way the logical subject of a transitive clause can be relativized is as a final Absolutive in a Retreat clause (48b). Other examples are given in (49)-(54).

(49) **Li cuink** li x -Ø -a'bi- n- k r -e li son
the man that tns-B3-hear-R-asp A3-Dat the music

x -Ø -x -bicha.
tns-B3-A3-sing
'The man who heard the song sang it.' (Ba,1976:88)

(50) **A'an** li qui-Ø -yo'obtesi-n chak k -e nak
that that tns-B3-create -R dir A1p-Dat that

nequ-Ø -e'x-c'oxla li cristian.
tns -B3-pA3-think the people
'The people think that that is what created us.' (E&C,KK.14)

(51) A'aneb len -Ø li c'u nequ-e'-chap -o- c r -e
they say-B3 the c'u tns- p -sustain-R-asp A3-Dat

li ruchich'och'.
the world
'They say that the c'u (mythological gods) are the ones that sustain the world.' (H,D:122)

(52) Qui-Ø -x-yeh r -e nak chi camsic
tns-B3-A3-tell A3-Dat that for the purp to be killed

li x - rabin ut r - ochben **li cuink** li
the his-daughter and her-companian the man the who

qui-Ø -c'am- o -c r -e.
tns-B3-take- R-asp A3-Dat
'He said to him, "May my daughter be killed along with the man that took her."' (E&C,MSS.55)

(53) Abanan **chixjunil-eb** li nequ-e'-yaba-n r -e li
but all -p that tns-p - ask-R A3-Dat the

x - c'aba' li kacua t - e'-col - e - k'.
his-name the our father tns- p -save-pass-asp
'But all those that pray to God will be saved.' (E&C,J.2:32)

(54) Qui- Ø -cam li cu<u>i</u>nk a'in li na -Ø -il -o-c
tns-B3-die the man this the who tns-B3-see-R-asp

r -e li has<u>i</u>end.
A3-Dat the hacienda (E&C,GG.2)
'This man, the one who watches the hacienda died.'

The nominal bearing the Rel relation in (48)-(54) heads an initial Erg arc and a final Abs arc. That the final subject of the Retreat clause bears a narrow overlay relation follows from the Retreat Subject Constraint.

4.2.2 Properties of Foci

The five diagnostics established for foci (in Chapter 3) can be used to distinguish nominals heading final Abs arcs from nominals heading final Erg arcs. It will be argued in Sections 4.2.2.1- 4.2.2.5 that these five properties characterize the final subject of a Retreat clause, but not the final subject of a transitive clause.

4.2.2.1 Preverbal Position

The final subject of a Retreat clause differs from the final subject of a transitive clause because the former <u>must</u> occur in preverbal position, and the latter <u>cannot</u> (see Section 3.2.2 in Chapter 3). Further, it is obligatory that the final subject of the retreat clause be overt. In contrast, nuclear term pronominal dependents are optional elsewhere.

(55)a. X - Ø -x-c'ub li tib li ixk ut <u>a'an</u>
tns-B3-A3-prepare the meat the woman and she

x - Ø -tzeca-n r - e chixjunil.
tns-B3- eat -R A3-Dat at once
'The woman prepared the meat and <u>she</u> ate it at once.'

(55)b.* X- Ø-x-c'ub li tib li ixk ut Ø x -Ø -tzeca-n
tns-B3-eat -R
r - e chixjunil.
A3-Dat at once
('The woman prepared the meat and Ø ate it at once.')

In (55a) the Retreat subject a'an occurs in preverba position. (55b) is ungrammatical because the Retreat subjec must be overt. By contrast, the corresponding subject of th transitive clause need not be overt (55c), and cannot occu in preverbal position (55d).

(55)c. X - Ø -x- c'ub li tib li ixk ut Ø
tns-B3-A3-prepare the meat the woman and

x - Ø -x -tzeca chixjunil.
tns-B3-A3-eat at once
'The woman prepared the meat and Ø ate it at once.'

d.* X-Ø-x-c'ub li tib li ixk ut a'an x -Ø -x -tzeca
she tns-B3-A3-eat

chixjunil.
at once.
('The woman prepared the meat and she ate it at once.')

The focus position is preverbal. The fact that the tran sitive subject cannot occur in this position reinforces ou earlier claim that a nominal heading a final Erg arc mus head an Abs arc in order to bear a narrow overlay relation A'an heads an initial Erg arc and a final Abs arc in (55a) Therefore, it may occur in preverbal position as focus. I (55d) a'an heads an initial Erg arc and a final Erg arc Therefore, it cannot occur in preverbal position. Finally that the subject of a Retreat clause must occur in preverba position (55b) provides independent evidence for the Retrea Subject Constraint (38).

4.2.2.2 Neg

The contrastive properties of foci are evidenced under negation. The Ergative Extraction Constraint claims that a final Erg can bear a narrow overlay relation only if it heads an Abs arc. Therefore, ergative foci circumfixed by the negative discontinuous morpheme moco...ta must head an Abs arc.

As evidenced in (56a) and (56b) final Absolutives may be foci, and as such they may be circumfixed by Neg for contrast. As exemplified in (56c) the final focused subject of a retreat clause may also be circumfixed by Neg. (56d) is ungrammatical because a nominal heading a final Erg arc may only bear a narrow overlay relation if it heads an Abs arc, as it does in (56e). Recall (Chapter 3, §3.3) that the subject of a reflexive clause heads an Abs arc in the initial 1:2 MA stratum. It therefore meets the condition of the Ergative Extraction Constraint and may be focused.

```
(56)a.[ Moco li  cuink ta ] na- Ø -alina a'ban li  al.
       neg  the  man neg  tns-B3-  run   but  the boy
      'It's not the man who runs, but the boy.'

    b. [ Moco li  cuink ta ] x- Ø-in-sac' a'ban li ixk.
                             tns-B3-A1-hit  but the woman
      'It's not the man that I hit, but the woman.'

    c. [ Moco li cuink ta ] x -Ø- sac'-o-c   cu-e .
                              tns-B3-hit-R-asp A1-Dat
      'It isn't the man who hit me.'

    d.*[ Moco li cuink ta ]  x- in- x- sac'.
                              tns-B1-A3- hit
      ('It isn't the man who hit me.')
```

(56)e. [Moco li cuink ta] x -Ø- x-toch' r -ib.
tns-B3-A3-hit A3-self
'That isn't the man who bumped himself.'

4.2.2.3 The Emphatic Particle Ha'

The emphatic particle ha' may introduce focused nominals. As predicted by the Ergative Extraction Constraint, ergative foci must head an Abs arc. Ergative nominals introduced by ha' must therefore head an Abs arc.

In this Section we will see that Unergs (57a), DOs (57b), Passive Subjects (57c), Retreat Subjects (57d), and the transitive subject of a reflexive clause (57f) may be introduced by ha', but the transitive subject of a nonreflexive clause (57e) may not be introduced by ha'. This follows from the Ergative Extraction Constraint and the notion of MA (as developed in Chapter 3).

(57)a. Ha' li cuink x -Ø - t'ane'.
emph the man tns-B3- fall
'That's the man who fell.'

b. Ha' li ic x - Ø - in- lok'.
emph the chile tns-B3- A1- buy
'That's the chile I bought.'

c. Ha' li ic x - Ø -lok'-e'.
emph the chile tns-B3-buy-pass
'That's the chile that was bought.'

d. Ha' li cuink x -Ø-lok'-o-c r-e li ic.
emph the man tns-B3-buy-R-asp A3-Dat the chile
'That's the man who bought the chile.'

e.* Ha' li cuink x - Ø- x -lok' li ic.
emph the man tns-B3-A3- buy the chile
('That's the man who bought the chile.')

(57)f. **Ha'** li cui̲nk x - Ø-x -toch' r -ib.
emph the man tns-B3-A3-hit A3-self
'That's the man who bumped himself.'

The nominals introduced by ha' are focused. Since the focused nominal must head an Abs arc, this provides further evidence that the subject of a Retreat clause heads a final Abs arc.

4.2.2.4 Demonstratives

Foci may co-occur with the demonstrative pronouns for emphasis. Given the Ergative Extraction Constraint, it is clear that ergative foci that co-occur with the demonstrative pronouns must head an Abs arc. Thus, we can predict that Retreat subjects will be able to co-occur with the demonstratives, but the corresponding subject in a transitive clause will not.

(58)a. **A'aneb** li mem aj al a'in x -e'-banu-n-c r- e.
they the stupid prt boy this tns-p-do -R-asp A3-Dat
'Those stupid boys did it.' (F,YB.70)

b. **A'in** li anum na- Ø -xebesi-n- c er-e.
this the ghost tns-B3-frighten-R-asp A2p-Dat
'This is the ghost that is frightening you (pl).'
(E&C,GG.16)

c. Li tz'i' **a'an** x -Ø- tiu -o-c cu-e.
the dog that tns-B3-bite-R-asp A1-Dat
'That's the dog that bit me.'

In (58a)-(58c) the focused Retreat subject co-occurs with the demonstrative pronouns for emphasis. The transitive subject can not co-occur with the demonstrative pronoun as focus (58d) unless it heads an Abs arc, as in (58e).

(58)d.* Li tz'i' a'an x -in-x -tiu.
the dog that tns-B1-A3-bite
('That's the dog that bit me.')

e. Li tz'i' a'an x -Ø -x-tiu r -ib.
the dog that tns-B3-A3-bite A3-self
'That's the dog that bit himself.'

These facts support the notion of MA and the conclusion that Retreat subjects head an Abs arc.

4.2.2.5 The Insistence Particle Pe'

Focused NPs may co-occur with the particle pe' for emphasis. Pe' must occur in clause second position; therefore, it may follow the preverbal NP, as NP pe', or if used in conjunction with the particle ha', it may precede the NP, as ha' pe' NP. As predicted by the Erg Extraction Constraint, if a nominal heading a final Erg arc co-occurs with pe', it must head an Abs arc.

In (59a) the intransitive subject is focused. In (59b) the DO is focused. In (59c) the Retreat Subject is focused. These nominals head final Abs arcs. The transitive subject in (59d) may not be focused because it heads an initial and final Erg arc. The transitive subject in (59e) may be focused because it heads an Abs arc in the initial 1:2 MA stratum. True to the prediction, only final Ergs heading Abs arcs may be focused, and thereby co-occur with pe'.

(59)a. { laat pe' x -Ø -yabac.
you pe' tns-B3-cry
ha' pe' laat
emph pe' you }
'You are the one who cried.'

(59)b. { laat pe' / ha' pe' laat } t- at-in-muk r-iq'uin-eb li xul
tns-B2-A1-bury A3- with-p the animal

cui' t - e'-cam-k .
if tns- p - die-asp
'You are the one I will bury with the animals, if they die.'

c. { laat pe' / ha' pe' laat } ta -Ø -col -o- k cu-e.
tns-B3-defend-R-asp A1-Dat
'You are the one who will defend me.'

d. * { laat pe' / ha' pe' laat } t - in-a -col
tns - B1-A2-defend
('You are the one that will defend me.')

e. { laat pe' / ha' pe' laat } t -Ø -a -col acu -ib.
tns-B3-A2-defend your-self
'You are the one that will defend yourself.'

4.2.2.6 Summary

It has been argued that in a Retreat clause the initial Erg is the final Abs. The Erg Extraction Constraint (discussed in detail in Chapter 3) interacts with this claim.

Erg Extraction Constraint:
If a nominal heads a final Erg arc in a clause c and it also heads a narrow overlay (Q, Foc, or Rel) arc, it must head an Abs arc.

The first piece of evidence that the nominal heading the initial Erg arc heads a final Abs arc in a Retreat clause is that it can bear a narrow overlay relation, while the corresponding subject of a transitive clause can not (see Sections 4.2 and 4.2.1).

The second piece of evidence concerns the properties of foci. Five diagnostics established for foci were used (§4.2.2.1-4.2.2.5). It was shown that these five properties can characterize the final subject of a Retreat clause, but not the final subject of a transitive clause. Thus, the subject of a Retreat clause can occur in preverbal position and be circumfixed by the discontinuous negative form _moco...ta_ for contrast, the emphatic particle _ha'_, the demonstrative pronouns, or the insistence particle _pe'_ for emphasis. On the other hand, the subject of a transitive clause cannot occur in preverbal position, or be circumfixed by _moco...ta_, the emphatic particle _ha'_, the demonstrative pronouns, or the insistence particle _pe'_, unless it heads an Abs arc (in a 1:2 MA stratum).

In addition, it was also argued that the final subject of a Retreat clause _must_ bear a narrow overlay relation. This is stated in the Retreat Subject Constraint.

> _Retreat Subject Constraint:_
> If the initial DO is the final IO of a clause c, then the the nominal heading the final subject arc of clause c must also head a narrow overlay arc.

First, it was shown that the final subject of a retreat clause can be Foc (§ 4.1). This was evidenced in the sentence triplets in (5)-(8). It was then shown that the final subject of the retreat clause _must_ occur in the preverbal focus position. As predicted by the Retreat Subject Constraint, if the subject of the retreat clause occurs in its 'normal' subject final position, the sentence is ungrammatical (cf. the (c) sentences in (5)-(8)). Consistent with the claim in the Retreat Subject Constraint, it was also shown that the final subject of a retreat clause can be Q, or Rel (§ 4.2.1).

Further support for the Retreat Subject Constraint was evidenced in § 4.2.2.1. Pronominal nuclear terms need not be overt (Chapter 1, § 1.1.1). However, the pronominal subject of a retreat clause must be overt. This follows from the fact that the subject of a retreat clause must occur in preverbal position as Q, Foc, or Rel, and therefore must occur in surface structure.

4.2.3 Inanimate Nominals

The third argument that the nominal heading the initial Erg arc heads a final Abs arc in a retreat clause interacts with a condition on inanimate nominals. As discussed in Chapter 3 (§ 3.3.2), an inanimate nominal may be a final intransitive subject, DO, Passive subject, or the (transitive) subject of a reflexive, or retroherent unaccusative clause. However, there are passive clauses with no active transitive counterpart, as in (60) below. In these clauses the final 1 chômeur (introduced by -<u>ban</u>) is an inanimate nominal. Given a passive analysis, it is clear that the inanimate nominal heads an initial Erg arc. The problem is that there are no corresponding transitive clauses in which the nominal heading the initial Erg arc heads a final Erg arc. The condition proposed to account for this fact is given in (61), below.

(60)a. Qui- Ø-c'at-e' **x-ban** li ca̲k li x-jolom.
tns-B3-burn-pass A3-by the lightning the his-head
'His head was burned by the lightning.' (B,S7.87)

b.* Qui -Ø-x -c'at li x-jolom li ca̲k .
tns-B3-A3-burn the his-head the lightning
('The lightning burned his head.')

(61) Condition on Inanimate Ergs:
If an inanimate nominal heads a final Erg arc, it must head an Abs arc.

The condition in (61) accounts for the ungrammaticality of sentences like (60b), and it makes a further prediction: If an inanimate nominal is the final subject of a retreat clause, we should expect to find retreat clauses with no active transitive counterpart. The sentence pair in (62) illustrates this.

(62)a. Li ca̲k qui-Ø -c'at-o- c r -e li x-jolom.
the lightning tns-B3-burn-R-asp A3-Dat the his-head
'The lightning burned his head.'

b.* Qui-Ø -x -c'at li x -jolom li ca̲k.
tns-B3-A3-burn the his-head the lightning
('The lightning burned his head.')

The Inanimate Constraint claims that if an inanimate nominal is a final Erg, it must head an Abs arc. For this reason there are Passive clauses with inanimate 1 chômeurs (60a) and Retreat clauses with inanimate subjects (62a) that have no corresponding transitive counterpart (62b). The relational network in (63a) corresponds to the sentence in (60b) and (62b).

(63)a. *

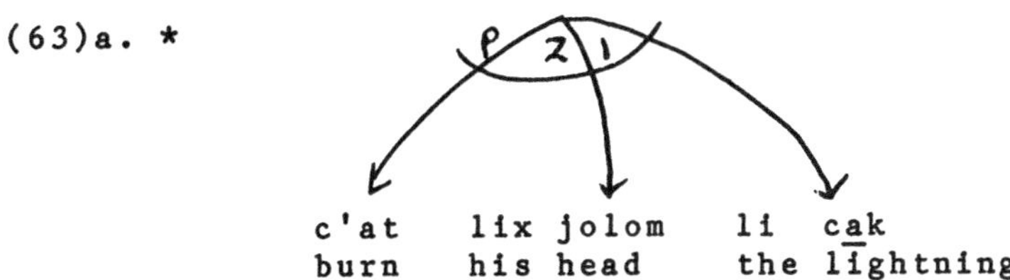

(63a) is ill-formed because an inanimate nominal heads a final Erg arc and it does not head an Abs arc.

The relational networks for the corresponding passive and retreat clauses have the same initial structure as (63a) above. The relational network corresponding to the passive clause in (60a) is presented in (63b), and the relational network corresponding to the retreat clause in (62a) is presented in (63c).

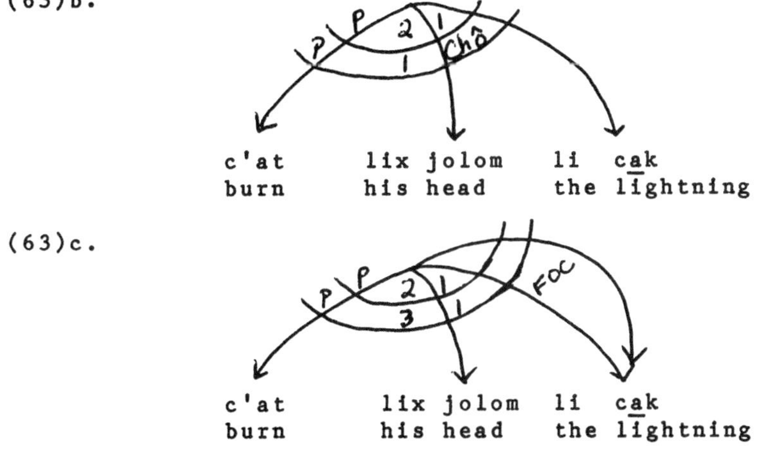

In (63b) the inanimate nominal heads an initial Erg arc and a final Chô arc in a passive clause. Since the inanimate nominal is not a final Erg, it need not head an Abs arc.

In (63c) the inanimate nominal heads an initial Erg arc and a final Abs arc in a Retreat clause. Because it is the final subject of a Retreat clause, it must bear a narrow overlay relation (Retreat Subject Constraint (38)).

Other Retreat clauses with no active transitive counterpart are given in (64)-(68).

(64)a. C'a'ru x -Ø -camsi-n r -e li cuink?
what tns-B3-kill-R A3-Dat the man
'What killed the man?'

b.* C'a'ru x- Ø -x- camsi li cuink ?
what tns-B3-A3-kill the man
('What killed the man?')

(65)a. Li ninki xox x - Ø -camsi-n r -e.
the big spot tns-B3-kill -R A3-Dat
'It's smallpox that killed him.'

b.* Li ninki xox x - Ø -x- camsi.
tns-B3-A3- kill
('Smallpox killed him.')

(66)a. Li hik qui- Ø -mich' -o- c r- e li che'.
the earthquake tns-B3-uproot -R-asp A3-Dat the trees
'It's the earthquake that uprooted the trees.'

b.* Li hik qui-Ø -x -mich' li che'.
tns-B3-A3-uproot the trees
('The earthquake uprooted the trees.')

(67)a. Li pec x -Ø -ch'em -o -c r -e li ch'ich'.
the rock tns-B3-nick - R-asp A3-Dat the machete
'The rock nicked the machete.' (H,D:143)

b.* X - Ø -x -ch'em li ch'ich' li pec .
tns-B3-A3-nick the machete the rock
('The rock nicked the machete.')

(68)a. Li hab ta- Ø -uk' -o- k r -e li ch'och'.
the rain tns-B3-flood-R-asp A3-Dat the land
'It's the rain that will flood the land.'

(68)b.* Ti -Ø -x-uk'   li ch'och' li hab .
tns-B3-A3-flood the land   the rain
('The rain will flood the land.')

The inanimate nominals in the (b) sentences head an initial Erg arc and a final Erg arc. As predicted by the Inanimate Condition (61), if an inanimate nominal is a final Erg, it must head an Abs arc. The (b) sentences are ungrammatical because the inanimate nominal does not head an Abs arc.

In the (a) sentences the inanimate nominals head an initial Erg arc and a <u>final Abs arc</u>. This follows from an analysis of 2-3 Retreat. That the inanimate nominal may be the final subject of a retreat clause, but can not be the final subject of a transitive clause supports our conclusion that it heads an Abs arc in the final stratum.

4.3 Initial DO is final IO

We have already seen two pieces of evidence that there is no final DO in a Retreat clause. First, as claimed in the Verbal Agreement Rules (§ 4.1.1.2): agreement is with the final Subject and DO of the clause. There is no agreement with the 'logical object' of the retreat clause because it is not a final DO. Second, as claimed in the Case Marking Rules (§ 4.1.1.4): final nuclear terms are unmarked. The 'logical object' of a retreat clause is expressed in a marked possessive construction because it is not a final DO.

These facts follow from an analysis of 2-3 Retreat. There is no final DO in a retreat clause because the initial DO is a final IO. With respect to the first claim then, the logical object of the retreat clause does not control verbal agreement because it is a final IO, and IOs don't control agreement. With respect to the second claim, the logical object of a retreat clause is expressed in a marked possessive construction because <u>all</u> final non-nuclear terms (except 2-chômeurs) are presented as possessors of a relational noun. An IO is a non-nuclear term, and as such, it is presented as possessor of the Dative relational noun stem -<u>e</u>.

Three additional arguments will be given which support the claim that the initial DO is the final IO of a Retreat clause.

4.3.1 Pronominal Dependents

As noted in Chapter 1, nonemphatic nuclear term pronominal dependents need not occur in surface structure. As predicted by this claim, the logical object of a transitive clause may or may not be overt, but the logical object of a retreat clause must be overt. This follows from the fact that a) the logical object of a transitive clause is a final DO, b) the logical object of a retreat clause is a final IO, and c) nonemphatic (pronominal) IOs must occur in surface structure.

(69)a. Lain x - Ø -in-sac'.
I tns-B3- A1-hit 'I hit her/him/it.'

b.* Lain x -in-sac'-o- c.
I tns-B1-hit -R-asp ('I hit her/him/it.')

In the transitive clause in (69a), the object is not overt. It is understood as third person singular by virtue of the verb agreement. In the retreat clause in (69b), the object cannot be understood as third person, since IO's do not control verb agreement. For this reason, non-nuclear term pronominal dependents must be overt. To express the pronominal object in (69b), the relational noun re is required, as in (69c).

c. Lain x -in-sac'-o- c r -e.
I tns-B1-hit -R-asp A3-Dat 'I hit her/him/it.'

In (70) below, the object is second person singular. This is cross-referenced by the Set B2 verbal affix -at in (70a) and by the Set A2 nominal prefix acu- in (70b). To express the person and number of the object in (70b), the Dative relational noun acue must be overt.

(70)a. Lain x- at -in-sac' (laat).
I tns-B2 -A1-hit you 'I hit you.'

b. Lain x -in-sac'-o- c acu -e (laat).
I tns-B1-hit-R-asp A2- Dat you 'I hit you.'

The final DO of a transitive clause, as in (69a) and (70a), need not be overt, but the final IO of a retreat clause, as in (69b), (69c), and (70b), must be overt. This follows from the fact that nuclear term pronominal dependents need not occur in surface structure, but non-nuclear term pronominal dependents must; thus providing further evidence that the initial DO is a final IO in a Retreat clause.

4.3.2 Reflexivization

The second argument that the initial DO is final IO in a retreat clause interacts with a condition on MA (Chapter 3, § 3.3.6). This condition is stated in (71).

(71) *MA Condition*
The only clause-internal MA that is well-formed is 1:2.

As argued in Chapter 3 (§3.3), clause-internal coreference is represented by multiattachment. The relational networks of reflexive clauses in K'ekchi involve a stratum in which a single nominal heads two neighboring arcs. It was also argued that reflexive clauses in K'ekchi are finally transitive. Two pieces of evidence confirm this. *First*, both the Set A and B affixes occur on the verb. (The rules for verbal agreement are given in §4.1.1.2). This is illustrated in (72), below.

(72)a. X - Ø -r- il r-ib li al sa' lem.
tns-B3-A3-see A3-self the boy in mirror
'The boy saw himself in the mirror.'

b. T -Ø -a̱cu-il a̱cu-ib sa' lem.
tns-B3-Ā2-see Ā2-self in mirror
'You will see yourself in the mirror.'

The nominal heading the final Erg arc controls Set A agreement, while the nominal heading the final Abs arc controls Set B agreement. And *second*, the intransitive aspectual affix may not occur in a reflexive clause. (The rules for aspect are given in § 4.1.1.3.) This is illustrated in (73).

(73)a.* X - Ø -r -il - c r-ib li al sa' lem.
tns-B3-A3-see-asp
('The boy saw himself in the mirror.')

b.* T - Ø -acu-il - k acu-ib sa' lem.
tns-B3-A2-see- asp
('You will see yourself in the mirror.')

As argued in §4.1.1.3, -<u>k</u> is obligatory in the incompletive aspect if the clause is finally intransitive. Since -<u>k</u> cannot suffix to the verb stem in a reflexive clause, this argues that reflexive clauses are finally transitive.

Consider the sentence pair in (74).

(74)a. Li ixk qui-Ø -x- takla li hu r- e laj Lu'.
the woman tns-B3-A3-send the letter A3-Dat art P
'The woman sent the letter to Pedro.'

b.* Li ixk qui-Ø -x-takla li hu r- e r -ib.
A3-Dat A3-self
('The woman sent the letter to herself.')

(74a) is a transitive clause. (74b) is ungrammatical because a reflexive may not head a 3-arc. The associated relational network in (75) is ill-formed because there is a 1:3 MA. This RN is ruled out by the MA Condition (71).

(75)*

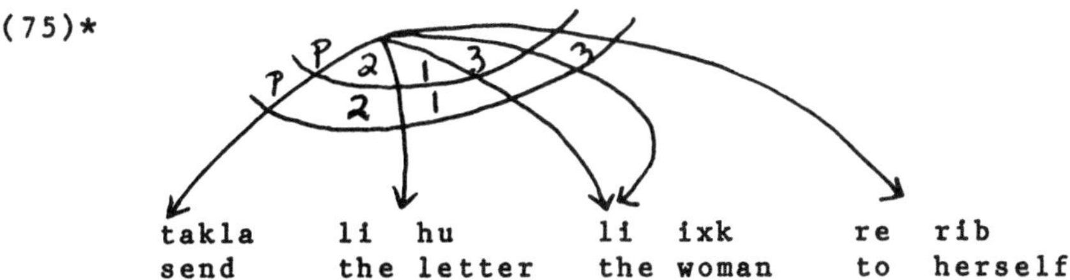

The MA Condition further predicts that the final 1 of a Retreat clause cannot be coreferential with the logical object of the clause, since that too would involve a 1:3 MA.

(76)a. L<u>a</u>in x -Ø -in-sac' cu-ib.
I tns-B3-A1-hit A1-self 'I hit myself.'

b.* L<u>a</u>in x -in-sac'-o-c cu-e cu-ib.
I tns-B1-hit -R-asp A1-Dat A1-self
('I'm the one who hit myself.')

(77)a. (77)b.*

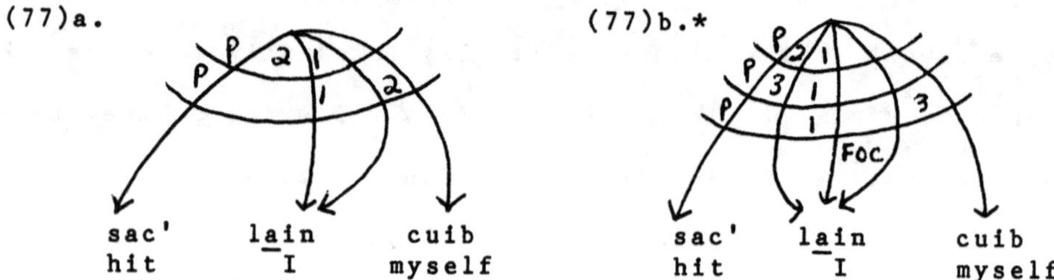

The relational network in (77a) is associated with the sentence in (76a). At the initial level of structure, the subject of the clause heads both a 1-arc and a 2-arc. At the final level of structure, the reflexive noun heads the 2 (Birth) arc and the subject heads the 1-arc.

The relational network in (77b) is associated with the sentence in (76b). At the initial level of structure the subject of the clause heads both a 1-arc and a 2-arc. At an intermediate level of structure the 2 demotes to 3. The multiattachment is resolved and the reflexive noun heads a 3 (Birth) arc. The final 1 of the retreat clause must head a narrow overlay arc (cf. (38)). The RN in (77b) involves a 1:3 MA stratum. As predicted by the MA Condition (71), only 1:2 MAs are well-formed. Thus, the relational network in (77b) is ill-formed.[5]

It was shown that retreat clauses may not have a reflexive object. The MA Condition provided further support that the logical object of the retreat clause is a final 3, since reflexives cannot head a 3-arc (74b, 76b).

4.3.3 Word Order

The third argument that the initial DO is final IO in a retreat clause is based on the word order principles and the predictions that they make with respect to focus. The Condition on Ergative Extraction, given earlier as (31), is repeated below.

(31) Condition on Ergative Extraction:
If a nominal heads a final Erg arc in a clause c and it also heads a narrow overlay (Q, Foc, or Rel) arc, it must head an Abs arc.

Now, consider the sentences in (78).

(78)a. X -o -e'x-tenk'a lao li cuink.
tns-B1p-pA3-help us the man. V-O-S
'The men helped us.'

b.* Ha' eb li cuink x- o -e'x-tenk'a lao.
emph p the man us *S-V-O

c.* Lao li cuink x - o- e'x- tenk'a. *O-S-V

(78a) is a finally transitive clause. The nominal heading the final Erg arc occurs in its nuetral sentence-final position. In (78b) and (78c), the nominal heading the final Erg arc occurs in a preverbal focus position. The S-V-O clause in (78b) is ungrammatical because the Erg cannot be focused unless it heads an Abs arc (31). The O-S-V clause in

(78c) is ungrammatical for the same reason. Interestingly, not all O-S-V clauses are ungrammatical. Consider the sentences in (79).

```
(79)a.* Li  tz'i'   li cuink   x - Ø- x-sac'.
        the dog     the man   tns-B3-A3-hit
        ('The man hit the dog.')

    b.  Li  tz'i'  li cuink   x -Ø -sac'-o- c   r -e.
        the dog    the man   tns-B3-hit -R-asp  A3-Dat
        'The dog, the man hit it.'
```

In (79a) the clause is finally transitive and the O-S-V word order is ungrammatical. However, a superficially similar word order in a retreat clause is grammatical, as evidenced in (79b). Since the final subject of a retreat clause heads an Abs arc, it may occur in the immediate preverbal position as Focus, while the final IO **li tz'i'** occurs in the S-initial position as Topic.

In the O-S-V clauses in (80)- (82) below, the final IO of the retreat clause is Topic and the final Subject is Focus. As with the clause in (79b), if the IO is third person and bears the Topic relation in a Retreat clause, the relational noun that cross-references it must occur in the IO position (after the verb).

```
(80) Li  bich a'in  ha'an  ta- Ø -bicha-n- k   r -e.
     the song this   he    tns-B3-sing -R-asp A3-Dat
     'This song, he will sing it.'

(81) A  trabaj a'in  cuink na- Ø-banu-n-k   r -e  sa' jalan
        work   this   men  tns-B3-do-R-asp A3-Dat in another
chic c'alebal.
     place
'This work, men do it in another place.'       (A&P,1976:33)
```

(82) Li po'ot lix Mar x -Ø -quem-o-c r -e.
the huipil ncl Mar tns-B3-sew -R-asp A3-Dat
'The huipil, Mary sewed it.'

It has been shown that O-S-V word order is not allowed in finally transitive clauses (78c), (79a), but is allowed in retreat clauses (79b), (80), (81), (82). This follows from an analysis of 2-3 Retreat in which the final stratum is intransitive, therefore allowing the subject to occur in preverbal position, when otherwise it is restricted from doing so. In addition, these facts provide further support for the Retreat Subject Constraint (38) and the Ergative Extraction Condition (31). That is, not only is it possible for the intransitive subject to occur in preverbal position, it must (38). In other words, the IO may not be Topic unless the final subject of the Retreat clause bears a narrow overlay relation (and occurs in preverbal position).

(83)a.* Li bich a'in ta -Ø -bicha-n- k r -e.
the song this tns-B3-song -R-asp A3-Dat
(' This song, he sang it.')

b.* Li bich a'in ta -Ø-bicha-n- k r-e ha'an.

c.* Li bich a'in ta -Ø-bicha-n- k ha'an r-e.

The sentences in (83) are ungrammatical because the final subject of the retreat clause does not bear a narrow overlay relation.

4.4 Initial IO is Final Chômeur

In this Section three pieces of evidence are presented which argue that the initial IO is a final chômeur in a

Retreat clause. This analysis has some interesting theoretical implications for syntactic theory. It will be shown that even though the Chômeur Law has been abandoned, the initial IO bears the chômeur relation in demotion construtions. The Chômeur Law and the Stratal Uniqueness Law (already discussed with respect to Passive, Chapter 2) interact with this claim. The Stratal Uniqueness Law claims that no two nominals can bear the same term relation in the same stratum. This is stated formally in (84), and the Chômeur Law is stated in (85).

(84) <u>Stratal Uniqueness Law:</u>
Let "$Term_x$" be a variable over the class of Term R-signs, that is, "1", "2", or "3". Then: If arcs A and B are both members of the c_kth stratum(b) and A and B are both $Term_x$ arcs, then A=B.

(85) <u>Chômeur Law:</u>
If an RN contains arcs of the form [$Term_x$(a,b) <c_u c_k c_y>] and [$Term_x$(c,b) <c_{k+1} c_z>], then it contains an arc of the form [Chô(a,b) <c_{k+1} c_w>].

In short, if a network contains a subnetwork of the form

(86)

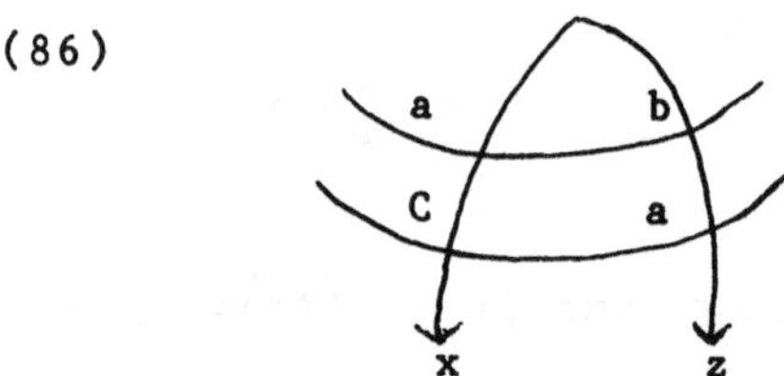

where a term relation (<u>a</u>) is borne by Nominal <u>X</u> in one stratum and Nominal <u>Z</u> in the next, then <u>C</u> is the chômeur relation. This is common in discussions of Passive and 3-2 advancements- both of which create chômeurs. It is shown here that the Chômeur Law is relevant to the class of demotions, as well. Specifically, the subnetwork in (87) is well-formed in K'ekchi.

(87)

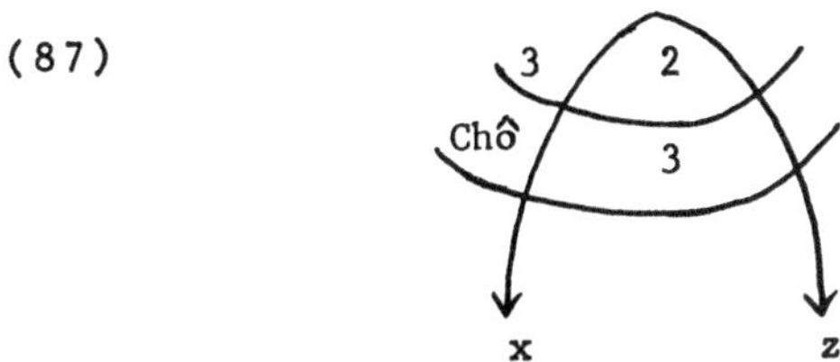

4.4.1 IO Word Order

The basic order of elements in a clause is stated in (88).

(88) V (2 chô) (3) (2) (3 chô) (Obl*) (1 chô*) 1 (*)

As discussed earlier, the position of the oblique and the 1 chômeur is not fixed with respect to the final Subject. That is, an oblique may precede or follow the final Subject. In addition to this variance, the IO and the DO are subject to some interchangeability. Despite this variance, I argue, based on two constructions involving IOs, that the position of a pronominal IO is immediately after the verb. I then show that in clauses with a final 3 and a 3-chômeur, only the final 3 may occur in the IO position.

The DO may precede the IO if the IO is a full NP, as in (89b).

(89)a. X - Ø -x-q'ue r -e lix Mar li utz'u'uj .
tns-B3-A3-give A3-Dat art M the flower V-IO-DO
'He gave the flowers to Mary.'

(89)b. X - Ø -x-q'ue li utz'u'uj r -e lix Mar.
the flower A3-Dat art M V-DO-IO
'He gave the flowers to Mary.' (not:V-DO-IO-S)
(not: 'Mary gave the flowers to her/him.')

In sentences of this type, speakers prefer (89a) but also accept (89b). The relational network for (89a,b) is given in (90). In general, the DO may not precede the IO if the IO is pronominal. For this reason, (89b) is not ambiguous. Re lix Mar is understood as a single IO constituent, not as: [re]$_{IO}$ [lix Mar]$_{S}$.

(90)

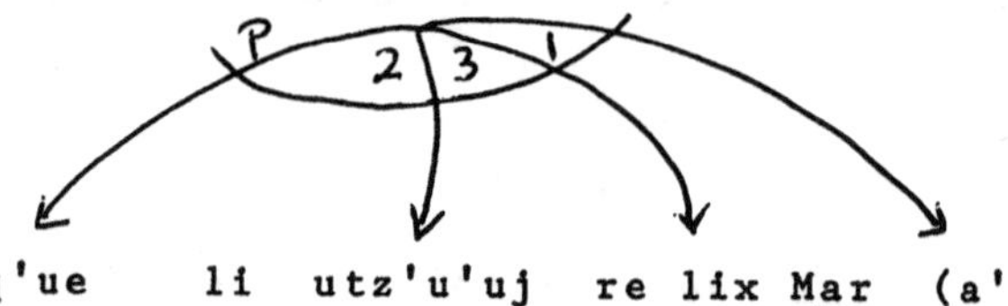

q'ue li utz'u'uj re lix Mar (a'an)
give the flowers to Mary he

The lack of ambiguity in sentences like (89b) suggests that the position of a pronominal IO is after the verb. This prediction is borne out in imperative clauses.

(91)a. Q'ue cu- e li ha'.
give A1-Dat the water (E&C,Gr:275)
'Give the water to me.'

b.*Q'ue li ha' cu-e

(92)a. Q'ue cu- e li x- hu laj Lu'.
give A1-Dat the his-book art P (H,Gr:86)
'Give Pedro's book to me.'

b.*Q'ue li x-hu laj Lu' cu- e

Finally, as evidenced in Section 4.3.3, when the IO is topicalized the relational noun must occur in the IO position, or more precisely, after the verb.

(93)a. Laat x -Ø -in-q'ue acu- e li tumin.
you tns-B3-A1-give A2-Dat the money
'To you I gave the money.'

b.*Laat x -Ø -in-q'ue li tumin acu-e.

Now observe the transitive clause (94a) and its retreat clause counterpart (94b). In the transitive clause the final (pronominal) IO occurs after the verb. In the corresponding retreat clause it does not. An analysis of 2-3 Retreat together with the chômeur relation provide an explanation for this fact.

(94)a. X -Ø-in-q'ue acu-e li tumin.
tns-B3-A1-give A2-Dat the money
'I gave the money to you.'

b. Lain x -in-q'ue-o-c r -e li tumin acu-e .
I tns-B1-give-R-asp A3-Dat the money A2-Dat
'I am the one who gave the money to you.'

The relational network associated with (94b) is given in (95). **Li tumin** 'the money' heads an initial 2-arc and a final 3-arc. Acue 'to you' heads an initial 3-arc and a final Chô-arc. There is no special morphological marking for a 3-chômeur. Rather, the 3-chômeur is cross-referenced as the possessor of the Dative relational noun stem -e, in the same way as a final 3.

Since the 'Dative' nounphrases do not differ with respect to nominal agreement or case marking, one might propose an alternative account of this data claiming that there are two IOs in (94b). Under such an analysis, the structure associated with (94b) would be (95b), instead of (95a).

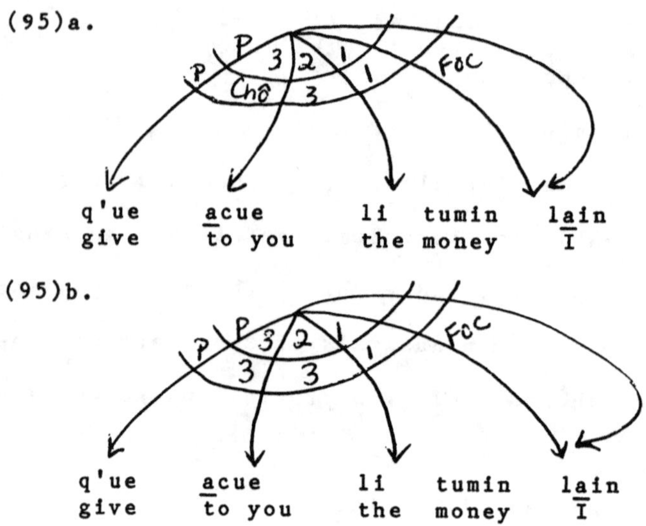

The relational network in (95b) is in violation of the Stratal Uniqueness Law because there are two 3-arcs in the <u>same</u> stratum.

The above generalization governing IO pronominal word order makes a prediction with respect to final 3-hood that can help distinguish between the proposed structures in (95a) and (95b). We have seen that the 'preferred' IO position is after the verb and that in certain cases, the pronominal IO <u>must</u> occur after the verb. If both acue and re li tumin are final 3s, then the position of the pronominal IO acue should be after the verb, however it cannot occur in that position. Compare (96) below to (94b) above.

(96)* Lain x -in-q'ue-o-c acu-e r -e li tumin.
I tns-B1-give-R-asp A2-Dat A3-Dat the money
('I'm the one who gave the money to you.')

The nominal corresponding to the initial IO cannot occur in the IO position, instead the nominal corresponding to the initial DO occurs in that position. These facts support an analysis of 2-3 Retreat and the proposed structure in (95a). (96) is ungrammatical because the IO chômeur acue occurs in the IO position after the verb. However, since re li tumin is the final IO, it should occur after the verb, as it does in (94b). Other examples follow.

(97)a. Lain x -in-q'ue-o-c r - e acu-e.
I tns-B1-give-R-asp A3-Dat A2-Dat
'I'm the one who gave it to you.'

b.*Lain x -in-q'ue-o-c acu- e r -e .

(98)a. Ani x -Ø-q'ue-o-c r -e li hu r- e li ixk?
who tns-B3-give-R-asp A3-Dat the book A3-Dat the woman
'Who gave the book to the woman?'

b.*Ani x -Ø-q'ue-o-c r -e li ixk r -e li hu ?

(99)a. Laj Manu' x -Ø -sih -o-c r-e li utz'u'uj acu-e
ncl Manu' tns-B3-give-R-asp A3-Dat the flowers A2-Dat
'It was Manuel who presented the flowers to you.'

b.*Laj Manu' x -Ø-sih-o-c acu-e r-e li utz'u'uj .

(100)a. Laat pe' li x -at-q'ue-o-c r-e li matan cu-e
you pe' that tns-B2-give-R-asp A3-Dat the gift A1-Dat
'You are the one that gave the gift to me.'

b.*Laat pe' li x -at-q'ue-o-c cu-e r-e li matan .

(101)a. Ma laat x -at-q'ue-o-c r-e li tumin r-e laj Lu' ?
Q you tns-B2-give-R-asp A3-Dat the money A3-Dat ncl Lu'
'Did you give the money to Pedro?'

b.*Ma laat x-at-q'ue-o-c r -e laj Lu' r-e li tumin ?

As indicated in the retreat clauses in (97)-(101) the position of the final IO (whether pronominal or not) is after the verb.

Summing up: two constructions were discussed that require the (pronominal) IO to occur after the verb: IO Topicalization and imperatives. It was then shown that in retreat clauses the initial 2/final 3 must occur after the verb and that the initial 3/final Chômeur could not. The fact that the nounphrase corresponding to the initial IO cannot occur in the IO position in a retreat clause supports our conclusion that it is a chômeur, as predicted by the Chômeur Condition[6].

4.4.2 IO Topicalization

It was claimed earlier, with respect to Passive, (Chapter 2), that a chômeur cannot bear the Topic relation. The fact that the final Subject in the passive clause in (102a) can be Topic, but the Subject Chômeur cannot (102b), is predicted by the Chômeur Constraint, given in (103).

(102)a. Li ixk x - Ø- saq'u- e' x-ban li cuink.
the woman tns-B3-hit -pass A3-by the man
'The woman was hit by the man.'

b.* X-ban li cuink x -Ø-saq'u-e' li ixk.
('By the man the woman was hit.')

(103) Chômeur Constraint: (Chapter 2, §2.3.3)
A Chômeur cannot head an overlay arc.

It will be argued that the final IO can be distinguished from the IO Chômeur in a retreat clause because only the former can be topicalized.

(104)a. X - Ø -in-q'ue r- e laj Lu' li tumin.
tns-B3-A1-give A2-Dat ncl Lu' the money
'I gave the money to Pedro.'

b. Lain x-in-q'ue-o-c r -e li tumin r -e laj Lu'.
I tns-B1-give-R-asp A3-Dat the money A3-Dat ncl Lu'
'I'm the one who gave the money to Pedro.'

The relational network associated with (104b) is given in (105). **Li tumin** heads an initial 2-arc and a final 3-arc and **re laj Lu'** heads an initial 3-arc and a final Chô-arc. The final 1 of the retreat clause heads a Foc-arc. Given the Chômeur Constraint (103), we can predict that the final 3 will be able to topicalize and that the 3-chômeur will not.

(105)

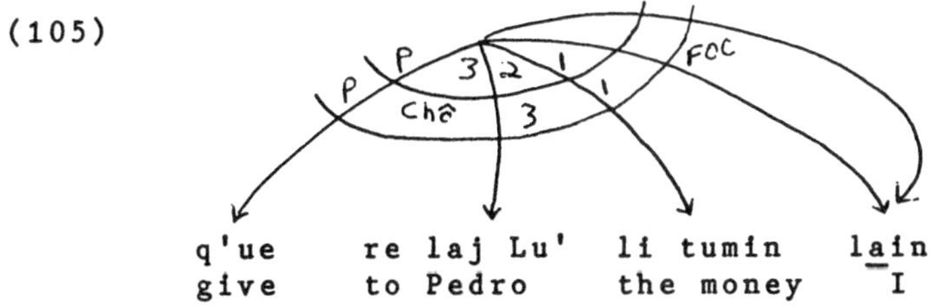

The sentences in (106) are an attempt to topicalize the initial 3/final Chômeur. Because these are retreat clauses, the final 1 must head a narrow overlay arc and occur in preverbal position (Retreat Subject Constraint (38)).

(106)a.* **Laj Lu'** lain x-in-q'ue-o-c r- e li tumin r-e.
ncl Lu' I tns-B1-give-R-asp A3-Dat the money A3-Dat
('Pedro, I gave the money to him.')

b.* **Laj Lu'** lain x-in-q'ue-o-c **r-e** r-e li tumin.
('Pedro, I gave him the money.')

c.* **Re laj Lu'** lain x-in-q'ue-o-c r-e li tumin.
('To Pedro, I gave the money.')

The relational network associated with (106) is given in (107). It is ill-formed because a final Chômeur cannot head a Topic arc.

(107)*

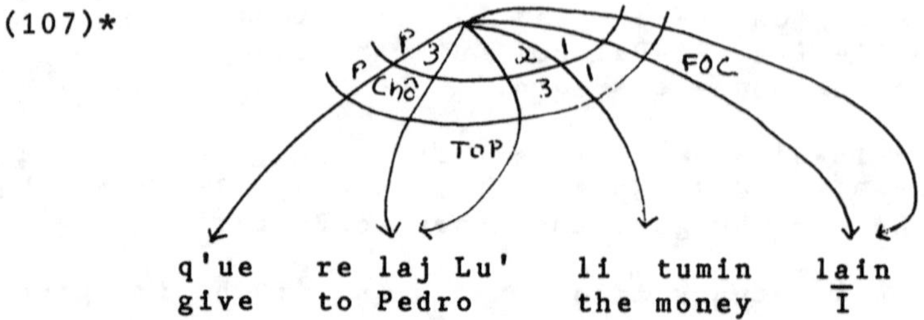

In contrast, the final 3 of the retreat clause can be Topic (108) and the associated relational network is well formed (109).

(108) **Li tumin** lain x -in-q'ue-o-c r-e acu-e.
the money I tns-B1-give-R-asp A3-Dat A2-Dat
'The money, I gave it to you.' (B,BNB.71)

(109)

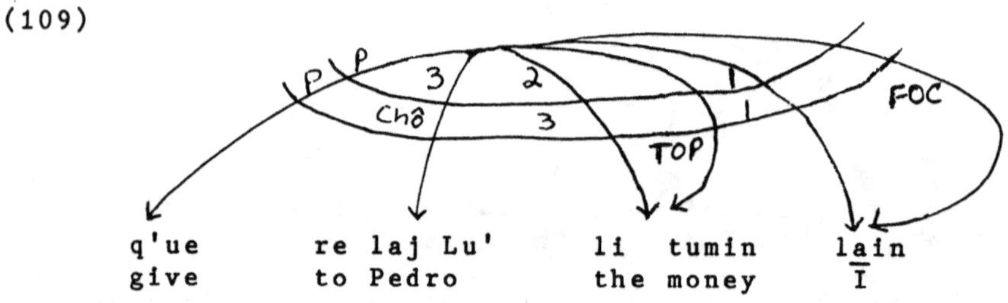

Consistent with the IO word order generalization (§ 4.4.1), the IO (relational noun) re must occur after the verb if the IO possessor li tumin is Topic. (110) is not grammatical because the chômeur acue occurs after the verb.

(110)* **Li tumin** lain x -in-q'ue-o-c acu-e r- e .
the money I tns-B1-give-R-asp A2-Dat A3-Dat
('The money, I gave it to you.')

Finally, note that pronominal first and second person IOs may be Topics (111a), but 3-chômeurs cannot (111b).

(111)a. **Acu-e** x - Ø-in-q'ue li tumin.
A2-Dat tns-B3-A1-give the money
'To you I gave the money.' (B,BNB.69)

(111)b.* **A̲cu-e** la̲in x- in-q'ue-o-c r- e li tumin.
A2-Dat I tns-B1-give-R-asp A3-Dat the money
('To you I gave the money.') (B,BNB.71)

As predicted by the Chômeur Constraint (103), the relational network associated with (111b) is not well formed.

(112)*

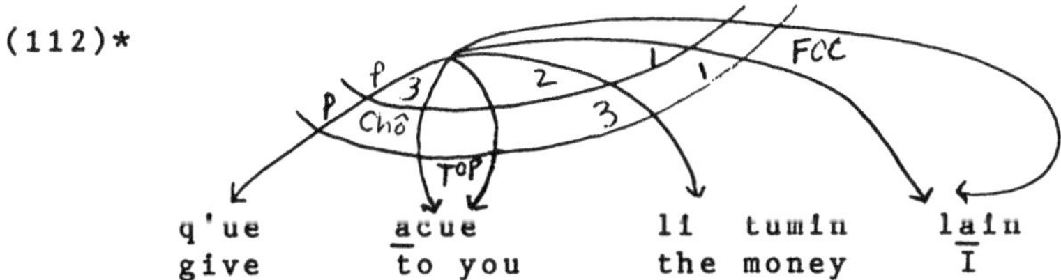

It has been shown that the final 3 of a retreat clause can bear the Topic relation, but the 3 chômeur cannot. This supports our conclusion that the initial 3 is a final chômeur in a retreat clause.

4.4.3 The Q Relation

In § 4.4.2 we saw that a chômeur could not bear the Topic relation. In this Section we will see that a chômeur can not bear the Q relation. This follows from the Chômeur Constraint, given in (103). I argue that a final 3 can head a Q arc, but a 3-chômeur cannot.

4.4.3.1 Questioning Non-Nuclear Terms

Non-nuclear term nounphrases may be questioned in a construction in which the relational noun appears in an unpossessed form and is preceded by the classifier aj. The questioning of a Dative nounphrase is exemplified in (113).

(113) **Ani aj e** x -Ø- a̲-q'ue la̲ - tumin ?
who aj Dat tns-B3-A2-give your-money (li + a̲ > la̲)
'To whom did you give your money?'

Other non-nuclear terms are questioned in (114) and (115). Since there is no single semantic function associated with these relational nouns, the literal translation appears in the gloss. Ix meaning 'back, behind, about' is most generally associated with the Comitative or Locative relations. Iq'uin meaning 'with' is commonly associated with the Locative, Comitative, and Instrumental relations.

(114) **Ani aj ix nequ-ex-atinac ?**
Who aj back tns-B2p-talk
'Who are you (p) talking about?' (H,G:114)
(lit. 'On whose back are you (p) talking?')

(115) **Ani aj iq'uin nequ-Ø -e -lok' chak e -may ?**
Who aj with tns-B3-A2p-buy dir A2p-cigarettes
'With whom did you (p) buy your cigarettes?' (H,G:34)

Given the Chômeur Constraint, we can predict that the final 3 of a retreat clause can head a Q-arc in the aj + (Dative) relational noun construction but, the 3 Chômeur cannot. This is exemplified in (116).

(116)a. **Caru aj e laat x -at-q'ue-o-c r -e laj Manu'?**
what aj Dat you tns-B2-give-R-asp A3-Dat ncl Manu'
'What did you give Manuel?' (B,BNB.81)

b.* **Ani aj e laat x -at-q'ue-o-c r-e li tumin?**
who aj Dat you tns-B2-give-R-asp A3-Dat the money
('To whom did you give the money?') (E&C,L.17)

In (116a) the final 3 of the retreat clause heads a Q-arc. In (116b) the final Chômeur cannot.

Since the final 1 of the retreat clause must head a narrow overlay arc (38), neither (116a) nor (116b) are grammatical if **laat** does not occur.

(117)a.* **Caru aj e** x- at-q'ue-o-c r-e laj Manu'?

b.* **Ani aj e** x- at- q'ue-o-c r-e li tumin?

It is concluded that the final 3 of the retreat clause can head a Q-arc, but the 3 chômeur cannot. This follows from the generalization that a chômeur cannot head an overlay arc (103). This explanation is possible within a relational framework that sanctions demotions and the chômeur relation, and as such provides support for these notions.

4.5 Summary

An analysis of retreat clauses in K'ekchi was given. Five constraints which interact with this analysis were discussed. These constraints are listed below.

I. <u>Ergative Extraction Constraint</u>:
If a nominal heads a final Erg arc in a clause c and it also heads a narrow overlay (Q, Foc, or Rel) arc, it must head an Abs arc.

II. <u>Retreat Subject Constraint</u>:
If the initial DO is the final IO of a clause c, then the nominal heading the final subject arc of clause c must also head a narrow overlay arc.

III. <u>Inanimate Erg Constraint</u>:
If an inanimate nominal heads a final Erg arc, it must head an Abs arc.

IV. <u>MA Constraint</u>:
The only clause-internal MA that is well-formed is 1:2.

V. <u>Chômeur Constraint</u>:
A chômeur cannot head an overlay arc.

Particular to the rule of 2-3 Retreat in K'ekchi is the fact that the final subject of a retreat clause must bear a narrow overlay relation (Constraint II). Constraint I, discussed in detail in Chapter 3, was found to interact with this claim since a final Erg must head an Abs arc in order to bear a narrow overlay relation. For this reason, the final subject of a retreat clause can be Q, Foc, or Rel, but the corresponding subject of a transitive clause cannot.

Four types of arguments were given as evidence for 2-3 Retreat. <u>First</u>, in § 4.1.1 four arguments based on the rules for Retreat Marking (§ 4.1.1.1), Verbal Agreement (§ 4.1.1.2), Aspect (§ 4.1.1.3), and Case (§ 4.1.1.4) provided evidence for the final intransitivity of retreat clauses.

<u>Second</u>, in § 4.2 three arguments were presented based upon narrow overlay relations (§ 4.2.1), properties of foci (Sections 4.2.2- 4.2.2.6), and inanimate nominals (§ 4.2.3) providing evidence that the initial Erg is a final Abs. These three arguments made similar predictions and all provided independent evidence for the notion of multiattachment (as it was developed in Chapter 3).

The first argument claimed that the final subject of a retreat clause could bear the Q, Foc, or Rel relation, but the corresponding subject of a transitive clause could not.

Interestingly, as pointed out in Chapter 3, the final subject of a (transitive) reflexive clause can bear the Q, Foc, or Rel relation. This follows from Constraint I and the notion of MA: I.e an Erg can bear a narrow overlay relation if and only if it heads an Abs arc. The transitive subject of a reflexive clause satisfies this condition because it heads an Abs arc at the initial level (in a 1:2 MA stratum). The intransitive subject of a retreat clause satisfies this condition because it heads a final Abs arc. However, the final subject of a (nonreflexive) transitive clause does not satisfy this condition and therefore cannot bear a narrow overlay relation.

The second argument (of § 4.2) is based upon five diagnostics for foci. It was shown that these five properties could be attributed to the final subject of a retreat clause, but not to the corresponding subject of a transitive clause. On the other hand, these five properties could be attributed to the (transitive) subject of a reflexive clause. Again, these facts follow from Constraint I and the notion of multiattachment.

The third argument (of § 4.2) is based on a condition on inanimate nominals. As discussed in Chapter 3, (§ 3.3.2) there are passive clauses with no active counterpart. In these clauses the inanimate nominal heads an initial Erg arc and a final Chô arc. Corresponding clauses in which the inanimate nominal heads an initial Erg arc and a final Erg arc are ungrammatical. Superficially, it appears to be the case that an inanimate nominal cannot head an Erg arc, but this is falsified by reflexive clauses which allow the final (transitive) subject to be an inanimate nominal. Constraint III together with the notion of MA captures the generalization: If an inanimate nominal is a final Erg, it must head an Abs arc. Constraint III makes the further prediction that there will be retreat clauses with inanimate subjects that have no transitive counterparts. This is discussed in §4.2.3, where it is shown that Constraint III, independently required to explain the passive and reflexive data, captures the generalization for retreat clauses as well.

All three arguments in § 4.2 provide independent evidence for the notion of multiattachment and all three arguments point to the same conclusion: The final subject of a retreat clause heads an initial Erg arc and a final Abs arc.

Third, in § 4.3 three arguments were presented based on pronominal dependents (§ 4.3.1), reflexivization (§ 4.3.2) and word order (§ 4.3.3) providing evidence that the initial DO is a final IO in a retreat clause.

For example, it was shown that a reflexive object in a transitive clause could head a 2-arc, but could not head a 3-arc. Constraint IV, independently required to rule out 1:Obl MAs (Chapter 3, § 3.3.6) was proposed to account for this. As predicted by Constraint IV, it was then shown that the logical object of a retreat clause could not head a reflexive arc because that would involve a 1:3 MA stratum; thus providing further evidence that the initial 2 is a final 3 in a retreat clause.

Fourth, in § 4.4 three arguments were presented based on IO word order (Section 4.4.1), IO topicalization (§ 4.4.2), and questioning non-nuclear terms (Sections 4.4.3- 4.4.3.1) providing evidence that the initial IO is a final chômeur, as predicted by the Chômeur Condition.

The arguments in § 4.4 were all designed to syntactically distinguish two nominals which were morphologically indistinguishable. It was first shown that in retreat clauses the nominal corresponding to the initial 2 could occur in the IO position after the verb, but the nominal corresponding to the initial 3 could not. This follows from the fact that word order rules are determined by final stratum relations and supports the conclusion that the initial 3 is a final chômeur.

Secondly, it was shown that a passive chômeur was unable to bear the Topic relation. The condition proposed to guarantee this was discussed in Chapter 2 and repeated as Constraint V. Interestingly, the class of chômeurs were found to behave alike with respect to overlay relations and only the final 3, but not the 3 chômeur was able to head an overlay arc.

A theory that did not recognize the chômeur relation would not be able to capture the generalization that 1) chômeurs of different types (passive chômeurs, retreat chômeurs) behave alike, and differently from both terms and non terms, with respect to overlay relations in K'ekchi, or 2) that two types of nominals behave alike with respect to case marking and nominal agreement, but differ from one another with respect to word order (§ 4.4.1), topicalization (§ 4.4.2), and questioning (§ 4.4.3.1).

Chapter 4 Footnotes

1. The verbal reflex -o, -n which occurs in retreat clauses also occurs in antipassive clauses (see Chapter 5). The rule presented in (9) is applicable to both.

2. There is a phonological rule effecting vowel length. Roughly, a vowel is lengthened if it precedes a final consonant cluster.

$$V \dashrightarrow VV \; / \; \text{-}[\; C_{+Nas}C \;] \; \#$$

This is the same rule that produces the vowel length of i in **cuinik** 'man'.

Returning to the phonological rule in (13), it is clear that if -c remains in final position and is preceded by a nasal, the preceding vowel will be lengthened. For this reason, the i in **sutinc** (16b) is long but, it is short in **sutin** (16a).

3. See footnote 2.

4. The case marking principle will be revised when constructions involving 2-chômeurs are considered.

5. Since little is known about MA strata in different languages, there is no **apriori** reason to assume that MA resolution be immediate. That is, it is not known whether this is a universal or language particular factor. However, I am assuming that MA resolution is not immediate and that relation changing rules may occur in an 'earlier' stratum. The languages in which MA has been attested support this assumption. For example, in Tzotzil (as discussed by Aissen 1982), there is an initial 1:3 MA, the 3 advances to 2 and MA is resolved by 2-cancellation. Evidence for 3-2 advancement is that the reflex -be occurs on the verb (see Aissen 1983). In Italian, Rosen (1981) has reported that there are constructions with initial 1:Obl MAs that involve Oblique advancement and, in these cases, the MA is resolved by cancellation of the object-arc. In K'ekchi, if we also assume that resolution occurs in a 'later' stratum, then (77b) is ill-formed because it violates the MA Condition (71). However, the MA Condition would not rule out the RN in (1) below, which could presumably be associated with the ungrammatical sentence in (76b) were MA resolution immediate.

(1) *

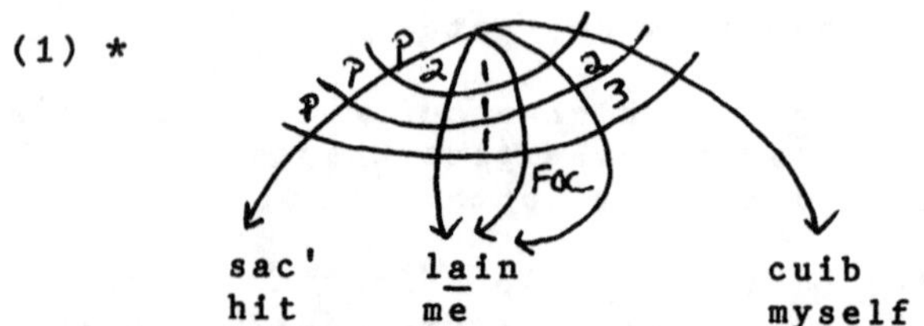

In (1), there is immediate resolution of the 1:2 MA by 2-birth, and demotion of the 2 to 3. The RN in (1) must still be ruled out even though there is not a 1:3 MA. In K'ekchi (1) is ruled out because the birth-arc must be a final 2 arc. The condition on MA resolution given in Chapter 3 (§3.3.6) was stated as: 'A 1:2 MA must be resolved by 2-birth'. A revision of that condition is given in (2) below.

(2) <u>Condition on Resolution</u>:
a) A 1:2 MA must be resolved by 2-birth.

b) The birth-arc must be a final 2-arc.

This revised version not only rules out the ill-formed network in (1), it also accounts for the impossibility of passives of reflexives like: 'Himself was hit by John' which would necessarily contain the subnetwork in (3).

(3) *

P
P
P
2
1
1
2
chô
1

-ib

Since I earlier compared a MA grammar to a no MA (NOMA) grammar (Chapter 3), it is useful to note that a grammar without MA would also require two statements to rule out the RNs in (1) and (3). I.e.:

<u>NOMA Condition on Reflexivization</u>:
a) The antecedent must be a final 1.

b) -<u>Ib</u> must be a final 2.

Therefore, this would not provide an argument for or against a MA grammar.

6. There is a surface structure constraint that prohibits strings of the form * <u>re</u> <u>re</u>. Therefore, if the final 3 is

third singular and pronominal, the 3 chômeur cannot be third person. For example, the sentences in (1) below are ruled out by the above surface structure rule.

(1)a.* L<u>a</u>in x -in-q'ue-o-c r- e r- e.
I tns-B1-give-R-asp A3-Dat A3-Dat
('I'm the one who gave it to him.')

b.* L<u>a</u>in x -in-q'ue-o-c r -e r- e laj Lu'.
I tns-B1-give-R-asp A3-Dat A3-Dat art P
('I'm the one who gave it to Pedro.')

This constraint is avoidable, if in such cases, the final 3 is presented as a full NP, as in (2).

(2)a. L<u>a</u>in x -in-q'ue-o-c r -e li tumin r- e.
I tns-B1-give-R-asp A3-Dat the money A3-Dat
'I'm the one who gave the money to him.'

b. L<u>a</u>in x -in-q'ue-o-c r-e li tumin r- e laj Lu'
I tns-B1-give-R-asp A3-Dat the money A3-Dat art P
'I'm the one who gave the money to Pedro.'

Notice that the order of the final 3 and the 3 chômeur cannot be reversed; even though that too, would conceivably avoid the <u>re</u> <u>re</u> constraint.

(3) * L<u>a</u>in x -in-q'ue-o-c r -e laj Lu' r -e.
I tns-B1-give-R-asp A3-Dat art P A3-Dat
('I'm the one who gave it to Pedro.')

(3) is ungrammatical because the final 3 of the Retreat clause must occur in the IO position after the verb and the 3 chômeur cannot.

Chapter 5

ANTIPASSIVE

5.0 Introduction

This chapter discusses a K'ekchi construction referred to as Antipassive (AP).[1] The sentences in (1-3) are antipassives. The logical object of this construction must be third person and nonreferential. It does not control verbal agreement. Verbal agreement is with the final (Absolutive) Subject of the clause.

(1) Inc'a' nequ-e'-ti'-o -c   ic.
     not   tns- p -eat-AP-asp chile
     'They don't eat chile.'

(2) X- at-sic' -o -c   cape.
     tns-B2-pick-AP-asp coffee
     'You pick coffee.'

(3) T - in-tz'ib<u>a</u>-n -k   hu.
     tns-B1-write -AP-asp letter
     'I will write letters.'

The first thing that should be noted about the clauses in (1)-(3) is the appearance of the verbal affix -<u>o</u>, -<u>n</u>. The rule that conditions this morphology was discussed in Chapter 4 in relation to Retreat clauses and is repeated below as (4):

(4) If a nominal <u>a</u> heads an Erg arc with tail <u>b</u> and coordinate c_k, and an Abs arc with tail <u>b</u> and coordinate c_{k+1}, then the verb of clause <u>b</u> has the suffix -<u>o</u> (if the verb is monosyllabic) or the suffix -<u>n</u> (if the verb has two or more syllables).

As is evident from (4), if a nominal heads an initial Erg arc and a final Abs arc, then the *-o*, *-n* verbal reflex is required. Since antipassive clauses require the *-o*, *-n* verbal reflex, this provides a strong argument for the *initial transitivity* of antipassive clauses. Other arguments for the *final intransitivity* of antipassive clauses depend on the rules for Verbal Agreement, and Aspect.

Two types of arguments are given for the multilevel structure of an AP clause in K'ekchi. *First*, it is argued that the nominal heading the initial Erg arc heads a final Abs arc in an AP clause. *Second*, it is argued that the nominal heading the initial 2-arc heads a final Chô arc.

Consider the relational network in (5). At the initial level of structure there is a 1 and a (nonreferential) 2. At the final level of structure there is a 1 and a (nonreferential) Chômeur. Strictly speaking, the RN in (5) is ill-formed, given (6).

(5)

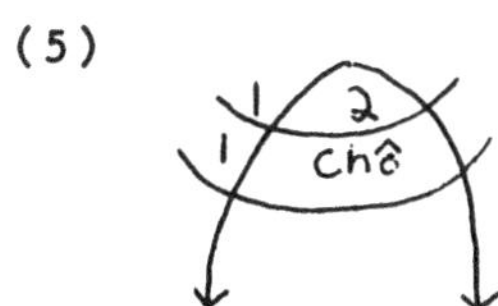

(6) *Motivated Chômage Law:*
If an RN contains an arc of the form [Chô(a,b) $< c_1 \; c_w >$], then it also contains distinct arcs of the form [Term_x (a,b) $< c_u c_{i-1} >$] and [Term_x(c,b) $< c_i c_z >$].

The Motivated Chômage Law rules out the possibility of 'unmotivated' or 'spontaneous' chômage. Basically, if a nominal heads a $Term_x$ arc in the c_i stratum and a Chô arc in the c_{i+1} stratum, then there must be a nominal heading a $Term_x$ arc in the c_{i+1} stratum. The possibility of having initial chômeurs is also ruled out by this Law.

The Motivated Chômage Law is violated in (5) because a nominal heads an initial 2-arc and a final Chô arc and no nominal assumes the 2 relation.

Postal (1977) has proposed an analysis of Antipassive clauses in which the initial and final grammatical relations agree with those postulated in (5) but which does not violate the Motivated Chômage Law. In this analysis, represented in (7), the initial Subject of the transitive stratum demotes to 2, placing the initial 2 en chômage, thereby satisfying the Motivated Chômage Law. This intermediate stratum is an unaccusative stratum (Chapter 3, § 3.3.2.1); the 2 of the unaccusative stratum advances to 1 via Unaccusative Advancement and is the Subject in the final stratum.

(7)

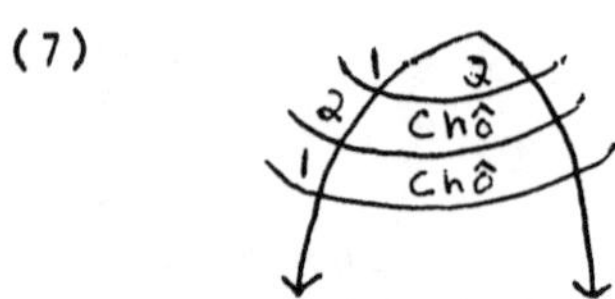

It will be assumed throughout the discussion that the analysis proposed by Postal is tenable for K'ekchi.

5.1 Evidence for Final Intransitivity

Three morphological facts attest to the final intransitivity of the AP clauses in (1)-(3). First, the verb does not bear a Set A affix, which must occur on finally transistems. Second, the verb (in (3)) bears the incompletive suffix -k which only occurs on finally intransitive stems. Third, the verb bears the -o/-n verbal reflex which only occurs on finally intransitive stems. These three facts will be discussed in turn.

5.1.1 Verbal Agreement

The predicate agrees with its subject and its direct object, if there is one. Thus, the defining morphological property of a transitive stem is the presence of a Set A and a Set B affix, while the defining morphological property of an intransitive stem is the lack of a Set A affix. The predicates in (1)-(3) agree with the final Subject of the clause and are cross-referenced by the Set B affix, as determined by the rules for person agreement and affix position in (8) and (9), below.

(8) Person Agreement:
  a. A nominal heading a final Erg arc determines Erg agreement in the verb.

  b. A nominal heading a final Abs arc determines Abs agreement in the verb.

(9) Set A and B Affix Positions:
  a. The affix which is determined by the nominal that heads a final Erg arc is immediately prefixed to the stem.

b. The affix which is determined by the nominal that heads a final Abs arc is suffixed to the stem in tenseless clauses and prefixed in tensed clauses.

The verbal morphology of the AP clauses in (1)-(3) support the claim that these clauses are finally intransitive.

5.1.2 Aspect

Incompletive aspect marking is conditioned by final (in)transitivity in K'ekchi. If an intransitive stem is affixed with either t(v)- 'future' or ch(v)- 'optative' T/A/M prefixes, -k must suffix to the stem.

(10)a. Ch- in-hilan- k sa' cu-ochoch.
A/M-B1-rest -asp in my-house
'that I may rest in my house' (E&C,GR:149)

b. Li Dios chi-Ø -osobtesi-n- k cu-e.
the God A/M-B3-bless -R-asp A1-Dat
'that God may bless me' (E&C,GR:150)

c. Ta -Ø-lok'-e' - k li caxlan x-ban li ixk.
fut-B3-buy-pass-asp the chicken A3-by the woman
'The chicken will be bought by the woman.'

The sentences in (10) are finally intransitive. The presence of the -k suffix is obligatory. -C may suffix in other tense/aspects if the clause is finally intransitive but, neither -c nor -k may be suffixed if the clause is finally transitive (refer to Chapter 1, § 1.3 for details). The aspect marking principle is presented in (11).

(11) Intransitive/Aspect Marking:
If the final stratum is intransitive, -k is suffixed to the verb stem in incompletive aspect, otherwise c- may suffix to the stem.

The optionality of the -c suffix is conditioned by the phonological rule represented in (12). If -c occurs in word final position, and is immediately preceded by a nasal or liquid, it may delete.

(12) optional:

$$c \longrightarrow \emptyset \, / \begin{bmatrix} +son \\ +cons \end{bmatrix} \_\_ \; \#$$

As predicted by (11), AP clauses in the incompletive aspect require the -k suffix, thereby supporting the conclusion that AP clauses are finally intransitive.

(13)a. T - e'-yiba-n - k poch li ixk.
fut-p- make-AP-asp tamales the woman
'The women will prepare tamales.'

b.*T -e'-yiba-n - c poch li ixk.

c.*T- e'-yiba-n poch li ixk.

(14)a. Inc'a' t - o- ti'-o - k tib sa' li cutan a'an.
not fut-B1p-eat-AP-asp meat on the day that
'We will not eat meat on that day.'

b.*Inc'a' t - o- ti'-o - c tib sa' li cutan a'an.

c.*Inc'a' t- o- ti'-o tib sa' li cutan a'an.

Finally intransitive stems in future and incompletive tense/aspects require the -k suffix, as exemplified in (10), (13) and (14). On the other hand, in non-future and completive tense/aspects, the -c suffix is optionally conditioned by the rule in (12). There are two AP suffixes -o and -n, and -n satisfies the phonological environment of (12). Therefore, in AP clauses (in non-future and completive tense/aspects) that require the -n suffix, -c aspect marking is optional. But, in AP clauses (in non-future and completive tense/aspects) that require the -o suffix, -c aspect marking is obligatory.

(15)a. X -e'-yiba- n- c poch li ixk.
pst-p-make -AP-asp tamales the woman
'The women made tamales.'

b.*X - e'-yiba- n- k poch li ixk.

c. X - e'-yiba- n poch li ixk.
'The women made tamales.'[2]

(16)a. Inc'a' x - o- ti'- o - c tib sa' li cutan a'an.
not pst-B1p-eat- AP-asp meat on the day that
'We did not eat meat on that day.'

b.*Inc'a' x - o -ti'- o- k tib sa' li cutan a'an.

c.*Inc'a' x- o - ti'- o tib sa' li cutan a'an.

For this reason, -c occurs optionally in (15) and obligatorily in (16). These facts follow from an analysis of AP clauses involving final intransitivity and the aspect marking rules in (11) and (12).

5.1.3 AP Marking

The rules for verbal agreement (§ 5.1.1) and aspect (§ 5.1.2) attest to the final intransitivity of AP clauses. The rule for AP marking is attestation not only of the final intransitivity, but also of the initial transitivity. This rule was presented as (4) and is repeated below as (17).

(17) AP Marking:
If a nominal a heads an Erg arc with tail b and coordinate c_k, and an Abs arc with tail b and coordinate c_{k+1}, then the verb of clause b has the suffix -o (if the verb is monosyllabic) or the suffix -n (if the verb has two or more syllables).

A retreat clause is detransitivized because an initial DO retreats to IO. An AP clause is detransitivized beacuse an initial Subject retreats to DO creating an unaccusative stratum which is resolved by unaccusative advancement.

Crucially, (17) captures what both Retreat clauses and AP clauses share. At the initial level the subject heads an Erg arc in a <u>transitive</u> stratum, and at the final level the subject heads an Abs arc in an <u>intransitive</u> stratum. For this reason, both constructions require the same verbal reflex. This morphology is <u>not</u> found in passive clauses (Chapter 2), even though passives also involve detransitivization.

For the sake of argument, the rule for retreat marking could be represented as it is in (18) below. This rule would correctly determine the -<u>o</u>/-<u>n</u> verbal reflex in Retreat clauses, but the occurence of this reflex in AP clauses would remain an anomaly.

(18) If a nominal <u>a</u> heads a 2-arc with tail <u>b</u> and coordinate c_k, and a 3-arc with tail <u>b</u> and coordinate c_{k+1}, then the verb of clause <u>b</u> has the suffix -<u>o</u> (if the verb is monosyllabic) or the suffix -<u>n</u> (if the verb has two or more syllables).

The rule in (17) captures what is common to both constructions. It is therefore evidence against the claim that AP clauses are initially and finally intransitive, and evidence for a syntactic analysis of AP clauses involving a multilevel structure.

5.2 Properties of the AP Subject

Despite the common verbal morphology, the AP subject is distinguishable from a retreat subject in four ways. First, the AP subject can occur in subject final position, the retreat subject cannot. Second, the AP subject can drop, the retreat subject cannot. Third, the AP subject can bear the Topic relation, the retreat subject cannot. Fourth, the AP subject may bear a narrow overlay relation, the retreat subject must bear a narrow overlay relation. These four differences follow from the fact that the subject of a retreat clause, but not the subject of an AP clause, is governed by the Retreat Subject Constraint (Chapter 4), repeated below.

(19) Retreat Subject Constraint:
If the initial DO is the final IO of a clause c, then the final subject of clause c must bear a narrow overlay relation.

The subject of an AP clause does not satisfy the condition of the constraint in (19). Therefore unlike a Retreat subject, an AP subject may be classified by the set of subject properties outlined above.

5.2.1 Position

The subject may occur in its normal postverbal position in an AP clause, as exemplified in (20) below.

(20)a. Ma x - Ø -lok'- o - c cua **laj Lu'** ?
Q tns-B3- buy -AP -asp tortillas ncl Lu'
'Did Pedro buy tortillas?'

(20)b. X - e' -sic'- o - c   cape   **li**   **cuink.**
tns-p- pick -AP-asp   coffee   the   man
'The men pick coffee.'

In contrast, the subject of a retreat clause must occur in the preverbal (focus) position (21a), and cannot occur in the postverbal subject position (21b).

(21)a. **Eb li**   **cuink**   x - e'-sic'-o -c   r- e   li   cape.
p   the man   tns-p -pick-R-asp   A3-Dat the coffee
'Those are the men who picked the coffee.'

b.*X - e'-sic'- o - c   r- e   li   cape   **(eb) li**   **cuink.**

5.2.2 Optionality

As stated earlier, nuclear term pronominal dependents are usually omitted in surface structure. (22) is exemplary.

(22)a.   Timil   t -in-alina- k.
slowly tns-B1-run   -asp   'I will run slowly.'

b.   T   -in-a -sac'.
tns-B1-A2-hit   'You will hit me.'

While AP subjects need not be overt, Retreat subjects must be overt. Compare the AP sentences in (23) to the Retreat sentences in (24).

(23)a. T - e' -yiba- n - k   poch.
tns-p -make -AP-asp   tamales
'They will make tamales.'

b. T - e'-cubsi -n - k   tumin re   x-lok'-bal
tns-p -donate-AP-asp money in order to A3-buy-nom

junak li   cuacax.
one   the cow
'They will contribute money in order to buy a cow.' (B,NP:4)

(24)a.* T- e'- yiba- n -k   r -e   li   poch.
tns-p-make - R -asp A3-Dat the tamales
('They will make the tamales.')

(24)b.* T- e'- cubsi-n -k r- e li tumin.
tns-p-donate-R-asp A3-Dat the money
('They will contribute the money.')

5.2.3 Initial Erg is Final Abs

Ergative extraction is governed by the constraint in (25) below. This constraint was discussed in detail in Chapters 3 and 4.

(25) Ergative Extraction Constraint:
If a nominal heads a final Erg arc in a clause c and it also heads a narrow overlay (Q, Foc, or Rel) arc, it must head an Abs arc.

The subject of an AP clause may head a narrow overlay arc, as exemplified in (26). The subject of the corresponding active transitive clause may not, as exemplified in (27). This provides evidence for the final intransitivity of an AP clause.

(26) Ha' li ma us aj musik'ej a'an nac-Ø-tz'ap -o -c
emph the not good ncl spirit that tns-B3-close-AP-asp

xic. 'That evil spirit makes people deaf.'
ears (lit. 'That evil spirit closes ears.')

(27)* Ha' li ma us aj musik'ej a'an na -Ø-x-tz'ap xic.
emph the not good ncl spirit that tns-B3-A3-close ears
('That evil spirit makes people deaf.')

The subject of the AP clause (26), heads an initial Erg arc and a final Abs arc. Consistent with (25), it may head a Foc arc. The subject of the corresponding transitive clause (27), heads an initial and final Erg arc. Consistent with (25) it may not head a Foc arc.[3]

The AP subject bears a narrow overlay relation in (28a-d), below. This supports the conclusion that it heads a final Abs arc.

```
(28)a. Ani ta - Ø-lok'-o -k   cua?
       who tns-B3-buy-AP-asp  tortillas
       'Who will buy tortillas?'

(28)b. nak  lain t - in-rak - o -k  atin, chan-Ø  li  Dios
       when  I    tns-B1-stop-AP-asp word said-B3 the God
       'when I judge, said God'                (E&C,J.2:31)
       (lit. when I stop words)

    c. A'an  na -Ø -numsi- n - c   cuink.
       she   tns-B3-pass -AP-asp   men
       'She fornicates.'
       (lit.'She passes through men.')                (H,D:239)

    d. Laat nac-at-il- o -c   coc'al.
       you  tns-B2-see-AP-asp children
       'You are a babysitter.' (lit. 'You watch children.')
```

Two points are relevant: First, unlike the final 1 of a retreat clause which is subject to the Retreat Subject Constraint (19) and _must_ bear a narrow overlay relation (21, 24), the final 1 of an AP clause may (26, 28a-d), or may not (23) bear a narrow overlay relation. Second, as exemplified in (27), the final 1 in the transitive counterpart of an AP clause _cannot_ bear a narrow overlay relation. This is predicted by the Ergative Extraction Constraint (25) and supports a multi-level analysis of AP clauses.

5.3 Properties of AP Object

Two properties of the AP object will be discussed in this section. First, the AP object must be third person.

Second, the AP object must be nonreferential. These two properties distinguish an AP object from both the final object in a transitive clause and the final object in a retreat clause.

Syntactically, the objects in an AP clause, transitive clause, and retreat clause have one thing in common. They each bear the initial DO relation. However, these three objects differ in the final grammatical relation that each bears to its clause. The AP object bears the final Chômeur relation, the transitive object bears the final DO relation, and the retreat object bears the final IO relation.

I argue that the AP object must be nonreferential, but that neither the final (direct) object in a transitive clause nor the final (indirect) object in a retreat clause is subject to this restriction.

5.3.1 AP Object Constraint

Morphologically, an AP chômeur is distinguished from other non-nuclear terms (IOs, Passive chômeurs, Retreat chômeurs, obliques, etc.) because an AP chômeur must be an unmarked bare noun. Thus the Case Marking principle (discussed earlier, Chapters 2, 3, 4) must be revised to capture this generalization.

(29) Case Marking

(a) Final nuclear terms and 2 chômeurs are unmarked.

(b) All other GRs are presented as possessors of a relational noun.

Even though both a final 2 and a 2 chômeur are 'unmarked', a final 2 must be *referential*, whereas a 2 chômeur must be *nonreferential*. The sentences in (30) are ungrammatical because the 2 chômeur is referential.

(30)a.* T - in-tenk'a-n - k laat .
fut- B1-help -AP-asp 2s pro ('I will help you.')

b.* X - at-tenk'a- n - c lao . ('You helped us.')
pst-B2-help -AP-asp 1p pro

Compare the AP objects in (30) above, to the direct objects in (31) and the indirect objects in (32), below.

(31)a. T -at-in-tenk'a laat.
fut-B2-A1-help 2s pro 'I will help you.'

b. X -o - a -tenk'a lao.
pst-B1p-A2-help 1p pro 'You helped us.'

(32)a. Lain t - in-tenk'a-n - k acu-e.
I fut-B1-help - R -asp A2-Dat
'I'm the one who will help you.'

b. Laat x -at-tenk'a- n - c k- e.
you pst-B2-help - R-asp A1p-Dat
'You are the one who helped us.'

The sentences in (30) are ruled out by the constraint in (33) below. A consequence of this constraint is that there are no first or second person AP objects. Another constraint that interacts with the nonreferentiality of nouns in K'ekchi is discussed in § 5.3.2. Before discussing that generalization, it is necessary to define what is meant by 'nonreferentiality' in K'ekchi.[4]

(33) <u>AP Object Constraint</u>:
The 2 chômeur in an AP clause must be nonreferential.

5.3.1.1 Referential versus Nonreferential

A nonreferential noun in K'ekchi cannot co-occur with a definite article, numeral, noun classifier, or possessive affix. As stated in (33), an AP 2 chômeur must be nonreferential. However, as will be shown below, a final 2 must be <u>referential</u>. Therefore, despite the fact that both final 2s and 2 chômeurs are 'unmarked' with respect to case (cf the Case Marking principle (29)), there are several morphological properties that distinguish the two GRs. For example, in (34) below, the AP 2 chômeur is a bare noun and the sentence is grammatical. In contrast, the DO in (35) below is a bare noun and the sentence is ungrammatical.

(34) X -at-ti' -o - c ic.
rec-B2-eat-AP-asp chile 'You ate chile.'

(35)* X - Ø -<u>a</u>- tiu ic.
rec-B3-Ā2-eat chile ('You ate chile.')

If <u>ic</u> 'chile' were preceded by a 'definitizer' in the transitive clause in (35), the sentence would have been acceptable, as in (36).

(36)a. X -Ø -<u>a</u>- tiu li ic.
rec-B3-Ā2-eat art chile 'You ate the chile.'

b. X- Ø -<u>a</u>- tiu **junak** ic.
art 'You ate a chile.'

c. X- Ø- a- tiu k -ic.
Alp-chile 'You ate our chile.'

d. X- Ø- a -tiu cuib ic.
two 'You ate two chiles.'

e. X- Ø- a- tiu li ic a'an.
the chile that 'You ate that chile.'

On the other hand, if a definitizer had occured in the AP clause in (35), the sentence would have been unacceptable, as in (37) below.

(37)a.* X -at-ti' -o -c li ic.
tns-B2-eat-AP-asp art chile ('You ate the chile.')

b.* X -at-ti'- o -c junak ic.
art ('You ate a chile.')

c.* X -at-ti' -o -c k -ic.
A1p ('You ate our chile.')

d.* X -at-ti'- o -c cuib ic.
two ('You ate two chiles.')

e.* X -at-ti'-o -c li ic a'an .
the chile that ('You ate that chile.')

Masculine proper nouns must be preceded by the definite article li plus the noun classifier aj, as in laj Lu' 'Pedro'. Feminine proper nouns are preceded by li plus the noun classifier ix, as in lix Rosa 'Rosa'. Aj must also precede the set of agentive nouns, as in aj ilonel 'the seer/ shaman' and may form a contraction with the definite article as in laj lok'onel 'the buyer'. As exemplified in (38), the noun classifiers aj and ix may precede a final 2 but, they may not precede a 2 chômeur (39).

(38)a. X- Ø -k -il laj Lu'.
tns-B3-A1p-see ncl Lu' 'We saw Pedro.'

b. X- Ø -k - il lix Rosa.
ncl Rosa 'We saw Rosa.'

c. X- Ø - k- il laj lok'onel.
ncl buyer 'We saw the buyer.'

(39)a.* X - o -il - o - c laj Lu'.
tns-B1p-see-AP-asp ncl Lu' ('We saw Pedro.')

b.* X - o -il - o - c lix Rosa.
ncl Rosa ('We saw Rosa.')

c.* X- o -il -o - c laj lok'onel.
ncl buyer ('We saw the buyer.')

So far we have seen that final 2s must be preceded by an article, a Set A affix, a numeral, or a noun classifier, and that 2 chômeurs cannot. We have also seen that a final 2 cannot be a bare noun and that a 2 chômeur can be a bare noun.

A 2 chômeur is further distinguished from a final 2: A 2 chômeur can occur with a preceding adjective or quantifier (40a)-(42a), and a final 2 cannot (40b)-(42b); unless it co-occurs with an article (40c)-(42c).

(40)a. L - in co ta -Ø-lok'-o - k **kanal** tul.
art-my daughter tns-B3-buy-AP-asp ripe bananas
'My daughter will buy ripe bananas.'

b.* L - in co ti- Ø - x -lok' **kanal** tul.
tns-B3-A3-buy
('My daughter will buy ripe bananas.')

c. L - in co ti -Ø - x -lok' **li kanal** tul.
the ripe bananas
'My daughter will buy the ripe bananas.'

(41)a. Ac x-in -lo- o -c **raxi** tul.
already tns-B1- eat-AP-asp green bananas
'I just ate green bananas.'

b.* Ac x- Ø -in-lou **raxi** tul.
tns-B3-A1-eat green bananas
('I just ate green bananas.')

c. Ac x - Ø -in- lou **li** **raxi** tul.
the green bananas
'I just ate the green bananas.'

(42)a. Ma x -Ø-lok'- o - c **na'bal** cua laj Lix?
Q tns-B3-buy-AP-asp many tortillas ncl Lix
'Did Andrés eat many tortillas?'

b.* Ma x -Ø-x - lok' **na'bal** cua laj Lix?
tns-B3-A3-buy
('Did Andrés eat many tortillas?')

c. Ma x -Ø - x-lok' **na'bal li** cua laj Lix?
many the tortillas
'Did Andrés eat many tortillas?'

The permissible forms of a final 2 and an AP 2 chômeur are summarized in Table I. The distinguishing feature of final 2s and AP 2 chômeurs is (non)referentiality. A final (unfocused) 2 must be referential. An AP 2 chômeur must be nonreferential. As such, it may be a noun or a noun compound (formed from a restricted set of adjectives and quantifiers plus noun). It may not co-occur with an article, Set A affix, numeral, or noun classifier.[5]

Table 1: The Forms of a Final 2 and an AP 2 Chômeur.

	Final 2	AP 2 Chômeur
def art + N	+	-
indef art + N	+	-
Set A + N	+	-
num + N	+	-
ncl + N	+	-
adj + N	-	+
Qu + N	-	+
N	-	+

5.3.2 A Restriction on Referentiality

Even though an AP 2 chômeur is distinguishable from a final 2 (see Table 1), it might be argued that AP clauses are _initially intransitive_ and that sentences like those in (35), (40b), (41b), and (42b) are ruled out simply because a nonreferential noun cannot head a 2 arc.

I argue that the (partial) condition stated in (43) below provides evidence for the _initial transitivity_ of antipassive clauses. At the same time, this condition entails that there will be antipassive clauses with an ungrammatical transitive counterpart.

(43) _Referentiality Constraint_: (partial statement)
If a (nonreferential) noun heads a final 2 arc, it must head an overlay arc.

It was shown earlier, in examples like (35), that an (unfocused) noun cannot bear the final 2 relation in a transitive clause. In this Section, it is shown that a bare noun, like _ic_ in (35) can bear the Topic (or Focus) relation in a transitive clause. This follows from the constraint in (43) and provides evidence for the initial 2-hood of nonreferential nouns-(since these 2s can occur as Topic or Focus in a transitive clause). As an example, compare the ungrammatical transitive clause in (44a) to the grammatical transitive clause in (44b).

(44)a.* X - Ø -ka-tz'iba hu .
tns-B3-A1p-write letters ('We wrote letters.')

b. Hu x - Ø -ka-tz'iba.
letters tns-B3-A1p-write 'Letters, we wrote.'

(44a) is ungrammatical because a nonreferential noun heads a final 2-arc and it doesn't head an overlay arc (43). On the other hand, (44b) is grammatical. The difference between (44a) and (44b) is expressed in the relational networks in (45a) and (45b), respectively.

(45)a.* P 1 2

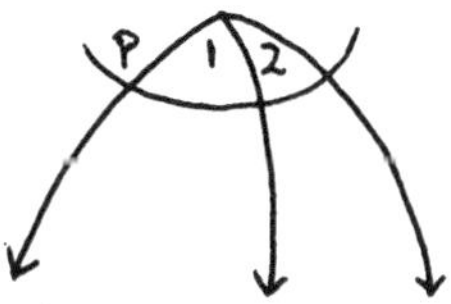

tz'iba la̲o hu
write we letters

(45)b. P 1 2 FOC

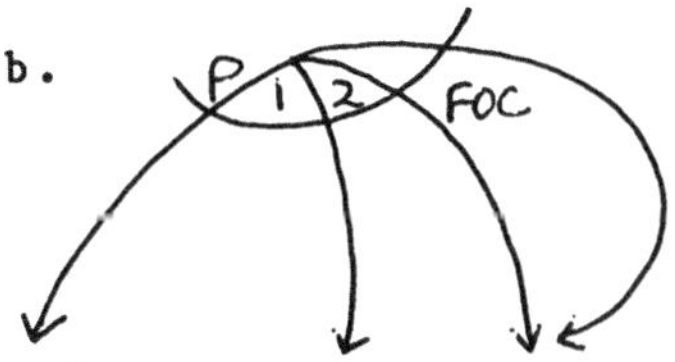

tz'iba la̲o hu
write we letters

In the relational network in (45a) the final 2 doesn't bear an overlay relation. As predicted by the constraint in (43), the relational network in (45a) is ill-formed because the final 2 is nonreferential.

The final 2 in the sentence associated with (45b) bears an overlay relation. Therefore, the (nonreferential) noun heads a 2-arc and a Foc arc. In accordance with the constraint in (43), the relational network in (45b) is well formed.

Since the nonreferential 2 can focus in transitive clauses (44b), there is evidence for positing initially transitive strata with 2 arcs headed by nonreferential nouns. The Referentiality Constraint (43), predicts that such RNs will be ill-formed unless the nonreferential noun heads an overlay arc. By extension, since the 2 chômeur in an antipassive clause must be nonreferential (Constraint

(33)), (43) predicts that the transitive counterpart of an antipassive clause will be ungrammatical, unless the non-referential noun is extracted. In accordance with this prediction (46a) below, is ungrammatical.

(46)a.* X -Ø -ka-tz'iba hu.
tns-B3-A1p-write letters ('We wrote letters.')

b. X- o - tz'iba- n hu.
tns-B1p-write-AP letters 'We wrote letters.'

The relational network associated with the transitive clause in (46a) is given in (45a). The relational network associated with the antipassive clause in (46b) is given in (47). At the initial level of structure, (45a) and (47) are identical, i.e. in each structure there is a nonreferential 2 at initial level. (46a) is unacceptable because the non-referential nominal heads a final 2 arc and it doesn't head an overlay arc, violating (43). (46b) is acceptable because the nonreferential nominal heads a final Chô arc.

(47)

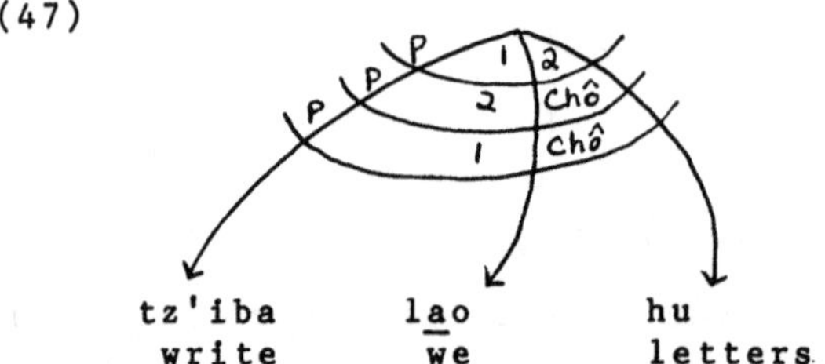

The Referentiality Constraint is not restricted to 2s. In fact, it is very general. In § 5.4 arguments will be presented which support the following revised version:

(48) Referentiality Constraint:(revised version of (43))
If a (nonreferential) noun heads a final nuclear term arc, it must head an overlay arc.

According to (48), if a nonreferential 1 or 2 bears a final nuclear term relation, it must also bear an overlay relation. I.e. it must extract.

5.4 Evidence for Initial Nonreferential Nuclear Terms

5.4.1 Evidence for Initial Nonreferential 2s

The first construction that provides evidence for positing nonreferential 2s at initial level is nonreferential DO Focus. In nonreferential DO focus clauses, a nonreferential noun heads an initial and final 2-arc in a transitive stratum. Consistent with the claim in (48), if the nonreferential noun in these constructions does not bear an overlay relation, the clause is ill-formed.

5.4.1.1 Nonreferential DO Focus

A final (non-focused) 2 must be 'referential', i.e. it must be preceded by an article, noun classifier, numeral, or Set A possessive affix (see Table I). The sentences in (49) and (50) are ungrammatical because the final 2 is a bare noun without modifiers.

(49)a.* X -Ø -in-q'ue acu-e **utz'u'uj** .
tns-B3-A1-give A2-Dat flowers
('I gave flowers to you.')

b.* X -Ø -in-q'ue acu-e **tumin** .
money
('I gave money to you.')

(49)c.* X -Ø -in-q'ue tumin acu-e.
('I gave money to you.')

(50)a.* X -Ø -in-bon t'icr.
tns-B3-A1-paint cloth
('I painted cloth.')

b.* X -Ø -in bon tz'ac.
floors
('I painted floors.')

As exemplified in (49) and (50), if a bare noun occurs in a post-verbal (non-focus) position, it may not head a final 2 arc. Furthermore, while a final 2 normally follows a pronominal IO (Chapter 4, §4.4.1), the bare noun in a transitive clause may not precede or follow it (49b,c).

On the other hand, if a bare noun occurs in preverbal (focus) position, it may head a final 2 arc. In (51) and (52) below, the bare noun heads a final 2 arc and a Foc arc.

(51) in response to the question:
C'a'ru x - Ø -a -q'ue r-e - eb ?
what tns-B3-A2-give A3-Dat-p
'What did you give them?'

a. Utz'u'uj x -Ø -in -q'ue acu-e.
flowers tns-B3-A1-give A2-Dat
'Flowers I gave to you.' (E&C,L.13)

b. Tumin x -Ø -in-q'ue r- e laj Manu'.
money A3-Dat art M
'Money I gave to Manuel.' (E&C,L.11)

(52) in response to the question:
C'a'ru x -Ø -a -bon?
what tns-B3-A2-paint
'What did you paint?'

a. T'icr x - Ø -in-bon.
cloth tns-B3-A1-paint
'Cloth I painted.'

(52)b. **Tz'ac** x -Ø -in-bon.
floors
'Floors I painted.'

As indicated by the ergative verbal agreement, the bare noun must head a final 2-arc since it controls Absolutive third singular agreement in a transitive clause. The difference between (50a) and (52a) is expressed in the relational networks in (53a,b).

(53)a.* b.

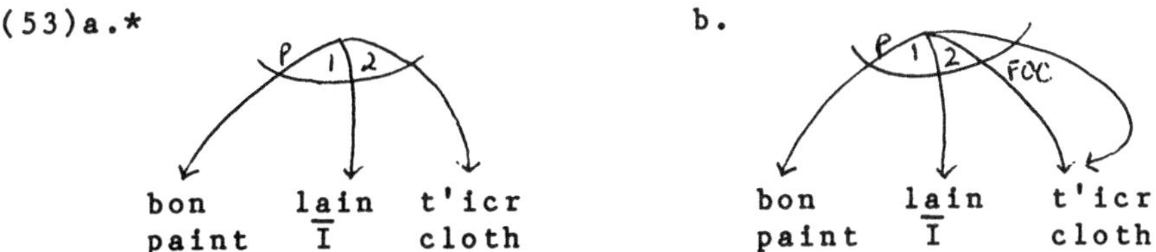

The sentence associated with (53a) is (50a). It is ruled out by Constraint (48) because a nonreferential noun heads a final nuclear term arc and it doesn't head an overlay arc. The sentence associated with (53b) is (52a). This sentence is grammatical because the bare noun heads a final 2 arc (accounting for the transitive verb agreement) and a Foc arc.

In (54a) and (55a), it is shown that the bare noun can topicalize out of a lower clause and bear an overlay relation. Furthermore, the verb of the lower clause must remain transitive, supporting our conclusion that the bare noun must head a final 2-arc. (54b) and (55b) are ungrammatical because the bare noun heads a Chô-arc in an AP clause and therefore cannot extract (cf. the Chômeur Constraint in (57) below)).

(54)a. **Quenk** ta- Ø- r -aj nak ti -Ø -x -tiu laj Manu'.
beans tns-B3-A3-want that tns-B3-A3-eat ncl Manu'
'Beans he wants Manuel to eat.'

b.* **Quenk** ta- Ø -r- aj nak ta -Ø -ti'-o -k laj Manu'.
tns-B3-eat-AP-asp
('Beans he wants Manuel to eat.')

(55)a. **Cua** t -Ø-incu-aj ti -Ø -x -lok' lix Mar.
tortillas tns-B3-A1-want tns-B3-A3-buy ncl Mar
'Tortillas I want Maria to buy.'

b.* **Cua** t - Ø-incu-aj ta -Ø -lok'-o- k lix Mar.
tns-B3-buy -AP-asp
('Tortillas I want Maria to buy.')

The relational networks associated with (54a) and (54b) are given in (56a) and (56b), respectively.

(56)a.

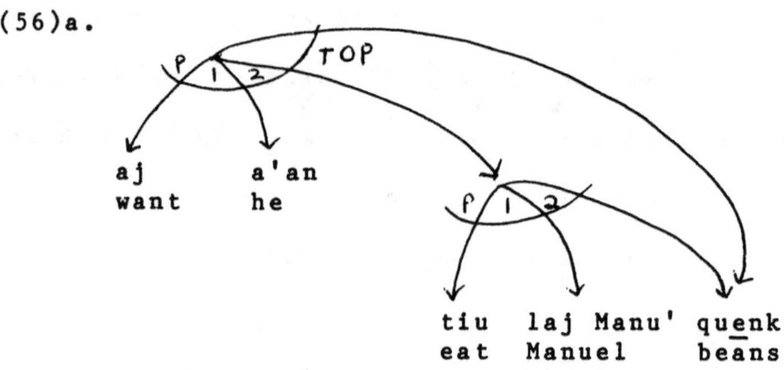

(56)b.*

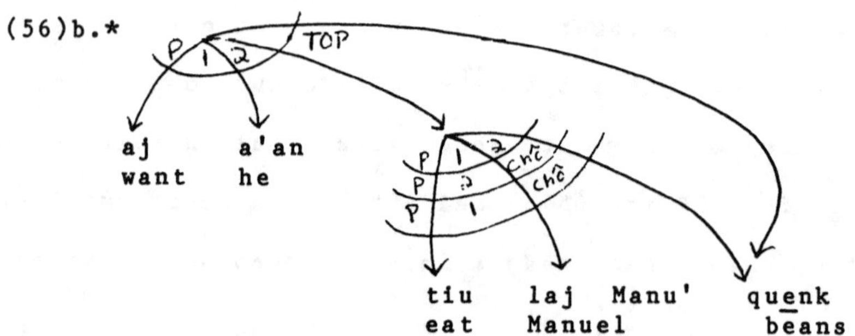

In (54a) the bare noun heads a final 2-arc and a Topic arc. As predicted by (48), the corresponding RN (56a) is well-formed. In (54b) the bare noun heads a final Chô arc and a Topic arc. The corresponding RN (56b) is ruled out by the Chômeur Constraint (discussed in Chapter 2 with respect to Passive 1 chômeurs and in Chapter 4 with respect to Retreat 3 chômeurs), given in (57).

(57) Chômeur Constraint:
A Chômeur cannot head an overlay arc.

The constraint in (57) is discussed in more detail in § 5.5. For now, it is important to note that the bare noun must be extracted from the lower transitive clause in sentences like (54a) and (55a), since it must head an overlay arc. (58a) and (58b) below are ungrammatical because the bare noun heads a final 2 arc and does not head an overlay arc.

(58)a.* Ta -Ø -r -aj nak ti -Ø -x-tiu quenk laj Manu'.
tns-B3-A3-want that tns-B3-A3-eat beans ncl Manu'
('He wants Manuel to eat beans.')

b.* T -Ø-incu-aj ti -Ø -x -lok' cua lix Mar.
tns-B3-A1-want tns-B3-A3-buy tortillas ncl Mar
('I want Mary to buy tortillas.')

This provides strong support for the Referentiality Constraint (48), since the nonreferential noun must extract from the transitive clause and bear an overlay relation. Failure to extract the nonreferential nuclear term violates (48). On the other hand, the bare noun cannot extract from the lower antipassive clause in sentences like (54b) and (55b), since it heads a final Chô arc. Thus, in contrast to (58a) and (58b) above, (59a) and (59b) below are grammatical because the bare noun heads a final Chô arc and extraction would violate the Chômeur Constraint (57).

(59)a. Ta- Ø -r- aj nak ta -Ø- ti'-o- k quenk laj Manu'.
tns-B3-A3-want that tns-B3-eat-AP-asp beans ncl Manu'
'He wants Manuel to eat beans.'

b. Ti- Ø -incu-aj ta- Ø-lok'- o - k cua lix Mar.
tns-B3-A1 -want tns-B3-buy-AP-asp tortillas ncl Mar
'I want Maria to buy tortillas.'

The distinction between (58) and (59) is expressed in the relational networks in (60).

(60)a.*

(60)b.

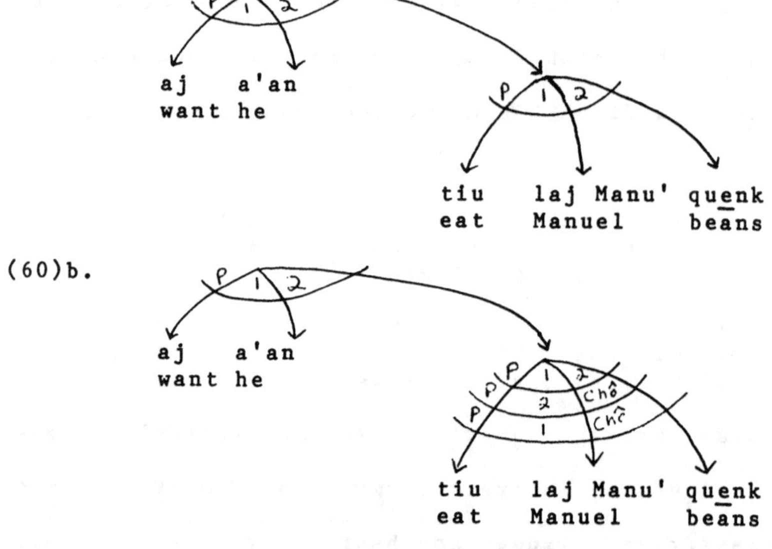

The RN associated with (58a) is represented in (60a). The bare noun heads a final 2-arc and it does not head an overlay arc. This violates the Referentiality Constraint (48) and is therefore ruled out. The RN associated with

(59a) is represented in (60b). The bare noun heads a final Chô arc and it does not head an overlay arc. In accordance with the predictions of (48) and (57), (60b) is well formed.

Summing up: It was shown that if a bare noun heads a final 2 arc, it must head an overlay arc. More precisely, since nonreferential 2 foci were able to control DO agreement in a finally transitive clause, it was argued that nonreferential 2s must be present at initial level.

It was also shown that the bare noun in an AP clause (unlike the bare noun in a transitive clause) was not able to head an overlay arc. This follows from an analysis of AP clauses in which the bare noun heads an initial 2 arc in a transitive stratum and a final Chô arc in an intransitive stratum (since chômeurs are unable to bear overlay relations (57)), thus providing further evidence for the initial transitivity of AP clauses. In addition, the Referentiality Constraint (48) together with the AP Object Constraint (34) and the Chômeur Constraint (57) provide an explanation for the otherwise odd fact that AP clauses lack a grammatical transitive counterpart in K'ekchi.

5.4.1.2 Nonreferential Passive Subjects

The second construction that provides evidence for nonreferential 2s at initial level is passive. There are passive K'ekchi clauses with nonreferential subjects that must bear an overlay relation. I argue that the initial nonreferential 2 advanced to 1 via passive. Since a noun heading a final nuclear term arc must head an overlay arc (48), the passive subject must extract.

In (61a) the passive subject li cuacax is definite and occurs in its normal postverbal position. In (61b) the anarthrous passive subject cuacax cannot occur in the postverbal position, and the sentence is ruled out by Constraint (48). However, in (61c) cuacax occurs as the focused subject of the passive clause.

(61)a. Ta -Ø -camsi - k li cuacax x -ban laj camsinel
tns-B3-kill=pass-asp the cow A3-by ncl butcher
'The cows will be killed by the butcher.'

b.* Ta- Ø-camsi - k cuacax x-ban laj camsinel.
('Cows will be killed by the butcher.')

c. Cuacax ta-Ø-camsi - k x-ban laj camsinel.
'Cows will be killed by the butcher.'

The relational network for (61b) is represented in (63), and the relational network for (61c) is represented in (64). In both relational networks the bare noun cuacax heads the initial 2 arc of a transitive stratum.

As exemplified in (62), cuacax cannot head a final 2 arc (see the sentences in (49)-(50)). And as exemplified in (63), cuacax cannot head a final 1 arc. However, in the sentence associated with (64), cuacax heads a final 1 arc and a Foc arc. This provides further support for the constraint in (48), and for positing nonreferential 2s at initial level.

(62)*

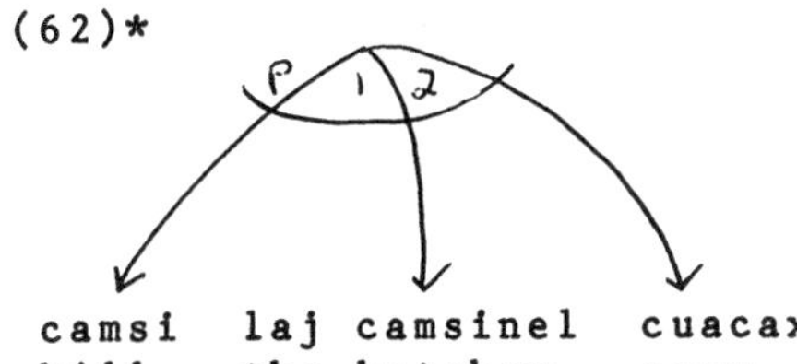

camsi laj camsinel cuacax
kill the butcher cows

(63)*

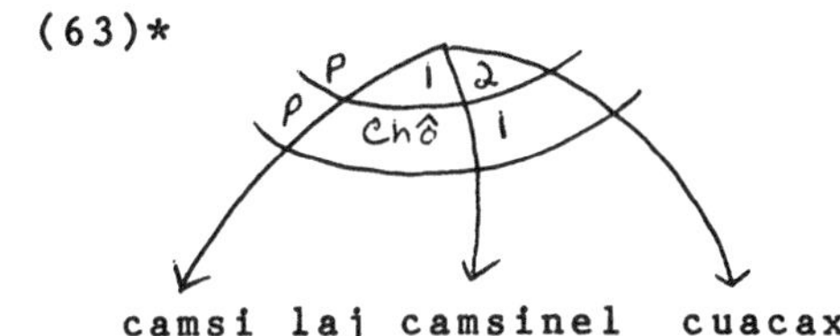

camsi laj camsinel cuacax
kill the butcher cows

(64)

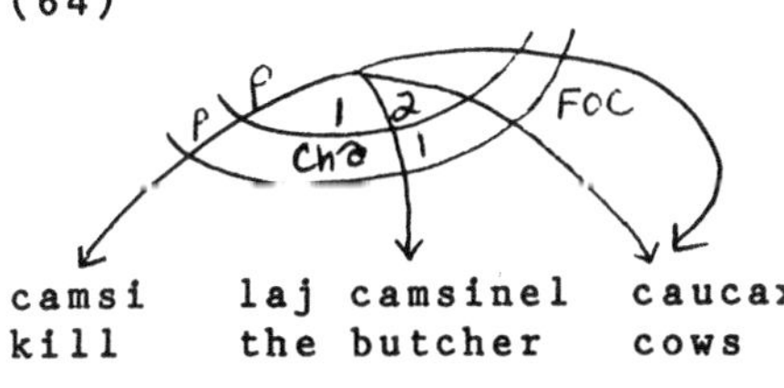

camsi laj camsinel caucax
kill the butcher cows

The sentences in (65) and (66) are further examples of bare noun subject focus in passive clauses. It should be pointed out that these sentences, like antipassive clauses, lack a grammatical transitive counterpart.[6]

(65) Hu ta- Ø -tz'iba - k x-ban-eb li popol.
letters tns-B3-write=pass-asp A3-by-p the authorities
'Letters will be written by the authorities.'

(66) Hix ta -Ø -camsi - k x- ban laj yo.
tigers tns-B3-kill=pass-asp A3-by ncl hunter
'Tigers will be killed by the hunter.'

In conclusion, it was argued that passive clauses in K'ekchi provide further evidence for positing nonreferential 2s at initial level. In particular, it was shown that a bare noun could not head a final 2 arc in a transitive clause, but it could head a final 1 arc and a Foc arc in the corresponding passive clause. And, as predicted by the Referentiality Constraint, if the noun did not head an overlay arc, the passive clause was ill-formed.

5.4.2 Evidence for Initial Nonreferential 1s

In this section evidence will be discussed which further supports the Referentiality Constraint (48), repeated below as (67).

(67) <u>Referentiality Constraint</u>
If a nonreferential noun heads a final nuclear term arc, it must head an overlay arc.

Two arguments will be presented which provide evidence for initial nonreferential Subjects. It will then be shown that if a nonreferential Subject heads a 1-arc, it must head an overlay arc.

5.4.2.1 Nonreferential Unergative Subjects

The definite nounphrases in (68a)-(70a) head an initial and final 1-arc in an intransitive clause. If the subject occurs as a bare noun in the 'neutral' post-verbal subject position, the sentences are ungrammatical; as evidenced in (68b)-(70b). However, if the subject occurs as a bare noun in preverbal Focus position, the sentences are grammatical; as evidenced in the (68c)-(70c).

(68)a. Nequ-e'-cuobac eb li tz'i' .
tns-p- bark p the dogs
'The dogs bark.'

b.* Nequ-e'-cuobac tz'i'
('Dogs bark.')

c. Tz'i' nequ-e'-cuobac.
'Dogs bark.'

(69)a. Nequ-e'-rupupic li tz'ic.
tns-p- fly the birds
'The birds fly.'

b.* Nequ-e'-rupupic tz'ic .
('Birds fly.')

c. Tz'ic nequ-e'-rupupic.
'Birds fly.'

(70)a. Nequ-e'-yabac li tz'ic .
tns-p-screech the birds
'The birds screech.'

b.* Nequ-e'-yabac tz'ic.
('Birds sreech.')

c. Tz'ic nequ-e'-yabac.
'Birds screech.'

The relational network associated with the (b) sentences in (68)-(70) is represented in (71). The relational network associated with the (c) sentences is represented in (72). In both structures the nonreferential noun heads an initial Abs arc. The structure in (71) is ruled out by the Referentiality Constraint because the noun heads a 1-arc and does not head an overlay arc. In contrast, the structure in (72) is not ruled out because the bare noun heads a final 1-arc and a Foc arc. Number agreement with the bare noun argues that it is a final 1, while word order argues that it is a focused nominal.

(71)*

(72)

P 1 Foc

cuobac tz'i'
bark dogs

5.4.2.2 Nonreferential Retreat Subjects

The second construction that provides evidence for non-referential 1s at initial level are Retreat clauses. First, I show that a nonreferential noun cannot head a final 1-arc in a transitive stratum. Then, I show that a nonreferential noun can head a final 1 arc and a Foc arc in a Retreat clause. As with Passive and AP, the point is that there are Retreat clauses with ungrammatical transitive counterparts. In this case, a noun cannot head a final Erg arc, but there is evidence that it must head an initial Erg arc since it can head a final 1 arc and a Foc arc in a Retreat clause.

As predicted by the Referentiality Constraint (67), a noun cannot head a final Erg arc and occur in its post-verbal subject position.

(73)a.* Nequ-Ø-e'x- sac' li r -ixaquil **calajenak.**
tns-B3-pA3-hit the their-wives drunks
('Drunks beat their wives.') (B,RNB:103)

b.* Nequ- Ø-e'r- au li ixim **cuink.**
tns -B3-pA3-plant the corn men
('Men grow the corn.') (B,RNB:103)

c.* Qu- in-e'x - tiu **hix.**
tns-B1-pA3 -bite jaguars
('Jaguars attacked me.') (B,RNB:104)

d.* Nequ-in -e'x -tiu **suk.**
tns- B1 -pA3-bite mosquitos
('Mosquitos bite me.') (B,RNB:106)

e.* Na- Ø -x -quet li c'al **xul.**
tns-B3-A3-eat the corn animals (B,BNB:100)
('Animals eat the corn (in the cornfield).')

Although the transitive sentences in (73a)-(73e) are ungrammatical, the corresponding retreat clauses with subject focus are grammatical.

```
(74)a. Calajenak nequ-e'-sac'-o-c   r-e    li  r-ixaquil.
       drunks    tns- p -hit- R-asp A3-Dat the their-wives
       'It's drunks who beat their wives.'        (B,RNB:103)

    b. Cuink   nequ-e'-au  -o -c   r - e  li  ixim.
       men     tns -p-plant-R-asp  A3-Dat the corn
       'It's men who grow the corn.'              (B,RNB:103)

    c. Hix     qu- e'-ti'- o - c   cu-e.
       jaguars tns-p-bite- R-asp   A1-Dat
       'They were jaguars that attacked me.'      (B,RNB:104)

    d. Suk       nequ-e'-ti- o -c   cu- e.
       mosquitos tns -p-bite-R-asp  A1-Dat
       'It's mosquitos that bite me.'             (B,RNB:106)

    e. Xul     na- Ø -quet-o -c   r - e  li  c'al.
       animals tns-B3-eat -R-asp A3-Dat  the corn
       'Animals eat the corn (in the cornfield).'
                                                  (A&P,1976:35)
```

The relational network associated with the sentence in (73a) is given in (75a), and the relational network associated with the sentence in (74a) is given in (75b).

(75)a.*

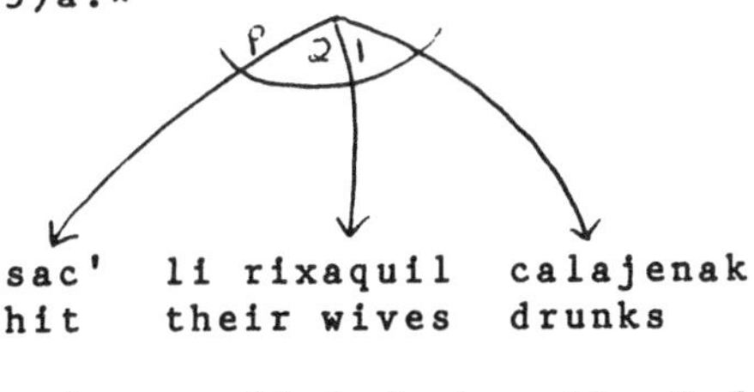

b.

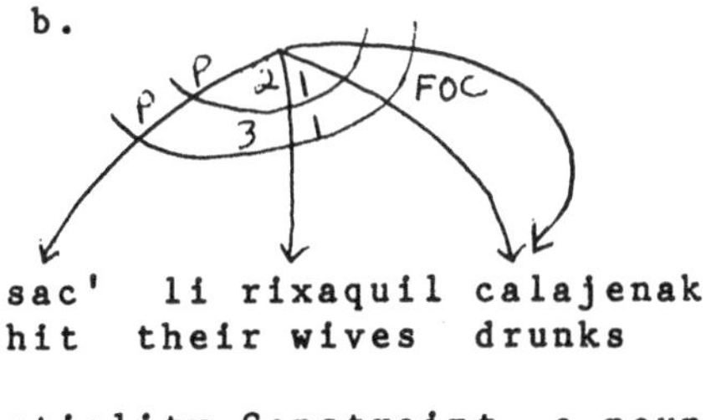

As predicted by the Referentiality Constraint, a noun cannot head a final 1 arc in a transitive clause (75a), but it can head a final 1 arc and a Foc arc in the corresponding Retreat clause (75b). This provides evidence for initial nonreferential 1s.[7]

5.4.3 Summary

Evidence for initial nonreferential nuclear terms was presented. Three arguments for initial nonreferential 2s were given based on Passive, AP, and DO focus clauses, and two arguments for initial nonreferential 1s were given based on Retreat and intransitive subject focus clauses. In each case, it was shown that a bare noun could head a final nuclear term arc only if it heads an overlay arc. This followed from the Referentiality Constraint.

It was argued that the Referentiality Constraint (67) could accurately predict the grammatical and ungrammatical sentences associated with the relational networks represented in (76)-(82) below, all of which posit an initial nonreferential nuclear term (x).

(76) Antipassive:

a.

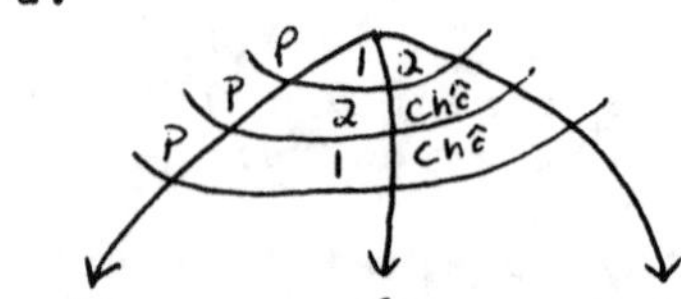

b.*

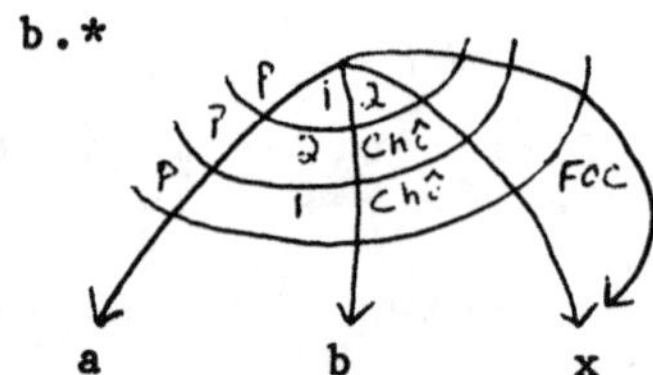

(77) Passive:

a.*

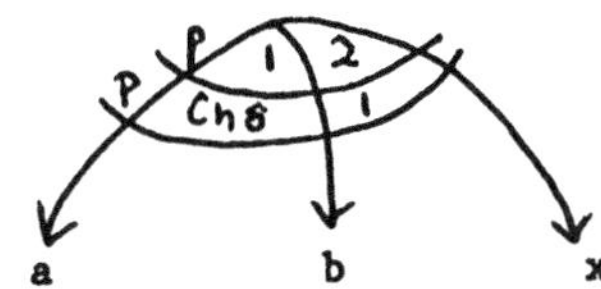

b.

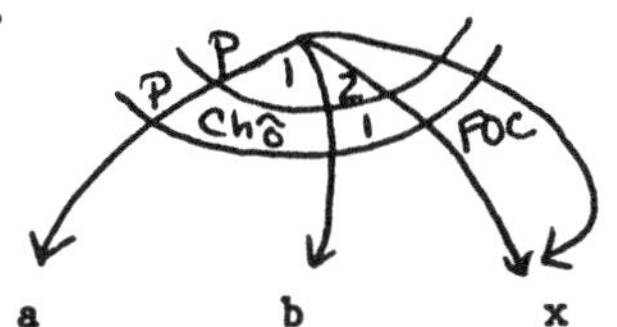

(78) Transitive/DO Focus:

a.*

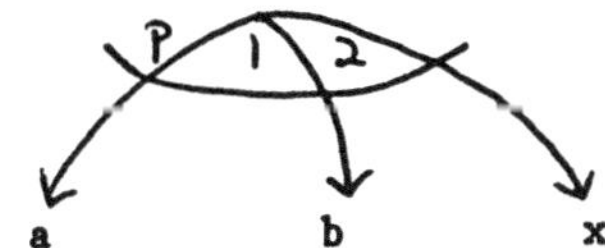

b.

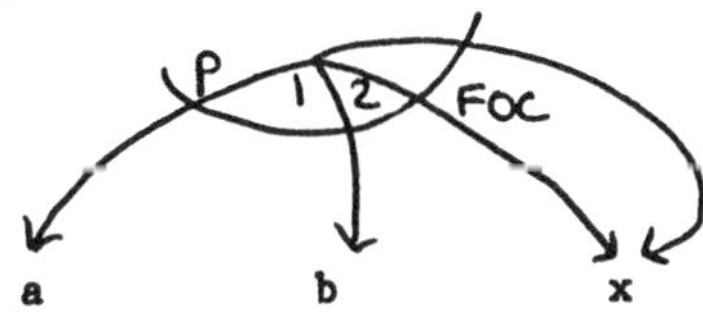

(79) 2-clause/lower transitive:

a.*

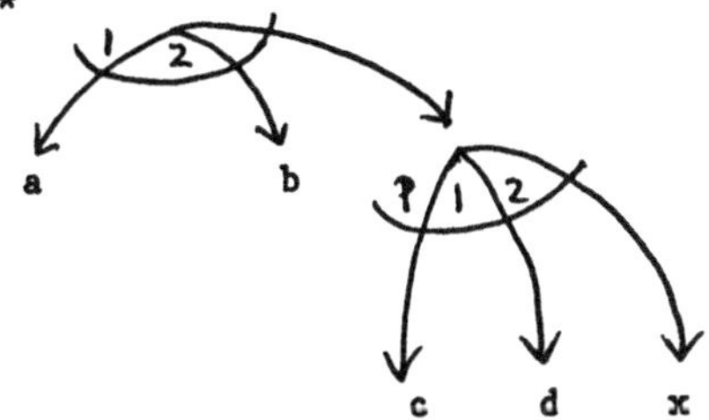

b.

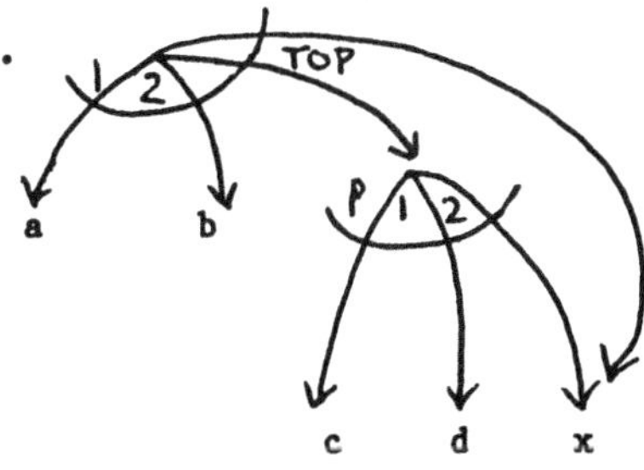

(80) 2-clause/lower AP:

a.

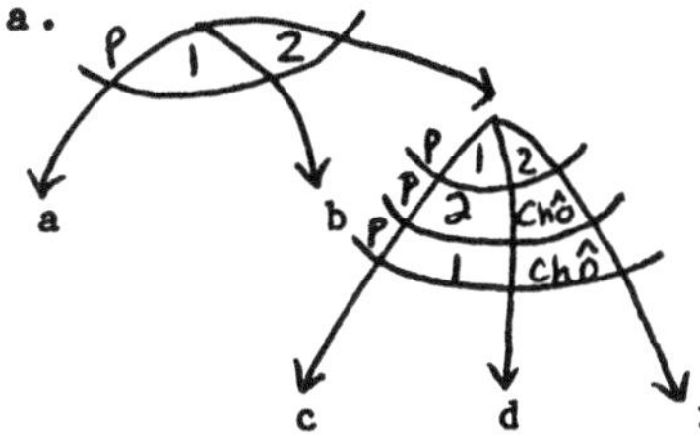

b.*

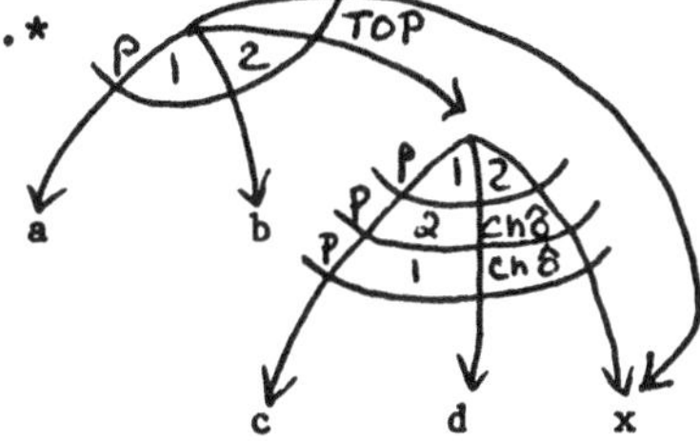

(81) Retreat:

a.*

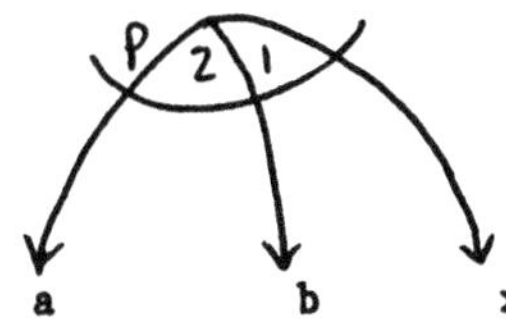

b.

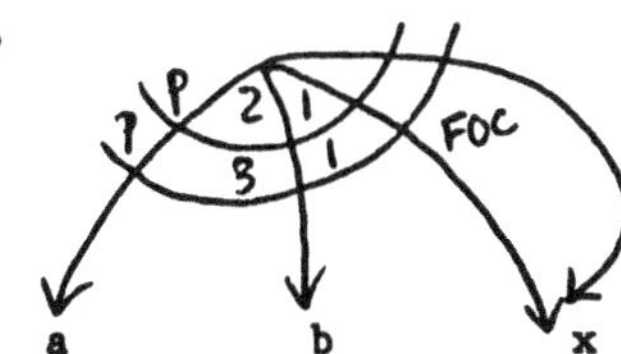

(82) Unergative:

a.* 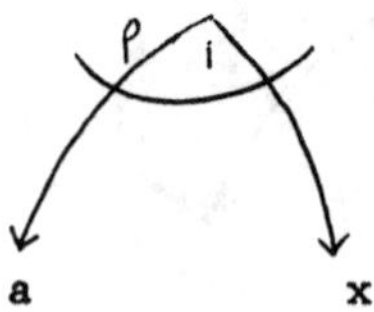

b. 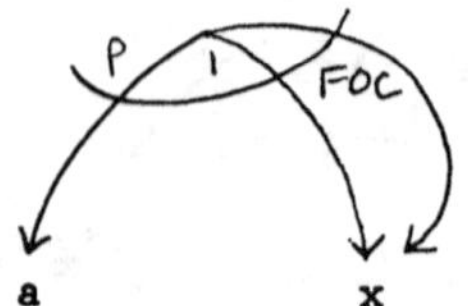

Consistent with the Referentiality Constraint, if a noun heads a final nuclear term arc, it must head an overlay arc, as it does in (77b), (78b), (79b), (81b), and (82b) providing evidence for its presence at initial level.

Consistent with the Chômeur Constraint, if a noun heads a final Chô arc, it cannot head an overlay arc, as evidenced in (76b) and (80b). This constraint will be discussed in more detail in the next Section.

5.5 Initial DO is Final Chômeur

In this section I argue that the initial DO is a final chômeur in an AP clause. It is shown that a final 2 can bear the Top, Foc, or Rel relation, but the object in an AP clause cannot. This follows from the Chômeur Constraint, given below.

(83) Chômeur Constraint:
A chômeur cannot head an overlay arc.

5.5.1 Object Topics and Foci

The logical object of the AP clause must occur in postverbal position. No other nominal may intervene between the verb and the AP object.

(84)a. T - in-q'ue- o - k **cua** r -e laj Lu'.
tns-B1-give-AP-asp tortillas A3-Dat ncl Lu'
'I will give tortillas to Pedro.'

b.* T -in-q'ue- o - k r-e laj Lu' **cua** .

(85)a. T - in -lok'-o- k **cua** sa' li c'ayil.
tns-B1-buy- AP-asp tortillas in the market
'I will buy tortillas in the market.'

b.* T - in -lok'-o- k sa' li c'ayil **cua** .

The object of an AP clause cannot bear an overlay relation. Compare the (a) and (b) clauses in (86)-(88).

(86)a. T -o -lok'-o -k **kanal tul** .
tns-B1p-buy-AP-asp ripe bananas
'We will buy ripe bananas.'

b.* **Kanal tul** t - o -lok'- o - k.
('Ripe bananas we will buy.')

(87)a. T - in -tz'iba- n **hu** .
tns-B1- wrute -AP letters
'I will write letters.'

b.* **Hu** t -in-tz'iba-n.
('Letters I will write.')

(88)a. X -at-sic' -o -c **cape** .
tns-B2-pick-AP-asp coffee
'You pick coffee.'

b.* **Cape** x -at-sic'-o -c.
('It's coffee you pick.')

As exemplified in the (b) sentences in (86)-(88), the bare noun in an AP clause cannot occur in preverbal position. This contrasts with the bare noun in a transitive clause (§5.4.1.1) which may occur in preverbal position as topic or focus. Thus, we can compare the bare noun of the transitive clause in (89) below to the bare noun in the AP clause in (87) and find that opposite generalizations hold.

(89)a.* T - Ø -in- tz'iba hu .
tns-B3-A1- write letters ('I will write letters.')

b. Hu t -Ø -in-tz'iba.
'<u>Letters</u> I will write.'

The bare noun heads a final Chô arc in (86)-(88). In contrast, the bare noun heads a final 2-arc in (89). That the bare noun can extract in (89) and cannot in (86)-(88) follows from the Chômeur Constraint, given in (83). Most importantly, this distinction follows from a constraint on chômeurs. It is not governed by referentiality since non-referential nuclear terms can focus, as evidenced in § 5.4 (with respect to DO focus, and Subject focus in passive and retreat clauses), and by (89).

The relational networks associated with (87a,b) are given in (90a,b). The relational networks associated with (89a,b) are given in (91a,b).

(90)a.

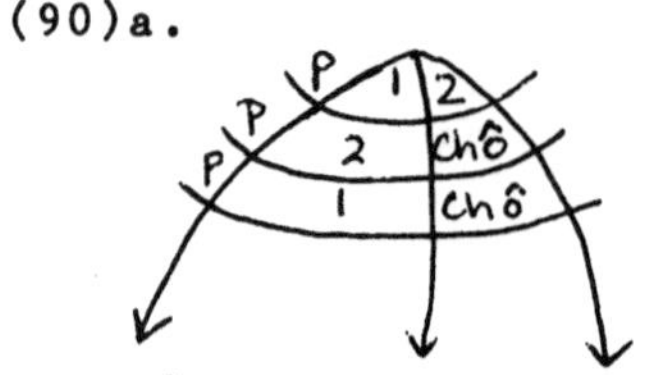

tz'iba laɨn hu
write I letters

b.*

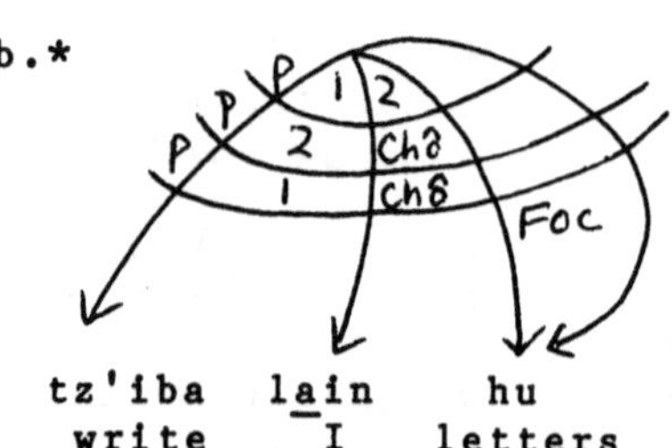

tz'iba laɨn hu
write I letters

(91)a.*

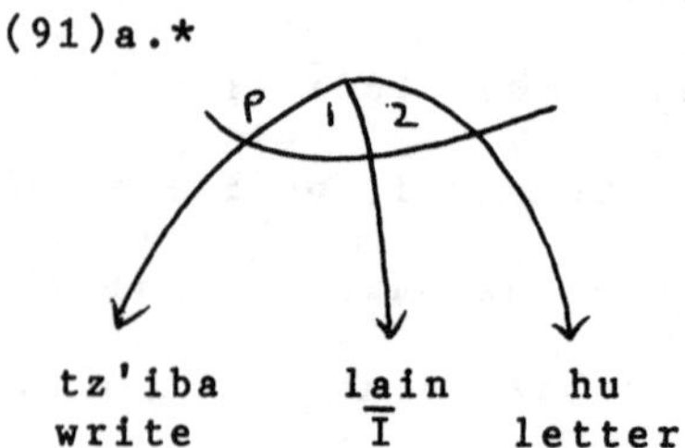

tz'iba laɨn hu
write I letter

b.

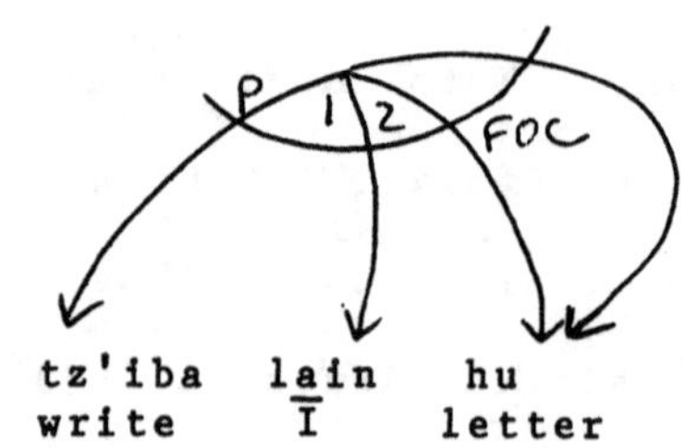

tz'iba laɨn hu
write I letter

Since 2 chômeurs occur without modifiers, 2 chômeurs and nonreferential nuclear terms are morphologically nondistinct, however the former cannot head an overlay arc and the latter must. Although these nouns are morphologically identical, syntactically they are not. This follows from the notion of chômeur. I argue that (90b) is ruled out by the Chômeur Constraint because a nominal heading a final Chô arc cannot head an overlay arc. On the other hand, (91a) is ruled out by the Referentiality Constraint because a nonreferential noun heading a final nuclear term arc must head an overlay arc.

The contrastive properties of foci are evidenced under negation. As is exemplified in (92), the final 2 can focus (92a), but the 2 chômeur cannot (92b).

(92)a. Entonces, moco **xul** **ta** li x - Ø -in-puba.
then neg animal neg that tns-B3-A1-shoot
'Then, it wasn't an animal that I shot.'(E&C,MSS.41)

b.*Entonces, moco **xul** **ta** li x - in-puba- n.
that tns-B1-shoot-AP
('Then, it wasn't an animal that I shot.')

Finally, in (93) we see that the final 2 of a transitive clause can bear the Rel relation (93a), but that the 2 chômeur of an AP clause cannot (93b).

(93)a. X - Ø -in-lok' **li cua** li x -Ø -x-cua laj Lu'.
tns-B3-A1-buy the tortillas that tns-B3-A3-eat ncl Lu'
'I bought the tortilla that Pedro ate.'

b.* X - in-lok'-o- c **cua** li x -Ø-x-cua laj Lu'.
tns-B1-buy-AP-asp tortillas
('I bought tortillas that Pedro ate.')

In this Section, it has been argued that the object of the AP clause cannot bear an overlay relation because it is a final chômeur. It was argued earlier that AP and 2-3 Retreat are distinct constructions, despite their common verbal morphology. Therefore, it should be noted that while the 'logical object' of an AP clause cannot bear the Topic relation, the 'logical object' of a Retreat clause can (Chapter 4, §4.3.3). This provides further support for the syntactic distinction between AP and 2-3 Retreat clauses. The 'logical object' of the AP clause bears the initial 2/final Chô relation and therefore cannot extract. The 'logical object' of a Retreat clause bears the initial 2/final 3 relation and therefore may extract like any other IO.

5.6 Conclusion

An analysis of K'ekchi AP clauses was given. Three constraints which interact with this analysis were proposed:

I. <u>AP Object Constraint</u>:
The 2 chômeur in an AP clause must be nonreferential.

II. <u>Referentiality Constraint</u>:
If a (nonreferential) noun heads a final nuclear term arc, it must head an overlay arc.

III. <u>Chômeur Constraint</u>:
A chômeur cannot head an overlay arc.

Five types of arguments were given as evidence for a multi-level AP analysis. First, in § 5.1 arguments based on verbal agreement (§5.1.1), and aspect (§5.1.2) provided evidence for the final intransitivity of AP clauses. In addition, the rule for AP marking (§5.1.3) provided evidence not only for the final intransitivity, but also for the initial transitivity of AP clauses.

Second, the properties of the AP subject were discussed (§ 5.2). It was shown that the subject of an AP clause was able to head a narrow overlay arc, but that the subject of the corresponding active transitive clause could not. That the final 1 of a transitive clause cannot head a narrow overlay arc follows from the Ergative Extraction Constraint (see Chapters 3 and 4). That the final 1 of the AP clause can head a narrow overlay arc supports the conclusion that AP clauses are finally intransitive.

Third, the properties of the AP object were discussed (§ 5.3). It was shown that an AP 2 chômeur must be nonreferential. This was stated as the AP Object Constraint (given in I above). It was then shown that nonreferential 2s could not occur in a postverbal (non-focus) position, but could occur in preverbal (focus) position. It was argued that this followed from the Referentiality Constraint (II above). Crucially, since the nonreferential DO could focus in transitive clauses, this provided evidence for positing initially transitive strata with 2 arcs headed by nonreferential nouns, and for an analysis of AP clauses with initially transitive strata.

Fourth, in § 5.4 further support for the Referentiality Constraint was given. Three arguments for initial nonreferential DOs were given based on Passive, AP, and DO focus clauses, and two arguments for initial nonreferential Subjects were given based on Retreat and intransitive subject focus clauses. The point of each argument was the same: A bare noun can head a final nuclear term arc only if it heads an overlay arc.

Fifth, in § 5.5 it was argued that the initial 2 is final chômeur in an AP clause. It was shown that a final 2 could bear an overlay relation, but the object in an AP clause could not. This followed from the Chômeur Constraint (given in III above) and provided additional evidence for the initial transitivity of AP clauses.

Finally, it should be pointed out that chômeur extraction is distinct from non-term extraction. A nominal heading a Chô arc cannot extract. However, a nominal heading a final Obl arc is not restricted in this way. As discussed earlier (Chapters 2 and 4), non-term possessors of relational nouns can bear an overlay relation, but 1 chômeurs and 3 chômeurs cannot, even though they too, are possessors of relational nouns. Finally, as just seen, bare nouns that are final nuclear terms <u>must</u> bear an overlay relation (Referentiality Constraint), but bare nouns that head a Chô arc cannot (Chômeur Constraint). A grammar without the notion 'chômeur' will not be able to capture the generalization that governs bare noun extraction, or be able to state what 1 chômeurs in Passive clauses, 2 chômeurs in AP clauses and 3 chômeurs in Retreat clauses have in common.[8]

Chapter 5 Footnotes

1. In the past, this construction has been labeled 'Absolutive Antipassive' by Mayanists.

2. The vowel length difference in examples (15b) and (15c) is due to a phonological rule (see footnote 2, Chapter 4).

3. As will be discussed in § 5.3.2, a final (unfocused) 2 must be 'referential' i.e. it must co-occur with an article, noun classifier, numeral, or possessive affix. Since the logical object in (27) occurs as a bare noun, it could be argued that (27) is ruled out by something other than the Ergative Extraction Constraint (25). However, as shown in (1) below, even if xic co-occurs with a definite article, the subject of the transitive clause cannot be focused.

(1)* Ha' li ma us aj musik'ej a'an na-Ø -x -tz'ap
emph the not good ncl spirit that tns-B3-A3-close

li xic.
the ears
('That evil spirit makes people deaf.')

4. The 2 chômeur in impersonal passive and impersonal unaccusative clauses is restricted to third person (Berinstein, in preparation). Therefore, it might be suggested that the relational networks associated with the sentences in (30) are ruled out by the 2 chômeur constraint in (1), below.

(1) 2 Chômeur Constraint:
A 2 chômeur must be third person.

Even though the 2 Chômeur Constraint is able to account for the ungrammaticality of the sentences in (30), it fails to predict the ungrammaticality of sentences like (2), below.

(2)* T -in- tenk'a - n - k a'an.
fut-B1-help -AP- asp 3s pro
('I will help her/him.')

In (2), the independent pronoun is third person and the sentence is ungrammatical. The ungrammaticality follows from the AP Object Constraint, given in (33).

5. In Chuj, a Mayan language of the Kanjobalan branch, Maxwell (1976) reports a similar split between the structure of direct objects and 'objects' of intransitive verbs derived in -w (an AP suffix). She discusses two dialects and notes that neither the San Sebastian nor the San Mateo dialect

allow the object of the intransitive verb to co-occur with an article, noun classifier, numeral, or possessor. She found that the two dialects differ in their treatment of modifying words and clauses, but that certain adjective-noun compounds were allowed as objects of intransitives in -w.

6. Notice that a remarkable parallel holds between subjects in Malagasy (also a verb initial and subject final language) and nonreferential nuclear terms in K'ekchi.

In Malagasy, (Madagascar, Malayo-Polynesian) subjects must be definite (Keenan 1976). Thus, an indefinite noun phrase marked by the absence of an article, cannot occur as subject in sentence final position.

(1)a.* Namono ny vehivavy **lehilahy** .
hit the woman man
('A man hit the woman.') (Keenan:1977)

Now consider the passive subjects in (2). These sentences are parallel to the K'ekchi clauses in (61a-c). In (2a) the passive subject is definite and it occurs in its normal postverbal position. The passive subject occurs without its article in (2b) and the clause is ungrammatical. In (2c) the anarthrous passive subject is focused and occurs in the preverbal position.

(2)a. Sasan- d Rasoa **ny lamba**
washed-by Rasoa the clothes
'The clothes are washed by Rasoa.' (Keenan,pc)

b.* Sasan-d Rasoa **lamba** .
washed-by Rasoa clothes
('Clothes are washed by Rasoa.')

c. **Lamba** no sasan- d Rasoa.
clothes foc washed-by Rasoa
'It was clothes that were washed by Rasoa.'

Structurally, lamba is a bare noun in (2b) and (2c), yet it can occur as subject focus in (2c), and not as subject in (2b). Similar to K'ekchi, the Malagasy subject constraint can be stated as:

(3) Nonreferential Subject Constraint (for Malagasy):
If a bare noun heads a final 1 arc, it must head an overlay arc.

7. The contrasting retreat clause without subject focus is ruled out independently by the Retreat Subject Constraint (Chapter 4), given below.

Retreat Subject Constraint:
If the initial DO is the final IO of a clause c, then the final subject of clause c must bear a narrow overlay relation.

(A)*

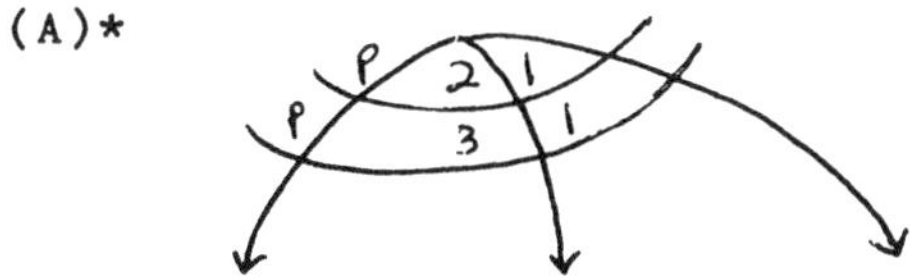

The structure in (A) is ruled out by the Retreat Subject Constraint i.e. irrespective of the subject's referentiality. The structure in (75a) is ruled out because of the subject's nonreferentiality. That (75b) is grammatical provides evidence for nonreferential subjects at initial level.

8. The Chômeur Constraint, as it is stated in III, accounts for all of the data discussed. Work that is in progress (Berinstein, in preparation) suggests that the generalization governing chômeur extraction may require revision when impersonal constructions are considered. Specifically, 2 chômeurs in impersonal unaccusative and impersonal passive constructions may head overlay arcs. Of importance, is that there is a principled reason for the difference between chômeur extraction in personal and impersonal constructions, namely: A brother-in-law of a final 1 behaves like a final 1 with respect to extraction. Notably, the final 1 in these constructions heads an Abs arc.

Chapter 6

CROSS-CLAUSAL MULTIATTACHMENT

6.0 Introduction

This chapter discusses cross-clausal multiattachments in equi and ascension constructions. The notion of cross-clausal MA was introduced in Chapter 3 (§ 3.3) and basically covers cases where a single nominal bears more than one central GR in distinct clauses.

First, it is shown that in simple retreat clauses, the final 1 must head a narrow overlay arc. This constraint was discussed in detail in Chapter 4 and is given in I below. It is then shown that complex clauses involving 2-3 Retreat must obey this same constraint. For example, in equi constructions, it is the 'controller' of the retreat infinitive that must bear the narrow overlay relation. This fact provides independent evidence for the notion of multiattachment. Specifically, complex clauses with non-finite retreat complements require obligatory extraction of the nominal in the matrix clause that is multiattached to the downstairs retreat subject. I argue that the controller of the retreat infinitive satisfies the condition in I because it also heads the final 1 arc in the retreat clause. This follows automatically from the hypothesized cross-clausal MA and the Retreat Subject Constraint.

I. <u>Retreat Subject Constraint:</u>
<u>If the initial DO is the final IO of a clause c, then the nominal which heads the final subject arc of clause c must also head a narrow overlay arc.</u>

6.1 Equi

6.1.1 Form of the Complement

There are three types of complements: a) full clause, b) infinitival, and c) nominalizations. Of the infinitives there are four types that will be discussed: AP, Retreat, Passive and base intransitive. There are no transitive infinitives in K'ekchi.

An infinitive may not be marked for person. A nominalization however, may register one participant as possessor. In K'ekchi, only final 1s can be equi victims. If the final 1 is equi victim in an intransitive complement, the result is an infinitive. If the final 1 is equi victim in a transitive complement, the result is a nominalization with the DO cross-referenced as possessor. As in other possessive constructions (Chapter 1, § 1.3.1), the possessor is cross-referenced with an affix from Set A.[1]

6.1.2 Full Clause Complements

Full clause complements are optionally introduced by the complementizer <u>nak</u> 'that, when'. <u>Re</u> 'in order to' or <u>re nak</u> 'in order that' may introduce purpose clauses. For example,

1)a. Ta - Ø -cu-aj nak t - at- xic.
tns-B3- A1-want that tns-B2-go
'I want you to go.'

1)b. Ma x - Ø -a -yeh r- e- eb nak inc'a' t - in-xic?
Q tns-B3-A2-say A3-Dat-p that not tns- B1-go
'Did you tell them that I wouldn't go?' (E&C,Gr.149)

c. Ch -Ø-a -tenk'a eb li coc'al re nak t - e'-
tns-B3-A2-help p the children in order that tns-p-

q'ui- k sa' li tiquilal.
grow-asp in the straightness (E&C,Gr.177)
'You may help the children so that they grow tall.'

d. Laj Juan qui- Ø -x -sic' li q'uim re nak ti-
ncl Juan tns-B3 -A3-hunt the straw in order that tns-

Ø - x-yib x-ben li r - ochoch.
B3-A3-fix its-top the his-house (E&C,Gr.177)
'Juan looked for straw in order to fix his roof.'

e. A'an na -Ø -x-sic' na'bal li mos ixk re
she tns-B3-A3-hunt many the servant women so that

t - e' -que'e- k.
tns-p- grind- asp (B,S11.44)
'She looks for many women servants so that they will grind.'

Excluding purpose clauses, it should be noted that if the subjects of the matrix and finite complement clause are coreferential, <u>nak</u> cannot occur. For instance, compare (2a) to (2b), and (3a) to (3b).

2)a. Ut anakcuan na- Ø -cu-aj nak t -o -xic.
and now tns-B3-A1-want that tns-B1p-go
'Now I want us to go.' (E&C,J.122)

b. T - Ø -incu-aj t -in-xic.
tns-B3-A1 -want tns-B1-go
'I want to go.'

c.* T - Ø -incu-aj nak t -in-xic.
('I want to go.')

3)a. Na- Ø -cu-aj nak t - Ø- a -tzol li K'ekchi.
tns-B3-A1-want that tns-B3-A2-learn the K'ekchi
'I want you to learn K'ekchi.'

b. T - Ø -incu-aj t - Ø -in- nau li K'ekchi.
tns-B3- A1 -want tns-B3-A1-know the K'ekchi
'I want to understand K'ekchi.'

3)c.* T - Ø-incu-aj nak t -Ø-in-nau li K'ekchi.
('I want to understand K'ekchi.')

If the complement subject and matrix subject are coreferential, the complement may be a full clause as in (2b) and (3b), an infinitive as in (4a), or a nominalization as in (4b).

4)a. T - Ø - incu-aj xic.
tns-B3- A1 -want go
'I want to go.'

b. T - Ø -incu-aj x -nau -bal li K'ekchi.
tns-B3-A1 -want A3-know-nom the K'ekchi
'I want to understand K'ekchi.'

The fact that <u>nak</u> does not introduce the complement in (4a) or (4b) is predicted by two facts. First, as already mentioned, <u>nak</u> may only occur if the subjects are <u>not</u> coreferential. Second, <u>nak</u> may only introduce full clause complements.

6.1.3 Infinitival Complements: Unerg Control

In order to understand the arguments based on cross-clausal MA, given in § 6.3, we must first see what determines the form of the complement. Three types of infinitival complements will be discussed: base intransitive, passive, and AP. Infinitives are not marked for tense, aspect, or person agreement. The form of the infinitive is <u>Vb + c</u>. The infinitival verb incorporates the revaluation marker which is independently motivated. Thus, the marker for the passive infinitive is determined by the same rule that determines passive morphology in full clauses (Chapter 2, § 2.1.2).

Similarly, the marker for AP infinitives is determined by the same rule that determines AP morphology in full clauses (Chapter 5 § 5.1.3), and so on.

Infinitival (and nominalized) complements are introduced by the preposition chi which is otherwise used to introduce oblique relations, as chirix (Loc) 'behind him', or chi che' (Inst) 'with a stick', etc. However, chi does not introduce either of the complements in (4a,b). This is because the presence of chi is determined by the GR that the complement clause bears to the matrix. In (4a,b), the complement bears the 2-relation and chi is not required. Chi introduces the complement only if it bears an oblique or chômeur relation to the matrix clause.[2] For example, in (5) below, chi introduces the intransitive infinitival complements.

5)a. Mas n -in- lub chi atinac.
much tns-B1-tire prep talk
'I'm very tired of talking.' (E&C,V.51)

b. C - o - oc chi yabac lao.
tns-B1p-enter prep cry we
'We began to cry.' (B,S14.15)

c. ...nak naqu-e'-xic chi auc laj auconel
when tns- p -go prep plant ncl planters
'when the planters go to plant' (Ac&P,107)

d. Qu-e'- oc chi hilanc rubel jun x-ton -al che'.
tns-p-enter prep rest under one its-trunk-poss tree
'They began to rest under a tree.' (E&C,P.13)

The matrix verb is fully inflected and agrees with the final 1 in person (5a,b) and number (5c,d). The final 1 may occur in sentence-final (subject) position, as in (5b,c).

The RN corresponding to (5b) is given in (6).

(6)

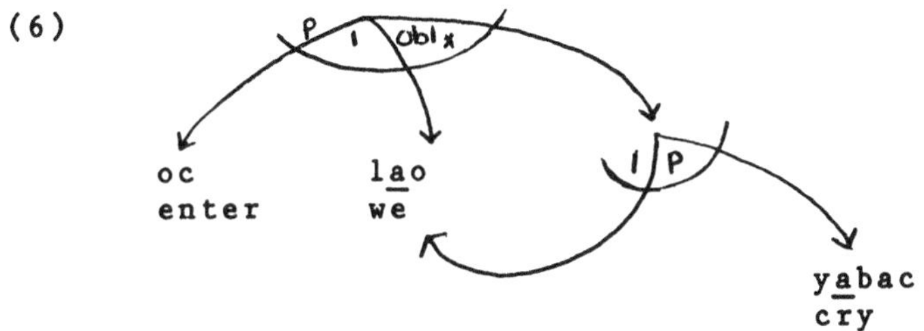

Under a MA analysis, a nominal may head more than one central GR arc in different clauses. For example, lao in (5b) heads a 1 arc in the matrix clause and a 1 arc in the complement clause. It is impossible for sentences like (5a-d) to contain a surface realization of the final 1 of the complement. I will refer to the nominal that can have no surface realization in the equi construction as the equi 'victim'. In these examples the equi victim is a final intransitive subject. I will refer to the nominal in the matrix clause that is understood as the subject of the infinitive as the 'controller'. Relevant to the surface realization of nominals in K'ekchi is the Highest Clause Constraint, given in (7) below.

(7) Highest Clause Constraint:[3]
If a nominal heads central GR arcs in more than one clause, only the highest clause in which it heads an arc is relevant to its realization.

In (8) below, chi introduces the passive infinitival complement. The passive marker is e'. The passive infinitive is not marked for tense or agreement, and -c is suffixed to the passive revaluation marker.

(8) T -in -xic chi bane'c.
tns-B1- go prep cure=Pass inf
'I will go to be cured.'

The RN associated with (8) is given in (9).

(9)

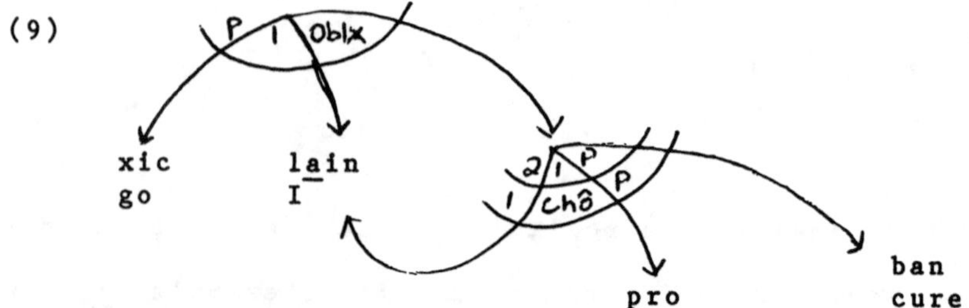

In (10) below, chi introduces the AP infinitival complements. The AP marker is -o if the verb stem is one syllable (and -n if the verb stem has more than one syllable). As in finite AP clauses, if the 2 chômeur is overt, it must be 'nonreferential'. I.e. it cannot occur with an article, noun classifier, possessive affix, or numeral. The bare nouns cacau in (10a) and ik in (10b) head Chô arcs in the AP complement. The AP infinitive occurs without any tense or agreement markers. The infinitival affix -c is suffixed to the AP revaluation marker -o.

(10)a. Nequ-e'-oc chi jec'oc cacau sa' coc'
tns- p-begin prep distribute=AP inf cacao in small

caki jom.
red bowls (B,S11.45)
'They begin to distribute cacao in small red bowls.'

b. T - in-xic chi c'amoc ik.
tns-B1-go prep carry=AP inf load
'I am going to carry loads.' (S,D.52)

c. Qui-Ø-oc chi tijoc li cuink.
tns-B3-begin prep pray=AP inf the man
'The man began to pray.' (E&C,V.37)

The RN associated with (10b) is given in (11).

(11)

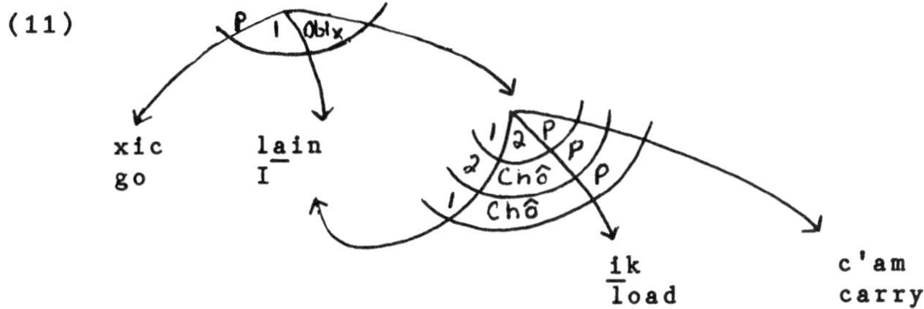

Summing up: We have seen three types of infinitival complements: base intransitive (5a-d), passive (8), and AP (10a-c). In all of these examples, the controller heads a final Abs arc, the victim is a final 1, the complement is introduced by <u>chi</u>, and the final 1 of the clause can appear in its 'normal' sentence-final position, as it does in (5b), (5c), and (10c). The conditions on controllers and victims are given in (11) and (12), below.

(11) <u>Condition on Controllers</u> (to be revised)
Final 1s of the matrix clause can control intransitive infinitival clauses.

(12) <u>Condition on Victims</u>:
Only final 1s can be equi victims.

6.1.4 Infinitival Complements: Erg Control

Consistent with the prediction in (11), the examples in (13) illustrate equi controlled by the final Erg. The complement is in all cases a final 2. Therefore, <u>chi</u> does not introduce it.

13)a. Qui -Ø-x-patz' oc sa' cuartel.
tns-B3-A3-ask enter in barracks
'He asked to enter the barracks.' (E&C,J.115)

13)b. Sa' in-ca'ch'inal inc'a' qui-Ø-cu-aj xic sa' escuel.
in my- youth not tns-B3-A1-want go to school
'In my youth, I didn't want to go to school.'(H,G.45)

c. Como mas k'emcun-Ø inc'a' na -Ø -r- aj cuaklic.
as very soft penis-B3 not tns-B3-A3-want arise
'Since he was very lazy, he didn't want to get up.'
(F,LJ.3)

The RN associated with (13a) is (14). The controller a'an heads a final Erg arc in the matrix clause. The complement heads a final 2 arc.

(14)

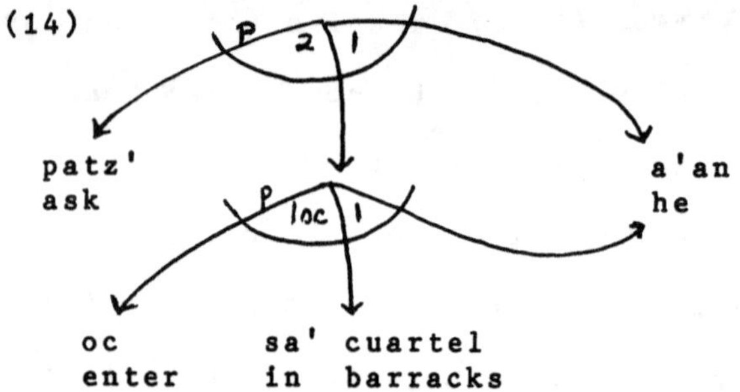

In (15) below, the controller heads a final Erg arc and the victim heads a final Abs arc in a Passive clause.

15)a. L -in ca'ch'in inc'a' na-Ø- r -aj cute'c.
the-my-child not tns-B3-A3-want inject=Pass inf
'My child didn't want to be vaccinated.' (H,D.105)

b. Na- Ø - ka-nau cole'c lao.
tns-B3-A1p-know save=Pass inf we
'We know how to be saved.'

The RN corresponding to (15b) is given in (16). Notice that, here too, it is possible for the final 1 to occur in its normal postverbal position.

(16)

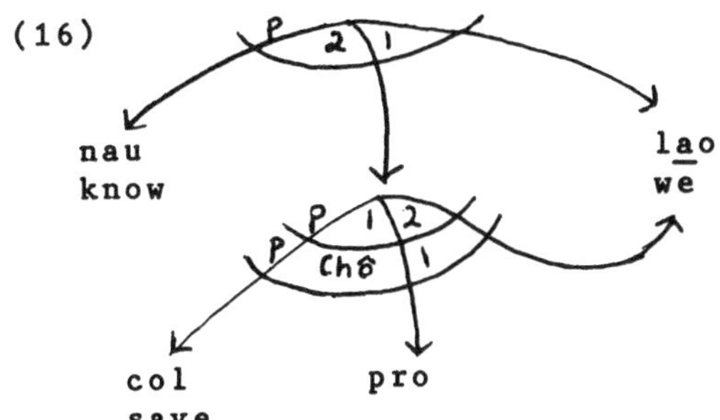

In the examples in (17) below, the controller heads a final Erg arc and the victim heads a final Abs arc in an AP clause. The RN associated with (17a) is given in (18).

17)a. Lain t -Ø -incu-aj lo'oc tul.
I tns-B3-A1-want eat=AP inf bananas
'I want to eat bananas.'

b. Laj Lu' na - Ø -x -nau bichanc.
ncl Lu' tns-B3-A3-know sing=AP inf
'Pedro knows how to sing.'

(18)

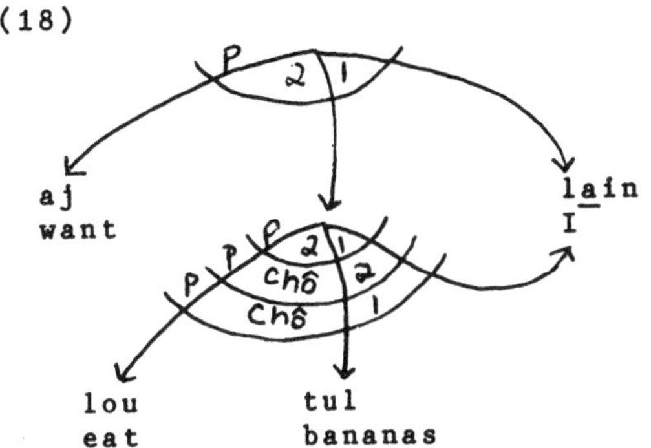

6.1.5 Infinitival Complements: DO Control

In this Section it is shown that the matrix DO can control equi into intransitive infinitival complements. The Condition on Controllers (11) is revised in (19) below, to capture this generalization.

(19) <u>Condition on Controllers</u>: (to be revised)
Final nuclear terms of the matrix clause can control intransitive infinitival clauses.

In (20a) and (20b) the controller heads a final 2 arc and the victim heads a final 1 arc. Since the complement is headed by a non-nuclear term arc, it must be introduced by <u>chi</u>.

20)a. Ch- o -a -tenk'a chi cuanc sa' x-yal -al.
tns-B1p-A2-help prep exist in its-truth-poss
'May you help us to live in peace.' (E&C,Gr.176)

b. Na -Ø- x-takla li al chi cuarc.
tns-B3-A3-send the boy prep sleep
'She sends the boy to sleep.'

c. Tons na -Ø -takla -c chi c'alec.
then tns-B3-send=pass-asp prep weed
'Then he is sent to weed.' (F,LJ.24)

The RN associated with (20c) is given in (21). The controller heads an initial 2/final 1 arc in a passive clause.

(21)

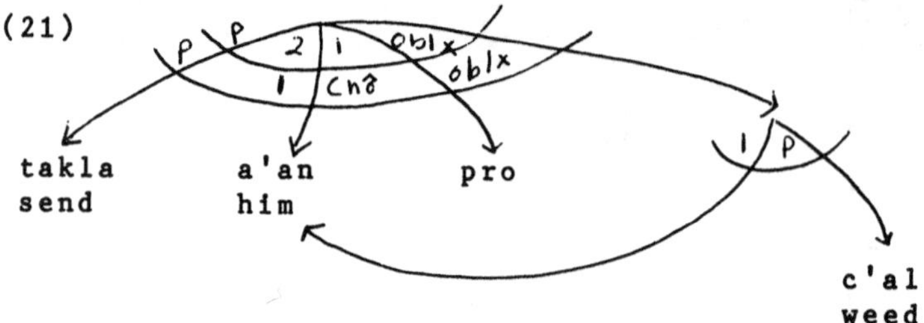

In (22) below the controller heads a final 2 arc and the victim heads a final 1 arc in a passive complement. The RN corresponding to (22b) is given in (23).

22)a. Bar x -Ø -e'x -c'am cui' li cuink chi bane'c?
where tns-B3-pA3-bring cui' the man prep cure=Pass inf
'Where did they bring the man to be cured?'

22)b. T -Ø -incu-aj t -Ø -in -nau bar t -Ø -in-q'ue
tns-B3-A1-want tns-B3-A1-know where tns-B3-A1-put

li cu-ak' chi puch'e'c.
the my-clothes prep wash=Pass inf
'I want to know where I should put my clothes to be cleaned.' (H,G.68)

(23)

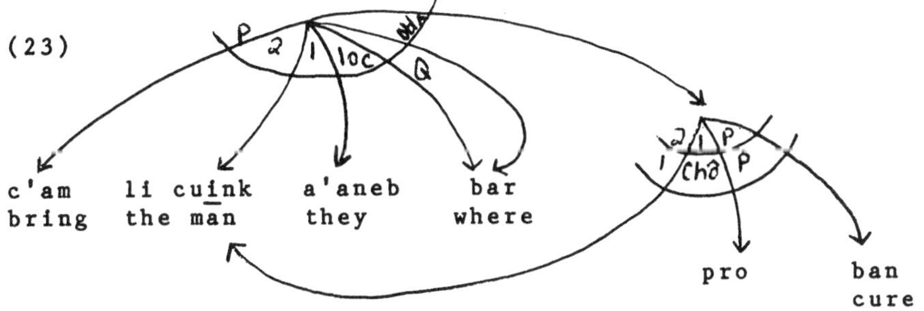

In (24) the controller heads a final 2 arc and the victim heads a final 1 arc in an AP clause. The bare noun cua heads a Chô arc in the AP complement. The RN corresponding to (24) is given in (25).

24) X - at -x- chakrabi chi lok'oc cua.
tns-B2 -A3-order prep buy=AP inf tortillas
'She ordered you to buy tortillas.'

(25)

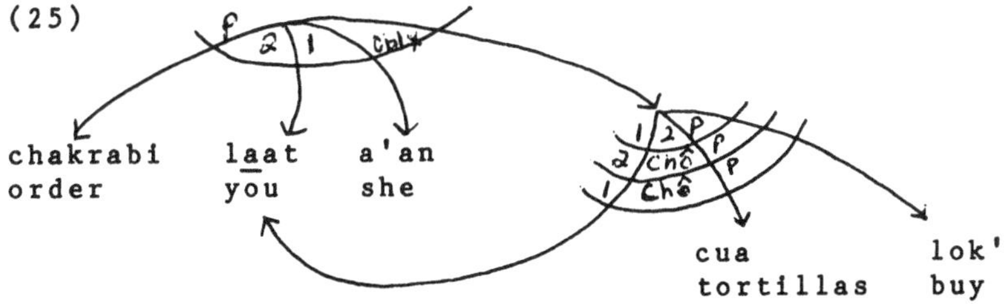

6.1.6 DO Nominalizations

There are two nominalizing suffixes that mark transitive nominalizations: -bal which is suffixed to root CV(C) (one syllable) stems and -(n)quil which is suffixed to stems with more than one syllable. The structure of a DO nominalization is: Set A + Vb + -bal/-(n)quil. For example, x-lok'-bal 'to buy it', x-camsi-nquil 'to kill it'.

In the examples that follow, the nominal heading a final Erg arc in the complement is multiattached (and coreferential with) a matrix nuclear term. In clauses in which the Erg is equi victim, the reduced embedded clause is a DO nominalization with the DO cross-referenced as possessor. Compare (26a) to (26b).

26)a. X -in-oc chi x -tz'iba-nquil li hu.
tns-B1-begin prep A3-write -nom the letter
'I began to write the letter.'

b. X - Ø -in- yo'ob x- tz'iba-nquil li hu.
tns-B3-A1-begin A3-write - nom the letter
'I began to write the letter.'

In (26a) the matrix verb oc is intransitive. The controller of the nominalization heads a final Abs arc. The complement heads a non-nuclear term arc and is introduced by chi. The third singular possessor of the nominalization x- is cross-referencing li hu 'the letter'. On the other hand, in (26b) the matrix verb yo'ob is transitive. The controller of the nominalization heads a final Erg arc. The complement heads a final 2 arc, and therefore it is not introduced by chi. The RNs for (26a) and (26b) are given in (27a) and (27b), respectively.

27)a.

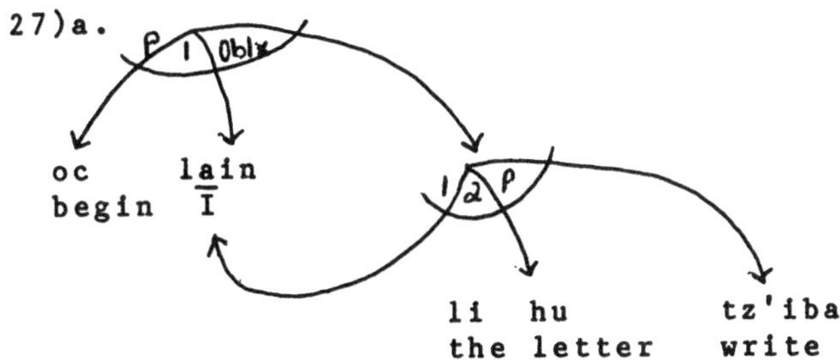

27)b.

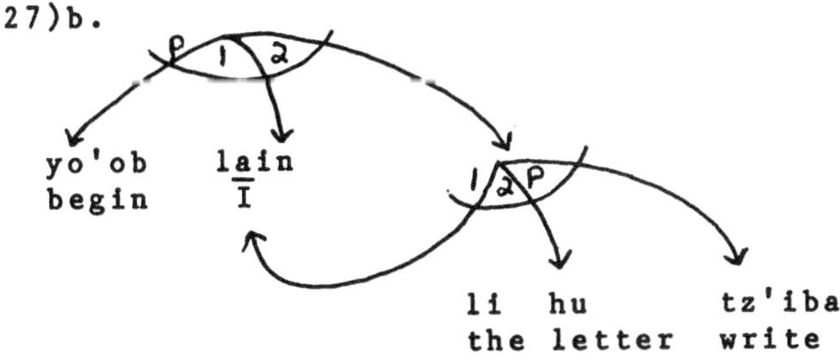

The sentences in (28) further exemplify nuclear term controlled nominalizations in transitive complements. In (28a-d) the nominal heading the final Erg arc (in the matrix clause) is the controller. In (28e-f) the nominal heading the final DO arc is the controller, and in (28g-i) the nominal heading the final Unerg arc is the controller. In all of these examples, the nominal heading the final 2 arc in the complement is cross-referenced as possessor of the nominalization.

28)a. Inc'a' na- Ø -ka-cuy r- isin-quil.
not tns-B3-A1p-endure A3-remove-nom
'We aren't able to remove it.' (H,G.50)

b. T - Ø- in-yal x-cuaclesin-quil.
tns-B3-A1-try A3-raise -nom
'I will try to raise her.' (H,G.51)

c. T -Ø -incu-aj acu-il -bal.
tns-B3-A1 -want A2-see-nom
'I want to see you.'

28)d. N - Ø -in-nau x - bon-bal.
tns-B3-A1-know A3-paint-nom
'I know how to paint it.' (F,P.105)

e. X -in-a-tenk'a chi x -lok'-bal l - in-ch'och'.
tns-B1-A2-help prep A3-buy -nom the-my-land
'You helped me to buy my land.'

f. X -at-x -chakrabi chi x-choy - bal li canjel.
tns-B2-A3-order prep A3-finish-nom the work
'He ordered you to finish the work.'

g. T -at-cana - k chi r -il- bal li k -ochoch.
tns-B2-stay-asp prep A3-see-nom the our-house
'You will stay to take care of our house.' (F,P.106)

h. X -Ø -chal chi x - camsin-quil li ak.
tns-B3-come prep A3- kill -nom the pig
'He came to kill the pig.' (F,P.107)

i. X - Ø -c'ay chi a - sac'-bal.
tns-B3-accustom prep A2-hit-nom
'He got use to hitting you.' (F,P.108)

Based on the class of complex clauses discussed so far, i.e. intransitive infinitivals and DO nominalizations, the conditions on possible controllers and victims in K'ekchi can be stated as:

29) Condition on Controllers:[4]
Final nuclear terms of the matrix clause can control DO nominalization and intransitive infinitival clauses.

30) Condition on Victims:
Only final 1s can be equi victims.

6.2 Ascensions

In this Section, I discuss infinitival and nominalized complements in an intransitive ascension construction.

Perlmutter and Postal (1983) have claimed that intransitive predicates that allow raising of dependents of their complements universally determine unaccusative initial strata. This is stated in (31).

31) Intransitive predicates governing Raising universally determine <u>unaccusative</u> initial strata.

(31) together with the Relational Succession Law (32) predicts that if the complement is an initial 2 of the matrix clause, the raisee will head a 2 arc in the matrix clause, thus placing the initial 2 (the complement) en chômage, as predicted by the Chômeur Law (33). As in other unaccusative strata (Chapter 3, § 3.3.2.1) in K'ekchi, the 2 (of the matrix clause) advances to 1, thus satisfying the Final 1 Law (34). The RN in (35) with the intransitive raising trigger <u>yo</u> 'continuative' is well-formed in K'ekchi.

32) <u>Relational Succession Law</u>:
An ascendee assumes within the clause into which it ascends the grammatical relation of its host NP (the NP out of which it ascends).

33) <u>The Chômeur Law</u>:
If an RN contains arcs of the form [Term_x (a,b) <c_u c_k c_y>] and [Term_x (c,b) <c_{k+1} c_z>], then it contains an arc of the form [Chô (a,b) <c_{k+1} c_w>].

34) <u>Final 1 Law</u>:
If there is a c_kth stratum of b and no c_{k+1}st stratum of b, we say that the c_kth stratum is the final stratum of b. Then: If b is a basic clause node, the final stratum of b contains a 1-arc.

35)

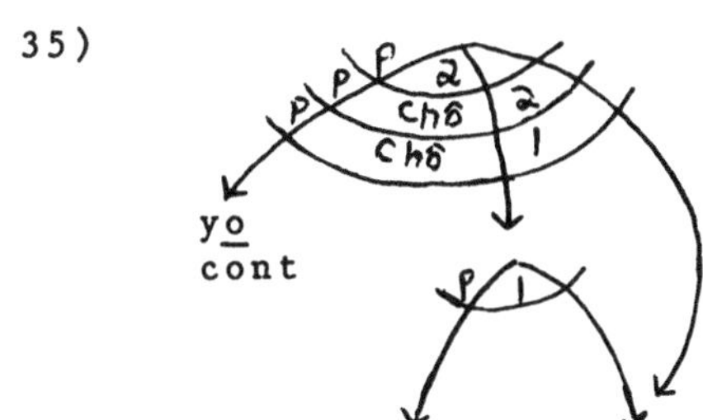

In K'ekchi, only final 1s can raise. Therefore, the RSL (32) predicts that the downstairs final 1 will assume the 2 relation in the matrix clause. Consistent with the prediction of the Chômeur Law, the complement is introduced like an oblique with the preposition chi, and consistent with the Final 1 Law, the ascendee controls (Absolutive) Set B person agreement with the matrix predicate. As in other intransitive complements, if the final intransitive subject is eliminated from its clause, the result is an infinitive. This is exemplified in (36).

```
36)a.  Yo - Ø    chi   cuarc  sa' li  muh.
       cont-B3   prep sleep  in  the shade
       'He would be sleeping in the shade.'          (F,LJ.30)

   b.  Yo  -qu-in  chi  alinac.
       cont-asp-B1  prep run
       'I am running.'

   c.  Yo- qu- eb  chi  taksinc  chi-r - u  li  tzul a'an.
       cont-asp-p  prep climb    on-its-face the mt. that
       'They were climbing the mountain.'          (E&C,P.13)

   d.  Yo - k -o    chi  trabajic nak  ta - Ø- chal- k   li
       cont-asp-B1p prep work     when tns-B3-arrive-asp the

   patron.
   boss
   'We will be working when the boss arrives.'  (E&C,Gr.257)

   e.  Yo  - Ø   chi  camc  li  x- soldados.
       cont-B3  prep  die   the his-soldiers
       'His soldiers were dying.'                  (E&C,J.152)

   f.  Yo -k-in   chi  cuaclic  lain.
       cont-asp-B1 prep stand    I
       'I will stand up.'
```

36)g. Bar cuan-qu-ex laex nak yo -qu-eb chi pletic
where exist-asp-B2p you p when cont-asp-p prep fight

li coc'al ?
the children
'Where were you when the children were fighting?'(H,G.41)

The partial RN in (35) is associated with the sentences in (36). It is claimed that the final subject of the embedded clause is also the final subject of the matrix clause. Arguments that the subject of the embedded clause is the final subject of the matrix clause are presented in Sections 6.2.1 and 6.2.2. An argument that the complement is not a final 2 is presented in § 6.2.3 and an argument that the complement is a 2 chômeur is presented in § 6.2.4. These arguments provide evidence for a raising analysis and for the subnetwork in (35).

6.2.1 Person Agreement

As predicted by the rules for person agreement, a verb must agree with its final subject and DO, if there is one. In (36) the matrix predicate bears a Set B person agreement marker and the complement is non-finite. An analysis that involves raising the subject of the embedded clause into the matrix clause accounts for the subject agreement in the matrix clause and provides an explanation for the form of the complement.

6.2.2 Number Agreement

A third plural final nuclear term may control number agreement in the verb. The rules determining number agreement were discussed in Chapter 1, § 1.5. If the third plural nominal heads a final 1 arc in a tenseless intransitive clause, and agreement is marked, then eb must suffix to the predicate. As evidenced in (36c) and (36g), yo agrees in number with the final third plural subject. Thus, the rule for plural agreement with eb provides evidence for the final intransitivity of the yo clause.

It should also be noted that consistent with the properties of subjects, the final 1 of the yo clause may drop, as in (36a)-(36d), or it may occur in sentence-final position, as in (36e)-(36g).

6.2.3 Final Intransitivity of Matrix

The universal laws outlined in (31)-(34) make the cross-linguistic prediction that clauses with intransitive predicates that allow raising will be finally intransitive. Arguments for the final intransitivity of the matrix clause provide support for the proposed RN in (35) and evidence against an analysis which might treat the embedded clause in constructions involving subject raising as a derived object (Munro 1976). That is, if the embedded clause headed a final 2-arc, the matrix clause would, by definition, be finally transitive. Therefore, arguments for the final intransitivity of the matrix clause provide support for the universal laws described above.[5]

Four facts attest to the final intransitivity of the matrix clause. First, as already noted, the subject person agreement affixes are determined by Set B-the Absolutive set. Second, the number marker -eb is determined by the third plural nominal heading a 1 arc in tenseless intransitive clauses and -eb cross-references the final 1 in (36c) and (36g). Third, yo is affixed with the aspectual suffix -k 'future' in (36d) and (36f) and -k must occur on finally intransitive stems (see Chapter 2, § 2.1.3). Fourth, -c/-qu may only occur on finally intransitive stems in 'non-future' aspects and it appears in (36b), (36c), and (36g).[6]

These four facts provide evidence for the final intransitivity of the matrix clause and in so doing provide evidence that the embedded clause is not a final 2.

6.2.4 GR of the Embedded Clause

We have just seen that the GR of the embedded clause can not be a final 2. In this section, I argue that the embedded clause is a chômeur, as predicted by The Chômeur Law. There are, however, two logical possibilities for the GR of the complement. Namely, the complement could be an oblique, or a chômeur, as in (37), below.

37)a.

b.

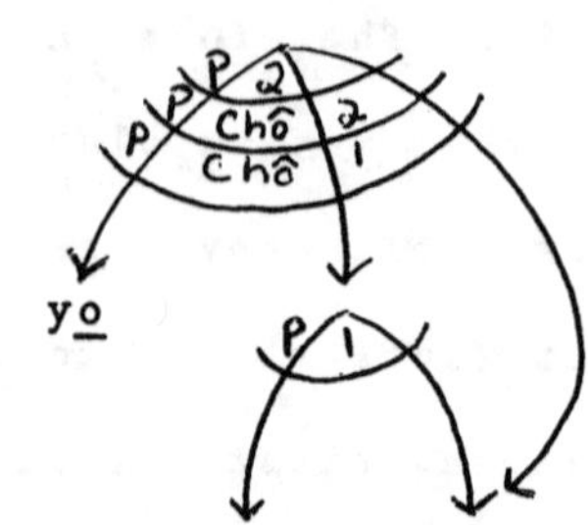

The structure in (37a) is in violation of the Oblique Law. It is therefore assumed that the structure in (37b) is the proper one and that chi may introduce clauses heading non-nuclear term arcs (i.e. obliques, as already evidenced in equi complements, and chômeurs).

6.2.5 Ascension Complements

Intransitive complements (passive and AP infinitives) are discussed in Sections 6.2.5.1 and 6.2.5.2 and transitive complements (DO nominalizations) are discussed in § 6.2.5.3.

6.2.5.1 Passive Infinitives

Only final 1s raise. If the final level of the complement clause is intransitive, the nonfinite complement must be an infinitive. It is argued that passive subjects may raise because they bear the final 1 relation and that the reduced embedded clause is a passive infinitive. Some examples of passive complements follow.[7]

38)a. Yo - Ø chi ile'c li ixk.
cont-B3 prep see=Pass inf the woman
'The woman was seen.'

38)b. Toj yo -qu- in chi ile'c x-ban li doctor.
still cont-asp-B1 prep see=Pass inf A3-by the doctor
'I am still being seen by the doctor.' (E&C,Gr.282)

c. Li ixim yo -Ø chi lok'e'c in-ban.
the corn cont-B3 prep buy=Pass inf A1-by
'The corn is being bought by me.'

d. Li cuink yo - Ø chi ch'ilac.
the man cont-B3 prep scold=Pass inf
'The man is being scolded.'

The passive complement in (38a)-(38d) is introduced by chi. As in other passive clauses, the passive marker is e' if the verb stem is one syllable and vowel length if the verb stem is more than one syllable. As in other infinitives, -c must be suffixed to the revaluation marker, if there is one, and the infinitive cannot be marked for person or aspect. The RN associated with (38b) is given in (39). The complement heads a Chô arc. It should be noted that the final 1 of the raising construction is cross-referenced by a Set B marker on the matrix verb yo, and that it may occur in its normal sentence-final position, as it does in (38a).

39)

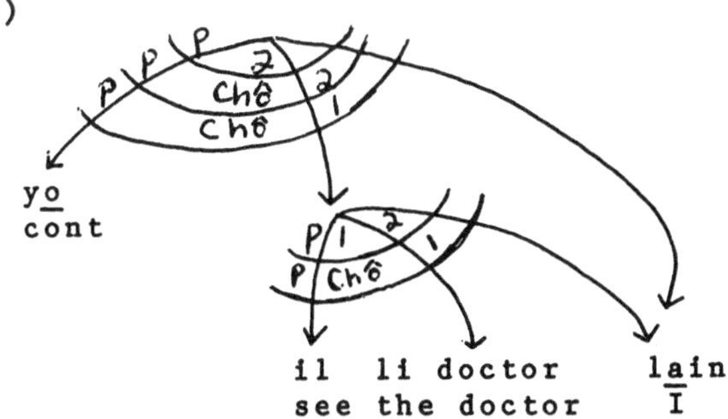

As (39) exemplifies, a passive analysis provides an explanation for the fact that the initial 1 of the complement is presented as a possessor of the relational noun -ban: it is a 1 chômeur. It also accounts for the passive morphology in the infinitive. Furthermore, given the condition on ascendees, i.e. that they must head a final 1 arc, it follows from a passive analysis that the initial 2/ final 1 of a passive complement will be able to raise. A subject raising analysis together with passive predicts that the complement will be infinitival and that it will be introduced by chi since it heads a Chô arc.

6.2.5.2 AP Infinitives

In (40) below, the infinitival complement is introduced by chi. The verb is not marked for tense or person agreement and it bears the AP suffix -o/-n plus the infinitival suffix -c. As exemplified in (40a) and (40b), the intransitive subject is third plural and the matrix predicate yo bears the suffix -eb in agreement with it. In (40c) the intransitive subject is first person plural and the matrix predicate displays the Set B affix -o in agreement with it.

40)a. Yo - qu -eb chi c'ayinc t'icr sa' c'ayil.
cont-asp-p prep sell=AP inf cloth in market
'They were selling cloth in the market.' (S,D.55)

b. Yo -qu -eb chi ximanc iyaj.
cont-asp-p prep dehusk=AP inf seed
'They were dehusking seed.' (Ac&P,106)

c. Yo -c - o chi lok'oc cua.
cont-asp-B1p prep buy=AP inf tortillas
'We were buying tortillas.'

The RN associated with (40a) is given in (41). It is claimed that the final 1 of the AP complement is raised into the matrix clause.

41)

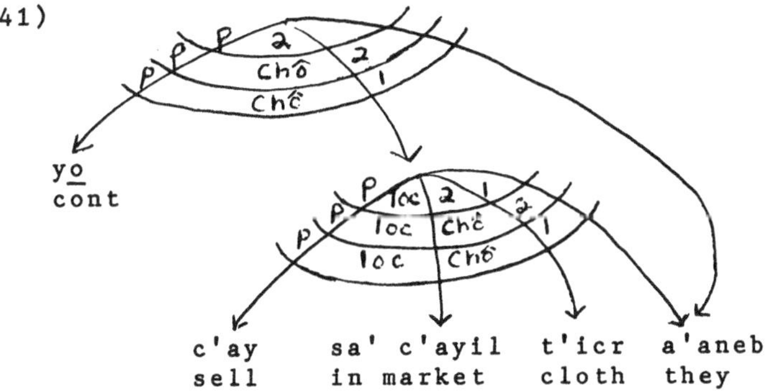

An AP analysis accounts for the AP -o/-n morphology in the infinitive and for the 2 chômeur (nonreferential noun) in the complement. It also accounts for the final intransitivity of the complement. This fact together with a subject raising analysis thus accounts for the nonfinite infinitival complement introduced by chi.

6.2.5.3 DO Nominalizations

In this Section, I discuss ascensions from transitive complements. If a nominal heading a final Erg arc ascends from its clause, the reduced embedded clause is a DO nominalization. In all of the sentences in (42a) -(42e) below, the final 2 of the complement is cross-referenced as possessor of the nominalization and the matrix predicate yo bears a person or number affix in agreement with a final intransitive subject.

42)a. Yo -qu -eb chi cu-il-bal.
cont-asp-p prep A1-see-nom
'They are (in the process of) watching me.'
(lit. 'They are on my watching.')

b. Yo -qu-in chi r -il -bal li ixk.
cont-asp-B1 prep A3-see-nom the woman
'I am (in the process of) watching the woman.'
(lit.'I am on the woman's watching.')

c. Yo -qu -eb ch -a -sic'- bal.
cont-asp-p prep-A2-hunt-nom
'They are seeking you.'

d. Ma yo -c -at chi cu- a'bin-quil ?
Q cont-asp-B2 prep A1 -listen-nom
'Are you listening to me?'

e. Yo - Ø chi r- uc'-bal li x - ha' li so'sol.
cont-B3 prep A3-drink-nom the his-water the buzzard
'The buzzard was drinking his water.' (B,S1.38)

A partial RN corresponding to (42e) is given in (43). Notice that the DO lix ha' is cross-referenced as third singular possessor of the nominalization and that the final subject li so'sol may occur in sentence-final position.

43)

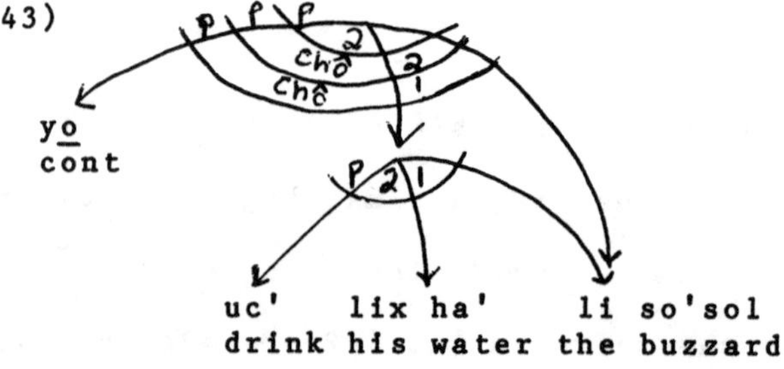

§ 6.2 presented a brief overview of the form of intransitive (passive and AP) and transitive (DO nominalization) complements in equi and ascension constructions. In § 6.3

below, equi and ascension clauses with retreat complements will be discussed.

6.3 Arguments for Cross-Clausal Multiattachment

In this Section complex clauses with retreat complements will be discussed. I argue that the same constraint that governed retreat subject extraction in simple clauses (44) is relevant to complex clauses. This follows automatically from the hypothesized cross-clausal MA (45).

44) <u>Retreat Subject Constraint</u>:
If the initial DO is the final IO of a clause c, then the nominal which heads the final subject arc in clause c must also head a narrow overlay arc.

The notion of cross-clausal and clause-internal MA was introduced in Chapter 3 § 3.3 and is repeated below.

45) <u>Multiattachment</u>:
a. Cross-clausal (or 'general') MA: Two or more overlapping arcs with distinct tails are headed by the same nominal.

b. Clause-internal (or 'reflexive') MA: Two or more parallel arcs sharing a coordinate are headed by the same nominal.

6.3.1 Equi Clauses with Retreat Complements: Unerg Control

Recall that in a simple retreat clause the final 1 may not drop or occur in its normal sentence-final position; rather, it must bear a narrow overlay relation. An example is given in (46).

46)a. **Li c'anti'** x -Ø -lop - o -c r- e li cuink.
the snake tns-B3-bite-R-asp A3-Dat the man
'It was the snake that bit the man.'

46)b.* X - Ø -lop -o -c r-e li cuink li c'anti' .
('The snake bit the man.')

c.* X - Ø -lop -o -c r -e li cuink.
('It bit the man.')

In (46a), li c'anti', the final 1 of the retreat clause, must bear a narrow overlay relation. As predicted by (44), if the final 1 of the retreat clause does not bear a narrow overlay relation, the sentence will be ungrammatical, as (46b) and (46c) illustrate.

In (47) below, an instance of equi, the retreat complement is non-finite and it is the matrix controller which must bear a narrow overlay relation. The RN associated with (47a) is given in (48).

47)a. Lain t -in -xic chi lok'oc r -e.
I tns-B1- go prep buy=R inf A3-Dat
'I'm the one who will go to buy it.'

b.* T - in -xic chi lok'oc r -e lain .
('I will go to buy it.)

c.* T - in -xic chi lok'oc r -e.
('I will go to buy it.')

48)

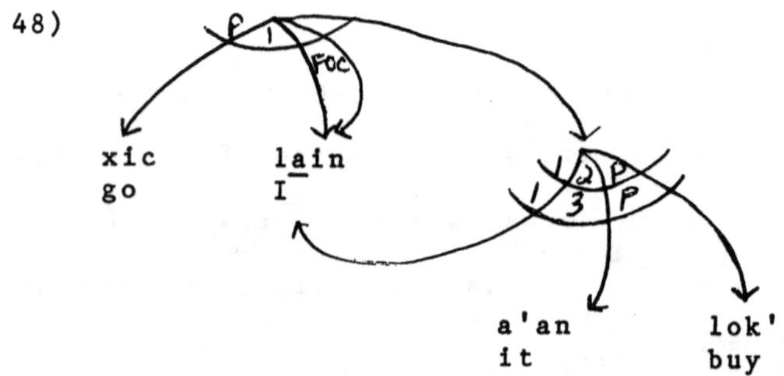

Lok'oc is a retreat infinitive. It is not marked for tense, aspect, or person agreement, but it bears the morphological reflex -o of Retreat. The non-finite complement is introduced by chi. The object of the retreat clause is final IO re. The subject of the Retreat complement is coreferential with the main clause Absolutive subject and it is the main clause subject that must extract and bear the Q, Foc, or Rel relation. (47b) and (47c) are ungrammatical because the controller of the retreat infinitive does not bear a narrow overlay relation. Therefore, we need to explain why the controller of the Retreat infinitive must bear a narrow overlay relation. In a grammar with the notion of MA, the explanation follows from the same principle that governs retreat subject extraction in simple clauses, namely (44). The reasoning is this: The coreference between victim and controller is represented through MA. The controller of the retreat infinitive also heads the final 1 arc in the retreat clause, thereby satisfying the condition in (44). Notice that this condition is only satisfied if the complement is a retreat infinitive. The controllers of the base intransitive (49a), passive (49b), and AP (49c) infinitives below are not subject to the Retreat Subject Constraint.

49)a. C - o -oc chi yabac lao.
tns-B1p-begin prep cry we
'We began to cry.'

b. T - in- xic chi bane'c.
tns-B1- go prep cure=Pass inf
'I will go to be cured.'

c. T - in -xic chi lok'oc cua.
tns-B1- go prep buy=AP inf tortillas
'I will go to buy tortillas.'

In (49), the final 1 may drop or occur in sentence-final position. Similarly, the final 1 may drop or occur in sentence final position if the complement is a DO nominalization, as (50) exemplifies.

50)a. T - in -xic chi x -lok'-bal la̲in.
tns-B1- go prep A3- buy -nom I
'I will go to buy it.'

b. T - in -xic chi x- lok' -bal.
'I will go to buy it.'

(47a) differs from (49a-c) and (50a-b) because the nominal heading the final 1 arc in (47a) must extract. However, all of these sentences share two properties. First, there is a 1:1 cross-clausal MA in each of the sentences. Second, the multiattached nominal that is realized, is the matrix subject. We know this from the form of the complement. The Highest Clause Constraint (7), repeated in (51) below, guarantees that in cases of cross-clausal MA in K'ekchi, only the highest clause in which the multiattached nominal heads an arc is relevant to its realization.

(51) Highest Clause Constraint:
If a nominal heads central GR arcs in more than one clause, only the highest clause in which it heads an arc is relevant to its realization.

In (52) below, there is a 1:1 cross-clausal MA. The Retreat Subject Constraint is applicable because the victim is the final 1 of a retreat clause. Consistent with the predictions of the Retreat Subject Constraint and the Highest Clause Constraint, the multiattached nominal in the matrix clause must also bear a narrow overlay relation.

52)a. Lain n - in-lub chi atinanc acu- e.
I tns-B1- tire prep talk=R inf A2-Dat
'I am tired of talking to you.'

b.* N - in -lub chi atinanc acu-e.

In (52a), lain heads a final 1 arc and a Foc arc. The relational network associated with (52a) is (53).

53)

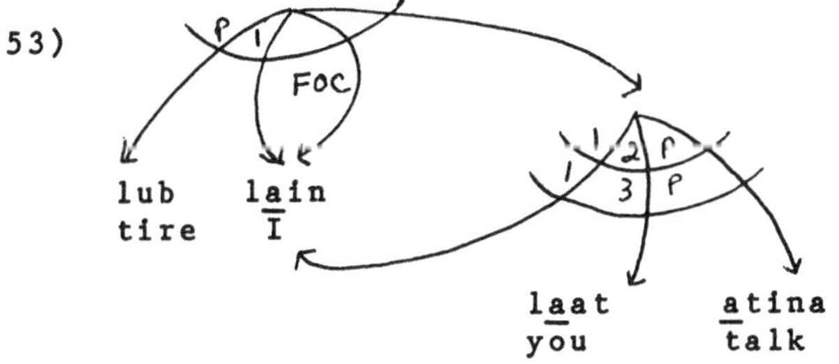

Lain is the controller of the retreat infinitive. Given the MA hypothesis, lain also heads the final 1 arc in the retreat clause. And as predicted by the Retreat Subject Constraint (44), it must bear a narrow overlay relation, as it does in (52a). In contrast, (52b) is ungrammatical because the controller of the retreat infinitive does not bear a narrow overlay relation.

In (54) below, there is a 1:1 cross-clausal MA. The complement clause is a retreat infinitive. As predicted by the Retreat Subject Constraint and the Highest Clause Constraint, the multiattached nominal in the matrix clause heads a narrow overlay (Q) arc.

54)a. Ani na- Ø -lub chi atinanc acu-e ?
who tns-B3-tire prep talk=R inf A2-Dat
'Who is tired of talking to you?'

b. Ani x - Ø -culun chi camsinc r -e li al ?
who tns-B3- come prep kill=R inf A3-Dat the boy
'Who came to kill the boy?'

54)c. Ani x - Ø -c'ay chi sac'oc acu-e ?
who tns-B3-accustom prep hit=R inf A2-Dat
'Who got used to hitting you?'

The relational network associated with (54a) is given in (55).

55)

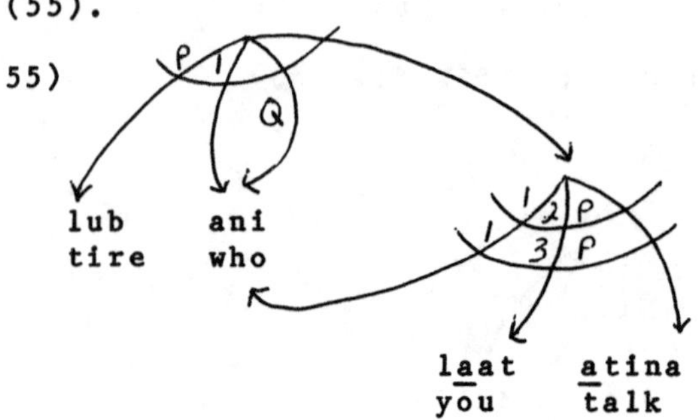

In this Section, we first saw that the final 1 of a retreat clause had to bear a narrow overlay relation. This constraint was stated as the Retreat Subject Constraint (44), repeated below. We then saw that in complex clauses with non-finite retreat complements, it was the controller of the retreat infinitive that had to bear the narrow overlay relation. It was argued that the hypothesized cross clausal MA plus the independently required Retreat Subject Constraint were able to account for the obligatory extraction of the Subject controller of the retreat infinitive. Specifically, the controller of the retreat infinitive satisfies the condition in (44) because it also heads the final 1 arc in the retreat clause. In a grammar without the notion of MA, like the NOMA grammar discussed in Chapter 3, it will be difficult to capture this generalization. At the very least, the Retreat Subject Constraint will be uneccessarily complicated, as (56) exemplifies.

(44) <u>Retreat Subject Constraint:</u>
If the initial DO is the final IO of a clause c, then the nominal which heads the final subject arc in clause c must also head a narrow overlay arc.

(56) <u>NOMA Retreat Subject Constraint:</u>
If the initial DO is the final IO of a clause c, then the nominal which heads the final subject arc in clause c, or the controlling nominal that is coreferential with the final subject of clause c must also head a narrow overlay arc.

This provides an argument against a no MA grammar and for a MA grammar.

6.3.2 Equi Clauses with Retreat Complements: DO Control

(57) shows that in DO controlled equi constructions with Retreat complements, it is the DO in the matrix that must bear the narrow overlay relation. Again, this follows from the fact that the DO is multiattached to the retreat subject and as predicted by the Retreat Subject Constraint, the nominal heading the final 1 arc of the retreat clause must head a narrow overlay arc.

57)a. Ca'ajcui' li x-na' na -Ø- x -takla chi
just the his-mother tns-B3-A3-send prep

abinc r -e.
listen=R inf A3-Dat (F,LJ.10)
'Always <u>his mother</u> he would send to listen to them.'

The relational network corresponding to (57) is given in (58). The matrix DO must control the subject.

58)

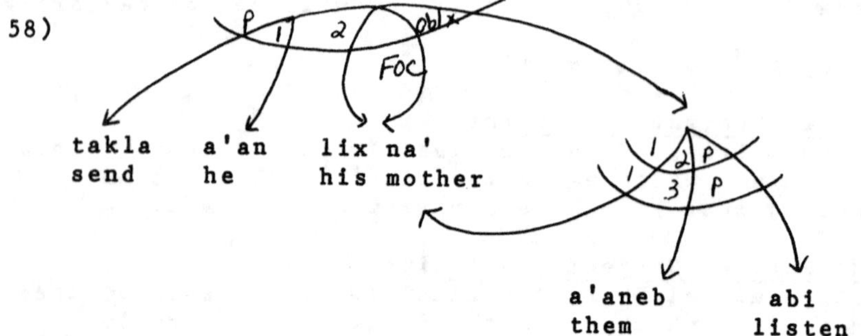

The matrix controller (in this case the DO), must bear a narrow overlay relation only if it is controller of a retreat infinitive. If the DO is controller of a nominalization, or a passive or AP infinitive, no such restriction applies.

In (59a) the DO controller of the retreat infinitive laj Lu' is focused. In (59b), it is not focused and the sentence is ungrammatical. However, as (59c) exemplifies, laj Lu' need not bear a narrow overlay relation if it is the controller of a nominalization.

59)a. Laj Lu' nequ-Ø -e'x -takla chi banunc r -e li
ncl Lu' tns-B3- pA3-send prep do=R̄ inf A3-Dat the
canjel.
work
'Pedro they send to do the work.'

b.* Nequ-Ø -e'x -takla laj Lu' chi banunc r-e li canjel.
('They send Pedro to do the work.')

c. Nequ-Ø -e'x-takla laj Lu' chi x-banun-quil li canjel.
tns-B3-p A3-send ncl Lu' prep A3-do- nom the work
'They send Pedro to do the work.'

In (60) below, the matrix NP that is multiattached to the Retreat subject must bear the narrow overlay relation.

(60b) is ungrammatical because the controller of the retreat infinitive does not bear a narrow overlay relation. On the other hand, (60c) is grammatical because the controller of the DO nominalization need not bear a narrow overlay relation.

60)a. Laat x -at-chakrabi - c chi choyoc r -e
you tns-B2-order=pass-asp prep finish R-inf A3-Dat

li canjel.
the work.
'You were ordered to finish the work.'

b.* X -at-chakrabi -c chi choyoc r-e li canjel.
('You were ordered to finish the work')

c. X -at - chakrabi - c chi x-choy-bal li canjel.
tns-B2- order =pass-asp prep A3-finish-nom the work
'You were ordered to finish the work.'

The relational network associated with (60a) is given in (61).

61)

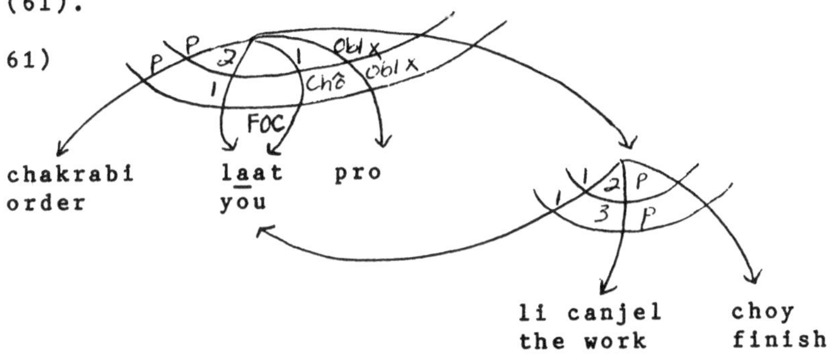

In the main clause the DO controller laat has advanced to Subject via Passive. The matrix verb bears the passive marker of final vowel length and a second singular Set B affix which is in agreement with the final 1 of the clause. Since laat also heads the final 1 arc in the retreat clause it must bear a narrow overlay relation, as predicted by the Retreat Subject Constraint.

Examples like (60a) also provide support for the Highest Clause Constraint since it is the initial 2/final 1 of the passive clause that must extract.

So far we have seen instances of Subject and DO controlled equi with Retreat complements. It was shown that if the matrix Subject is the controller then it must bear the narrow overlay relation in the matrix clause. If the DO is the controller, then it must bear the narrow overlay relation in the matrix clause. I argued that this followed from an analysis incorporating the notion of cross-clausal MA together with the Retreat Subject Constraint (44) and the Highest Clause Constraint (51). Most interestingly then, regardless of final GR (1, or 2), it is the nominal that is multiattached to the retreat subject which must bear the narrow overlay relation.[8]

6.3.3 Equi clauses with Retreat Complements: Erg Control

In this Section, consistent with the Retreat Subject Constraint, I argue that an Erg controller of a retreat infinitive must bear a narrow overlay relation. This fact provides independent evidence for the notion of multiattachment in two ways: First, complex clauses with retreat infinitivals require obligatory extraction of the nominal in the matrix clause that is multiattached to the downstairs retreat subject. Second, the extractee, consistent with the Ergative Extraction Constraint (see Chapters 3 and 4), given in (62) below, must head an Abs arc. This condition is satisfied because the controlling nominal heading the final Erg arc in the matrix clause also heads an Abs arc in the lower retreat clause. It should be noted therefore, that this is the only time a nominal can head a final Erg arc and a narrow overlay arc in a 'non-reflexive' clause (see Chapter 3) and that this follows from an analysis involving cross-clausal multiattachment.

(62) <u>Ergative Extraction Constraint:</u>
If a nominal heads a final Erg arc in a clause c and it also heads a narrow overlay (Q, Foc, or Rel) arc, it must head an Abs arc.

In (63) below, the complement is a retreat infinitive. It is not introduced by <u>chi</u> because it heads a final 2 arc. The controller of the infinitive heads a final Erg arc and a Q arc. The RN corresponding to (63) is given in (64).

63) Ani ta- Ø -r -aj lok'oc r- e li tib ?
who tns-B3-A3-want buy=Rinf A3-Dat the meat
'Who wants to buy the meat?'

64)

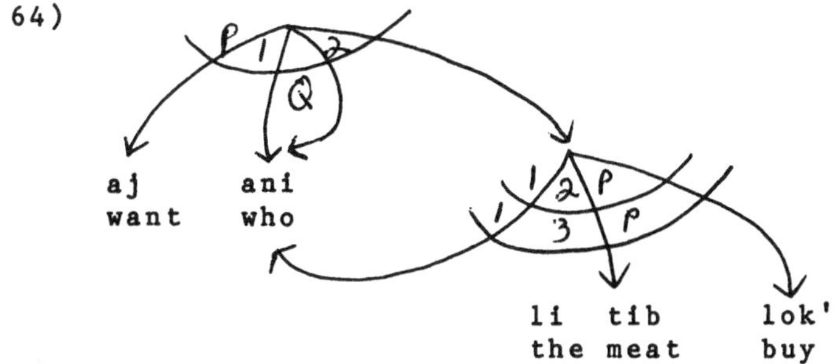

In a grammar with the notion of MA, extraction of ani in (63) is sanctioned because it heads an Abs arc in the retreat complement. Furthermore, this fact is predicted by the Ergative Extraction Constraint and the Retreat Subject Constraint- both of which are independently required. In a grammar without MA, extraction of ani does not follow from any principle. According to the NOMA grammar, as described in Chapter 3, a nominal heading a final Erg arc can head a narrow overlay arc only if it is subject of a 'reflexive' clause, a 'reflexive' clause being defined as one in which -ib heads a final 2 arc. Since (63) is not a reflexive clause, the NOMA grammar cannot account for the grammaticality of sentences like (63) without some additional ad hoc statement. (65) and (66) below provide some indication of what the NOMA grammar would require.

65) NOMA Condition on Ergative Extraction:
A nominal heading a final Erg arc can head a narrow overlay arc if it is subject of a 'reflexive' clause or if it is coreferential with a nominal that heads an Abs arc.

66) NOMA Condition on Reflexivization:
A clause c is a 'reflexive' clause if -ib heads a final 2 arc in clause c.

In addition, the NOMA grammar will require the disjunctive version of the Retreat Subject Constraint, given in (56), and repeated below.

56) NOMA Retreat Subject Constraint: (to be revised)
If the initial DO is the final IO of clause c, then the nominal heading the final subject arc of clause c, or the controlling nominal that is coreferential with the final subject of clause c must also head a narrow overlay arc.

Under the NOMA grammar there is no generalization that characterizes the class of ergative extractees, nor is there a generalization that explicitly characterizes retreat subject extraction.

Under the MA grammar there is a generalization that characterizes the extraction of nominals heading final Erg arcs. Namely, a nominal heading a final Erg arc can bear a narrow overlay relation only if it also heads an Abs arc. Thus, in a MA grammar, the final Erg in a reflexive clause can bear a narrow overlay relation because the Abs arc in the initial 1:2 MA stratum satisfies the condition in (62). The final Erg in a retroherent unaccusative clause can bear a narrow overlay relation because the Abs arc in the non-initial 1:2 MA stratum satisfies this condition. And as just shown, the Erg controller of a retreat infinitive must head a narrow overlay arc: the 1:1 cross-clausal MA satisfying the condition in (62) and the obligatory extraction of the controlling nominal satisfying the condition in (44). These facts follow from the hypothesized cross-clausal MA plus the conditions on ergative extraction (62) and retreat subject extraction (44) which were independently required in simple clauses.

The extraction of ergative controllers in K'ekchi therefore provides additional evidence against a NOMA grammar and for a MA grammar.

6.3.4 Ascension Clauses with Retreat Complements

In this section it is argued that in ascension clauses with Retreat complements, the ascendee must bear a narrow overlay relation. I argue that this follows from the Retreat Subject Constraint (44) and the hypothesized cross-clausal MA.

First, recall that the (subject) ascendee in yo clauses with Passive (67a), AP (67b), base intransitive (67c), and DO nominalization (67d) complements can drop, or occur in sentence-final position (§ 6.2) as:

```
67)a.  Yo -Ø  chi  ile'c           li ixk .
       cont-B3 prep see=Pass inf the woman
       'The woman was seen.'

   b.  Yo -qu- eb  chi iximanc        iyaj.
       cont-asp-p prep dehusk=AP inf seed
       'They were dehusking seed.'

   c.  Yo -qu-in   chi  alinac ( lain ).
       cont-asp-B1 prep run        I
       'I am running.'

   d.  Yo -Ø  chi   r- uc'  -bal li  x -ha'    li  so'sol .
       cont-B3 prep A3-drink-nom the his-water the buzzard
       'The buzzard was drinking his water.'
```

However, as shown below, the subject cannot drop or occur in sentence-final position if a retreat clause is complement to yo. This supports the claim that the final 1 of a Retreat clause must bear a narrow overlay relation (44).

68)a. **Na'bal li tenamit** y<u>o</u> -qu- eb chi sic'oc <u>a</u>cu-e.
many the people cont-asp-p prep look=R inf A2-Dat
'<u>Many people</u> are looking for you.' (E&C,SM.1:35)

b.* Yo -qu-eb chi sic'oc acu- e **na'bal li tenamit** .
('Many people are looking for you.')

but:

c. Y<u>o</u>- qu -eb ch- <u>a</u>- sic'-bal **na'bal li tenamit** .
cont-asp-p prep-A2-look-nom many the people
'Many people are looking for you/on your looking.'

The relational network associated with (68a) is given in (69). The final 1 of the retreat complement ascends to 2 (in accordance with the RSL) and advances to 1 via unaccusative advancement. Since this is an ascension there is no coreference involved; however, as predicted by the Retreat Subject Constraint and the Highest Clause Constraint the final 1 of the matrix clause must head a narrow overlay arc. Crucially, the ascendee <u>na'bal li tenamit</u> heads the narrow overlay arc and it also heads the final 1 arc of the retreat clause, thereby satisfying the condition of the Retreat Subject Constraint. (68b) violates the Retreat Subject Constraint because the ascendee of the retreat complement does not bear a narrow overlay relation. In contrast, (68c) is grammatical because the complement is a DO nominalization and the ascendee doesn't have to extract.

69)

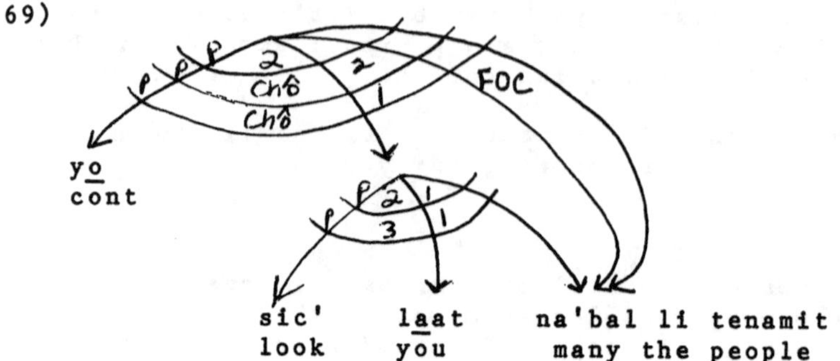

The fact that the ascendee of retreat complements to yo must bear a narrow overlay relation follows from the Retreat Subject Constraint and an analysis that assumes the notion of cross-clausal MA. In a grammar without MA, like NOMA, even the modified version of the Retreat Subject Constraint given in (56) cannot account for the ungrammaticality of sentences like (68b) since no coreference is involved. Under the NOMA grammar there isn't a generalization that accounts for the obligatory extraction in a) simple retreat clauses, b) Subject and DO controlled retreat infinitivals, and c) retreat ascensions. Rather, the Retreat Subject Constraint must be stated as a disjunction accounting for the extraction of the nominal heading the final 1 arc in the retreat clause in each of these constructions separately. An attempt to do this is given in (70), below.

70) NOMA Retreat Subject Constraint:
If the initial DO is the final IO of clause c, and the final 1 of clause c 'ascends', then it must head a narrow overlay arc in the highest clause in which it bears a central GR. If it does not ascend, then the nominal heading the final subject arc of clause c, or the controlling nominal that is coreferential with the final subject of clause c must also head a narrow overlay arc.

The ascension evidence thus provides a third argument against a NOMA grammar and for a MA grammar.

6.3.5 Summary

Ascensions and equi cross-clausal MAs have been described with intransitive and transitive complements. Three arguments for cross-clausal MA were given. These arguments were based on 1) Subject and DO controllers of retreat infinitives and the Retreat Subject Constraint, 2) Ergative controllers of retreat infinitives and the Ergative Extraction Constraint and 3) ascensions from retreat complements. It was argued that the Retreat Subject Constraint (44) which holds in simple clauses also holds in complex clauses. For example, in equi constructions with retreat complements, the controller must bear a narrow overlay relation in the matrix clause. This follows from an analysis incorporating the notion of cross-clausal MA. Crucially, MA is distinct from 'coreference' since as indicated by unaccusative ascensions, the <u>ascendee</u> (downstairs retreat subject) must bear a narrow overlay relation in the main clause and no coreference is involved.

A grammar without the notion of MA, will not be able to capture this generalization about K'ekchi extraction.

Chapter 6 Footnotes

1. I am ignoring intransitive nominalizations where a subject may register as possessor when nothing has happened, as in (1) below.

1) sa' x - ticla- jic chak li ruchich'och'
   in A3- begin- nom dir the world
   'in the beginning of the world' (S,D:147)

The nominalizing suffix in intransitive nominalizations is -(j)ic. -Ic is suffixed to stems ending in a consonant.

2. Another way of stating this generalization is to say that chi introduces the complement if the 'controller' heads an Abs arc. While this is an accurate statement, it is not a sufficient one since chi also introduces the complement in ascension constructions (as will be discussed in Sections 6.2 and 6.3) and there is no 'controller'.

3. (7) is a language-specific constraint. Others have dealt with this in a more general way. For example, Johnson and Postal (1980) capture this in terms of the erase relation between arcs. Rosen (1984) captures it in terms of the 'Realization Hypothesis'. The difference between these proposals is not relevant here.

4. The condition on controllers will have to be revised when 'inversion nominals' are considered. That data (see Berinstein 1984b) suggests that the condition on controllers is:

I. Working nuclear terms of the matrix clause can control DO nominalization and intransitive infinitival clauses.

5. Actually, the Chômeur Law is no longer claimed to be a linguistic universal (Perlmutter and Postal 1983a). It happens that in K'ekchi, there are no counterexamples to it.

6. As noted in Chapter 2, § 2.1.3, there are certain environments in which the presence of -c/-qu is optional. It should be noted therefore that -c must occur if followed by a vowel, i.e. by a Set B first or second person affix, or the number marker, but it does not occur if Set B is Ø, as in (36a) and (36e). This is distinct from -k future aspect which, as mentioned earlier, is obligatory and must occur on all finally intransitive stems, third singular included, as: yok 'it will be'.

7. As noted in Chapter 2, footnote 1, there is a phonological rule which is expressed informally as (1) below.

1) V ʔ C # --> V C ʔ # where C= [k, q]

The environment for (1) is satisfied in passive clauses with the reflex e' in the incompletive aspect (where e' is followed by -k) and in passive infinitives with the reflex e' (where e' is followed by -c). Thus, the passive infinitives in (38a-c) are phonetically [ilek'] and [loq'ek'] and are sometimes written as ilec' and lok'ec' to reflect this.

8. As argued in Berinstein (1984b), inversion nominals (i.e. nominals heading initial 1/final 3 arcs) may also control retreat infinitives (see footnote 4). And as predicted by the Retreat Subject Constraint and the Highest Clause Constraint, it is the inversion nominal heading the final 3 arc in the matrix clause that must bear the narrow overlay relation.

CONCLUSION

7.0 Results of the Study

This thesis treats aspects of the syntax of K'ekchi, and in so doing contributes to our understanding of Mayan languages. In Chapter 1, I present an outline of the K'ekchi agreement, and tense/aspect system. I also argue that there is a set of plural markers that constitute a third set of agreement affixes alongside Set A and Set B.

In Chapter 2, I present arguments that the initial DO may be final Subject of a Passive clause. In addition, a constraint on chômeurs is introduced: a chômeur may not head an overlay arc. Consistent with the prediction of this constraint, the initial Subject/final chômeur in a Passive clause may not extract. In contrast, the final Subject of a Passive clause may extract.

The most important theoretical contribution that this thesis makes is that it provides arguments for multiattachment. Chapter 3 discusses two conditions on final Ergs (the Condition on Ergative Extraction and the Condition on Inanimate Ergs) and provides arguments for clause-internal multiattachment. A grammar with the notion of MA is compared to a grammar without MA, and the latter is rejected.

In K'ekchi, Ergatives are distinct from Absolutives in their extractibility. While a final Abs can freely focus question, or relativize, a final Erg does so only in 'reflexive' clauses. A Condition on Ergative Extraction is proposed: if a nominal heads a final Erg arc in a clause c and it also heads a narrow overlay arc, it must head an Abs arc. That Ergs extract just in reflexive and retroherent unaccusative clauses follows from an analysis that posits (clause-internal) MA in these clauses. The 1:2 MA stratum in these constructions satisfies the Ergative Extraction Condition. Additional evidence for MA is based on constructions with inanimate subjects. An inanimate nominal can head a final Abs arc, but cannot head a final Erg arc unless it is subject of a 'reflexive' clause. A Condition on Inanimate Ergs is proposed: if an inanimate nominal heads a final Erg arc, it must head an Abs arc. That an inanimate nominal can head a final Erg arc in retroherent unaccusative clauses follows from an analysis that posits clause-internal MA in these clauses. The notions of MA and unaccusative thus find corroboration in K'ekchi.

There are two other important results of this chapter. First, I present evidence that syntactic levels are needed in order to account for K'ekchi reflexive and retroherent unaccusative clauses. Second, I present evidence for pronoun birth. Crucially, K'ekchi reflexive and retroherent unaccusative clauses are finally transitive. A 1:2 MA must be resolved by 2-birth. Arguments that the final Erg heads a 2 arc (at some level) in these constructions rests on evidence based on extraction and inanimate nominals.

Chapter 4 presents arguments that the initial DO may be final IO in a 2-3 Retreat clause. Particular to this construction in K'ekchi is that the final subject of a Retreat clause must extract and bear a Q, Foc or Rel relation. This is stated in the Retreat Subject Constraint: if the initial DO is final IO of a clause c, then the nominal heading the final Subject arc of clause c, must also head a narrow overlay arc. Further, it was argued that the initial IO bears the chômeur relation in this demotion construction. Three kinds of evidence distinguish a final IO from an IO chômeur, despite their common morphological properties. This provides additional evidence for the chômeur relation and for the representation of grammatical relations at more than one syntactic level.

In Chapter 5, I present evidence that the initial DO is final chômeur and that the initial Erg is final Abs in an Antipassive construction. Of importance to the description of Mayan languages is the distinction between this legitimate AP construction (which has been referred to as 'Absolutive AP' by Mayanists) and 2-3 Retreat (which has been referred to as 'Agentive AP' by Mayanists). I argue that both of these constructions have the same verbal morphology because this particular morphology occurs in clauses in which the initial Erg is final Abs. On the other hand, based on independently motivated conditions on Subject extraction, Referentiality, and Chômeurs, I also argue that these two demotion constructions are syntactically distinct.

Particular to AP clauses is the fact that there is no active transitive counterpart. Arguments for the initial transitivity of these clauses therefore provides important evidence for the multi-level structure proposed. The first piece of evidence depends on the rule for the verbal morphology, which, as just mentioned, requires an initially transitive stratum and a finally intransitive stratum. The second piece of evidence depends on a condition on nonreferential (bare) nouns in K'ekchi which states that if a nonreferential noun heads a final nuclear term arc, it must head an overlay arc. It is shown that a nonreferential noun cannot head a final 2 arc unless it is extracted. This provides evidence for positing initially transitive strata with 2 arcs headed by nonreferential nouns, and for an analysis of AP clauses with initially transitive strata. Crucially, the bare noun DO must be present at initial level since it can head a final 2 arc and a Foc arc in a transitive clause (or a final 1 arc and a Foc arc in a Passive clause). The third piece of evidence for initial transitivity interacts with the Chômeur Constraint (first presented in Chapter 2) and the above Referentiality Constraint. The 2 chômeur in an AP clause must be a bare noun. As predicted by the Chômeur

Constraint, the initial 2/final chômeur in an AP clause cannot head an overlay arc. Of interest is the following fact: bare nouns that are final nuclear terms must head an overlay arc (Referentiality Constraint), but bare nouns that head a Chô arc cannot. A grammar without syntactic levels and the notion 'chômeur' will not be able to capture the generalization that governs bare noun extraction in K'ekchi. In addition, a theory that did not recognize the chômeur relation would not be able to capture the generalization that chômeurs of different types- 1 chômeurs in Passive clauses, 2 chômeurs in AP clauses, and 3 chômeurs in Retreat clauses- behave alike, and differently from both terms and nonterms, with respect to overlay relations in K'ekchi.

In Chapter 6, arguments for cross-clausal multiattachment are presented. It is shown that the same constraint that governs subject extraction in simple Retreat clauses also governs extraction in complex clauses with Retreat complements. For example, in equi constructions, it is the controller of the Retreat infinitive that must extract, and in ascension constructions, if the retreat subject ascends, it is the ascendee in the matrix clause that must extract. That the controller of the Retreat infinitive and that the Retreat ascendee must extract and bear a narrow overlay relation follows from an analysis that posits cross-clausal MA in these constructions. Crucially, the controller and/or the ascendee of a Retreat complement satisfies the condition of the Retreat Subject Constraint because it also heads the final subject arc in the retreat clause. In contrast, the controller of a Passive or Antipassive infinitive, or the ascendee of a Passive or Antipassive complement need not extract. It is further argued that a grammar without MA cannot capture these generalizations about K'ekchi extraction.

REFERENCES

Ac Caal, Flora, and Sandra Pinkerton. 1976. Li k'alek, li a:wk, ut li q'olok. International Journal of American Linguistics. Native American Texts Series. vol. 1, no.1: 32-9. University of Chicago Press: Chicago.

Aissen, Judith. 1980. Review of papers in Mayan linguistics, ed. by Nora England, Journal of Mayan Linguistics, vol. 2.1.

Aissen, Judith. 1982. Valence and coreference, Syntax and Semantics 15: Studies in transitivity. eds. Paul Hopper and Sandra Thompson, Academic Press: New York.

Aissen, Judith. 1983. Indirect object advancement in Tzotzil, In D. Perlmutter, 1983:272-302.

Bacon, Marlys. 1976. K'ekchi clause structure. Studies in K'ekchi, ed. by S. Pinkerton, The University of Texas: Austin.

Bell, Sarah. 1983. Advancements and ascensions in Cebuano, in D. Perlmutter, 1983:143-218.

Berinstein, Ava. 1978a. A cross-linguistic study on the perception of stress. Journal of the Acoustical Society of America, vol. 63, V8.

Berinstein, Ava. 1978b. Acoustic correlates of stress in K'ekchi. Journal of the Acoustical Society of America. vol. 64, no.3.

Berinstein, Ava. 1978c. Instrument focus and subjectivization processes in K'ekchi, paper presented at the III Taller Maya, Cobán, Guatemala.

Berinstein, Ava. 1979. A cross-linguistic study on the perception and production of stress. Working Papers in Phonetics 47, University of California, Los Angeles, 59 pp.

Berinstein, Ava. 1980. Antipasivo y democión: Evidencia pragmática y sintáctica para dos reglas distintas, paper presented at the V Taller Maya, Universidad Rafael Landivar, Guatemala, Guatemala.

Berinstein, Ava. 1981. A re-analysis of third plural agreement, paper presented at the West Coast Mayan Symposium, Santa Barbara, California.

Berinstein, Ava. 1983a. 2-3 retreat and multiattachment in K'ekchi, paper presented at the Grammatical Relations Festival, Cornell University.

Berinstein, Ava. 1983b. Complex clauses and absolutive 'binding' in K'ekchi (Maya), paper presented at the Regional Conference on Linguistics, Indiana University of Pennsylvania.

Berinstein, Ava. 1984a. Absolutive extractions: Evidence for clause-internal multiattachment in K'ekchi. Cornell Working Papers in Linguistics, no. 5: 1-65.

Berinstein, Ava. 1984b. Impersonal inversion: Evidence for cross-clausal multiattachment in K'ekchi, paper presented at the Symposium on Grammatical Relations, SUNY at Buffalo.

Berinstein, Ava. (in preparation). Impersonal constructions and 2 chômeurs in K'ekchi.

Burkitt, Robert. 1902. Notes on the Kekchí language. American Anthropologist 4:444-63.

Burkitt, Robert. 1920. The hills and the corn. Philadelphia, The University Museum.

Campbell, Lyle. 1974. The theoretical implications of Kekchi phonology. International Journal of American Linguistics 40:269-78.

Campbell, Lyle. 1976. Kekchi linguistic acculturation: a cognitive approach. Mayan Linguistics 1, ed. Marlys McClaran, 90-1. University of California, Los Angeles: American Indian Studies Center.

Campbell, Lyle. 1977. Quichean linguistic prehistory. University of California, Publications in Linguistics 81, Los Angeles.

Carlson, Ruth, and Francis Eachus. 1977. The Kekchi spirit world. Cognitive Studies of Southern Mesoamerica. eds. Helen L. Neuenswander, and Dean E. Arnold. SIL Museum of Anthropology, Texas, 36-65.

Carter, William E. 1969. New lands and old traditions Kekchi cultivators in the Guatemalan lowlands. University of Florida Press: Gainesville.

Craig, Colette. 1977. The structure of Jacaltec. Austin: University of Texas Press.

Craig, Colette. 1980. The antipassive and Jacaltec. Papers in Mayan Linguistics. ed. by Laura Martin, 137-163 Lucas Brothers Publishers: Columbia, Missouri.

Davies, William. 1981. Choctaw clause structure, Ph.D. dissertation, University of California at San Diego.

Davies, William. 1982. 2-3 Retreat, the notion 'absolutive', and levels of grammatical relations. Working Papers in Relational Grammar, University of California at San Diego: La Jolla.

Davies, William. 1984. Antipassive: Choctaw Evidence for a universal characterization, in D. Perlmutter and C. Rosen, 1984: 331-376.

DeCormier, Christopher. 1979. Kekchi particle čaq: Relations in time and space. International Journal of American Linguistics 45: 291-98.

Eachus, Francis, and Ruth Carlson. 1966. Kekchi. Languages of Guatemala. ed. by Marvin K. Mayers. The Hague: Mouton. 110-124.

Eachus, Francis, and Ruth Carlson. 1971. Kekchi texts. According to our ancestors: Folk texts from Guatemala and Honduras. ed. by Mary Shaw, SIL Publications, no.32: 151-66, 389-410.

Eachus, Francis and Ruth Carlson. 1980. Aprendamos Kekchi. Instituto Lingüístico de Verano: Guatemala.

Freeze, Ray. 1970a. Case in a grammar of K'ekchi' (Maya). Ph.D. dissertation, University of Texas.

Freeze, Ray. 1970b. K'ekchi' predicate nominals. Chicago Linguistics Society 6: 107-13.

Freeze,Ray. 1976a. Possession in Kekchi (Maya). International Journal of Linguistics, vol. 42, no.2: 113-125.

Freeze, Ray. 1976b. K'ekchi' texts. International Journal of American Linguistics Native American Texts Series, vol. 1 no. 1: 21-31. ed. by Louanna Furbee-Losee, University of Chicago Press.

Freeze, Ray. 1978. Review of Studies in Kekchi, by S. Pinkerton, International Journal of American Linguistics, vol. 44, no. 4: 350.

Gerdts, Donna. 1981. Object and absolutive in Halkomelem Salish. Ph.D. dissertation, University of California at San Diego.

Greenberg, Joseph. 1963. Some universals of grammar with particular reference to the order of meaningful elements. Universals of language. ed. by Joseph Greenberg, 73-113, MIT Press: Cambridge.

Grimes, James L. 1971. A reclassification of the Quichean and Kekchian (Mayan) languages. International Journal of American Linguistics 35: 20-25.

Haeserijn, Esteban. 1966. Ensayo de la gramática del K'ekchi'. Suquinay, Purulhá, Baja Verapaz, Guatemala.

Haeserijn, Esteban. 1972. Guia para aprender a hablar y a escribir el K'ekchi'. San Juan Chamelco, Alta Verapaz, Guatemala.

Haeserijn, Esteban. 1979. Diccionario K'ekchi' Español. Guatemala.

Harris, Alice. 1981. Georgian syntax: A study in relational grammar. Cambridge University Press: Cambridge.

Johnson, David, and Paul Postal. 1980. Arc pair grammar. Princeton University Press: Princeton.

Kaufman, Terrence Scott. 1976a. New Mayan languages in Guatemala. Sacapultec, Sipacapa, and others. Mayan Linguistics 1, ed. by Marlys McClaran, 67-89. University of California, Los Angeles: American Indian Studies Center.

Kaufman, Terrence Scott. 1976b. Projecto de alfabetos y ortografiás para escribir las lenguas mayances. Guatemala: Ministerio de Educación Publica. 161 pp.

Keenan, Edward. 1976. Toward a universal definition of subject. Subject and Topic. ed. by Charles N. Li, New York: Academic Press.

Keenan, Edward. 1977. The syntax of subject-final languages. UCLA ms.

Klokeid, Terry. 1978. Nominal inflection in Pamanyungan: A case study in relational grammar. Valence, semantic case and grammatical relations. (Studies in Language, Companion Series, 1.) ed. by Werner Abraham, Benjamins B.V.: Amsterdam.

Li, Charles N., and Sandra A. Thompson. 1976. Subject and topic: A new typology of languages. Subject and Topic. ed. by Charles N. Li, 457-487, New York: Academic Press.

McQuown, Norman Anthony. 1956. The classification of Mayan languages. International Journal of American Linguistics 22:191-5.

McQuown, Norman Anthony. 1964. Los origenes y la diferenciación de los mayas segun se infiere del estudio comparativo de las lenguas mayanas. Desarrollo cultural de los mayas. Special publication of the Seminario de Cultura Maya, eds. E. Vogt and A. Ruz, 49-80. Mexico.

Mondloch, James. 1978. Disambiguating subjects and objects in Quiche, Journal of Mayan Linguistics, vol. 1, no. 1: 3-19.

Monro, Pamela. 1976. Subject raising, auxiliarization, and predicate raising: The Mojave evidence. International Journal of American Linguistics 42: 99-112.

Norman, William. 1978. Advancement rules and syntactic change: The loss of instrumental voice in Mayan. Proceedings of the Fourth Annual Meeting of the Berkeley Linguistics Society: 458-476.

Norman, William. 1979. Class lectures on Quichean syntax, University of California at San Diego.

Özkaragöz, İnci. 1980. Evidence from Turkish for the unaccusative hypothesis. Proceedings from the Sixth Annual Meeting of the Berkeley Linguistics Society: 411-22.

Özkaragöz, İnci. 1982. Transitivity and the syntax of middle clauses in Turkish. Working Papers in Relational Grammar, University of California at San Diego: La Jolla.

Perlmutter, David M. 1978. Impersonal passives and the unaccusative hypothesis. Proceedings of the Fourth Annual Meeting of the Berkeley Linguistics Society: 157-89.

Perlmutter, David M. 1979. Predicate: A grammatical relation, Linguistic Notes from La Jolla 6. University of California at San Diego.

Perlmutter, David M. 1981. Syntactic representation, syntactic levels and the notion of subject. The nature of syntactic representation. eds. P. Jacobson and G. Pullum, Reidel: Dordrecht and Boston.

Perlmutter, David M., ed. 1983. Studies in Relational Grammar 1. University of Chicago Press: Chicago.

Perlmutter, David M. (to appear). Multiattachment and the unaccusative hypothesis: The perfect auxiliary in Italian.

Perlmutter, David M., and Paul Postal. 1974. Lectures from the LSA Summer Institute.

Perlmutter, David M., and Paul Postal. 1977. Toward a universal characterization of passivization. Proceedings of the Third Annual Meeting of the Berkeley Linguistics Society: 394-417. Reprinted in Perlmutter 1983.

Perlmutter, David M., and Paul Postal. 1983a. Some proposed laws of basic clause structure. In D. Perlmutter 1983: 81-128.

Perlmutter, David M., and Paul Postal. 1983b. The relational succession law. In D. Perlmutter 1983:30-80.

Perlmutter, David M., and Paul Postal. 1984. Impersonal passives and some relational laws. In D. Perlmutter and Rosen eds. 1984:126-170.

Perlmutter, David M., and Carol G. Rosen., eds. 1984. Studies in relational grammar 2. University of Chicago Press: Chicago.

Pinkerton, Sandra. ed. 1976a. Studies in K'ekchi. Texas Linguistic Forum 3. Department of Linguistics, University of Texas: Austin.

Pinkerton, Sandra. 1976b. Ergativity and word order in K'ekchi. Studies in K'ekchi. ed. by Sandra Pinkerton, 48-66, University of Texas, Austin. Also appeared as Word order and the antipassive in K'ekchi. Papers in Mayan Linguistics. ed. by Nora England, no. 6, 1978:169-187. University of Missouri, Columbia, Mo.

Postal, Paul. 1977. Antipassive in French, NELS 7: 275-313.

Postal, Paul. 1981. Some arc pair grammar descriptions. The nature of syntactic representation. eds. P. Jacobson and G. Pullum, Reidel: Dordrecht and Boston.

Robertson, John. 1976. The structure of pronoun incorporation in the Mayan verb complex. Ph.D. dissertation, Harvard University.

Rosen, Carol. 1981. The relational structure of reflexive clauses: Evidence from Italian. Ph.D. dissertation, Harvard University.

Rosen, Carol. 1984. Degrees of finiteness in equi, ascension, and union complements, paper presented at the Symposium on Grammatical Relations, SUNY at Buffalo.

Sapper, Karl. 1906. Spielender Kekchi-Indianer. Boas anniversary volume: anthropological papers written in honor of Franz Boas, ed. Berthold Laufer, 283-9. New York: G.E. Stechert and Co.

Sedat, Guillermo S. 1955. Nuevo diccionario de las lenguas K'ekchi' y Española. Alianza para el Progreso: Chamelco, Alta Verapaz, Guatemala.

Shaw, Mary, and Helen Neunswander. 1966. Achi. Languages of Guatemala. ed. by M. Mayers, 15-48. The Hague: Mouton.

Smith-Stark, Thom. 1976a. The antipassive in Jilotepequeño Pocomam, unpublished ms., Tulane University.

Smith-Stark, Thom. 1976b. Notes on Proto-Mayan verb morphology, paper presented at the American Anthropological Association, Washington D.C.

Stewart, Stephen. 1980. Gramática Kekchí, Editorial Academica Centroamericana, Guatemala.

Stoll, Otto. 1896. Die Maya-Sprachen der Pokom-Indianer. nebsteinem arhang: die Uspanteca. Leipzig.

Swadesh, Morris. 1960. Interrelaciones de las lenguas Mayanses, Anales del Instituto Nacional de Antropologia e Historia, Mexico, 13: 231-267.

Williamson, Janis. 1979. Patient marking in Lakhota and the unaccusative hypothesis, Chicago Linguistics Society 15: 353-65.

For Product Safety Concerns and Information please contact our EU representative GPSR@taylorandfrancis.com
Taylor & Francis Verlag GmbH, Kaufingerstraße 24, 80331 München, Germany

www.ingramcontent.com/pod-product-compliance
Lightning Source LLC
LaVergne TN
LVHW020615110826
845149LV00002B/478
* 9 7 8 1 1 3 8 6 9 9 7 2 4 *